LIBRARY AND INFORMATION TECHNOLOGY

Library and Information Technology

Prashant Kaushik

ANMOL PUBLICATIONS PVT. LTD.
NEW DELHI - 110 002 (INDIA)

ANMOL PUBLICATIONS PVT. LTD.
H.O.: 4374/4B, Ansari Road, Daryaganj
New Delhi - 110 002
Ph.: 23261597, 23278000
B.O.: No. 1015, Ist Main Road, BSK III Stage
III Phase, III Block
Bangalore - 560 085 (India)
Visit us at: www.anmolpublications.com

Library and Information Technology

First Published, 2006

ISBN 81-261-2629-9

PRINTED IN INDIA

Published by J.L. Kumar for Anmol Publications Pvt. Ltd., New Delhi - 110 002 and Printed at Mehra Offset Press, Delhi.

Contents

Preface

"Library and Information Technology" as a paper is being taught at B.L.I.Sc. and M.L.I.Sc. in 'Library Science' at various universities and institutions. This book is designed as an introductory text to the above paper, encompassing vital information on all pertinent aspects. Thus the material presented here would be of interest as well as of great use to the students, teachers and professionals of Library Science. This book will provide complete knowledge of the information technology, computer in library, hardware and software aspects, communication network, fundamentals of telecommunication and videocassettes etc. to the students.

The major topics dealt in this book are—Introduction to Information Technology; Computer Architecture; Software Aspects; Technical Services; Computer in Library Management; Communication Network in Library; Fundamentals of Teleommunication; Use of Videocassettes in Library etc.

It is hoped that all those will benefit from the contents of this book for whom it is meant. The author will feel amply rewarded, if motive is achieved.

Editor

1

Introduction to Information Technology

In so far as control over information forms the basis of managerial authority, the technologies which process it are inherently political. Indeed, business organizations are under pressure to change their decision-making structures as a direct consequence of information technology implementation. These 'subversive' effects on organizational structures are not immediately obvious to management. They arise as the new technology changes the established work practices and consequently creates different relationships on the organization's information network. Management is then faced with a dual threat:

1. A new pool of knowledge outside its formal control structures. Employees are able to access information without hindrance.
2. Power is shifting from line managers to those who control the information technology, such as the technicians in the departments or knowledgeable users.

Management's response has been weak and incremental. The control of information generated by computer technologies increasingly reflected the new power structures that these technologies established. On the one hand, functional control (allocation, budget, etc.) remains with general management. On the other, operational control (how and what is processed) is left to the technicians in the DP departments. The pervasive nature of the technology spreading through all levels of the organization established those who controlled it as important powerbrokers or gatekeepers. Newcastle Business School research has shown that senior managers are often unwilling to become involved. They served their apprenticeship in computerless or, at best, early mainframe-driven organizations and therefore do not always fully understand or appreciate the new technologies. Despite the obvious need for new control structures the traditional methods are adhered to.

The dichotomy between the established management structures and the changed (and changing) technological structures is therefore maintained and often worsened. Such opposing forces create a complex environment and place considerable constraints on management action. The dichotomy quickly becomes institutionalized. Lack of management action causes other user employees to perceive themselves as powerless in any dealings with the new technologies. This serves to enhance the influence of the technicians and is built into the organization's structures. Business action then tends to become increasingly inflexible; user managers are reluctant to take risks in an environment they do not understand, and many operational decisions are left to the technicians. This area of decision-taking is also built into the firm's task structure. Meanwhile the new networked systems demand increasing flexibility in order to work but are instead being faced with increasingly inflexible and decision-shy managements.

To appreciate the nature of this threat and how profound its impact can be on the organization, it is essential to grasp the characteristics of technology, in particular its integrative nature with any social entity whether it be an organization or something else. Explore this area, but it also then distinguishes between different types of technology, highlighting the perceptual characteristics of information technology. It concludes that to control information technology we must realize that we cannot treat it as just another piece of machinery.

The relationship between technology and an organization has, indeed, been thoroughly explored. It is obvious that a firm's structure is characterized by the many forces emanating from its operating environment. What is perhaps not so obvious is that technology is one of those forces. This is because it is quite often seen as a locally owned, physical resource. The machine on the shopfloor is just that and not part of a more complex social process. Within the framework of this perspective technology is a tool, totally predictable and controllable by management.

The physical technology alone (*e.g.* machinery or computers) will not explain how organizations are affected by it. As Weizenbaum suggested, a computer or telecommunication system (or any form of technology) is merely junk without the people to relate to them. It is how those people relate to their technology, how they use it, their perceptions of it, and so on, that are important. These aspects govern not only the technological process but also the characteristics of the organization structure. In the same way, structure should not be seen merely in a physical sense. The dividing of a firm into departments and functions, although of interest does not capture the essence of an organization, which is to be found within the minds of its employees. The relationship between technology and structure is thus not physical but perceptual because it is within people's minds that the links are made. Our understanding of such techno behavioural forces is not great. This is partly because of the hegemonic view of business 'Organizations as hierarchies in organization theory. It would seem, therefore, that we have not as yet learnt to examine organizations in an appropriate dimension which can highlight the effects of information and its technology.

The traditionalist's view of an organization is typically presented by Schein as a rational co-ordination of activities. This emphasizes the hierarchical and functionally-bound aspects. Butler, on the other hand, discussed the lack of understanding of such models determining that all the interrelationships are not adequately identified. They tend to portray firms as static entities without the turbulence of opposing forces. In particular, technology is seen as a side issue, if at all, and not central to the fundamental mechanisms of an organization.

A more appropriate model in Butler's mind is Udy's, which puts technology at the centre of an interactive environment of production objectives, social setting, physical exigencies and work organization. Technology, not the structure, sets the constraints ('trade-offs' as Butler calls them) upon an organization. Thus, a certain structure can be considered suitable for a given technology. For example, a company using mass production techniques, such as Ford, will best be structured to suit the needs of mass production technology. The relationship does not end there, however, as in Pugh's model, because he suggests that it is technology which drives the organization.

Where this model fails is in not identifying with sufficient clarity the perceptual aspects of an organization's technology. It is only within this domain that useful links can be established between technology and structure. The perceptual aspects of structure must also be emphasized for this to be successful since within any physical domain technology can only be seen as a resource and structure as a functional framework. It will then demonstrate that employees' perception of their structure determines the consequent structural characteristics. This chapter also suggests, however, that the relationship is two-way, in that an established structure can itself influence and change the perception of the employees. The impact of information technology is then again introduced. Already it has been established that such technology can change the way that individuals perceive their environments. A link with the present chapter is that since an employee's perception of the environment can be changed through information technology, his/her perception of the firm's structure must also change. The post-implementation structure that emerges may be profoundly different from any previous structure.

This control-theoretic view of information technology's impact is particularly relevant to the devolution of management authority. The impact of the new technology may radically affect the power structure or the political relationships between management and staff (but not the functional relationships) thus creating an imbalance between the perceptual and physical aspects of the organization. Through the perceptual domain, information technology has also infiltrated the cultural base of organizations and has thus had the potential to alter cultural objectives, which are the consequence of existing value systems. For example, it may be the formal objective of one firm to produce good quality products at the expense of higher profits. This objective has arisen from the organization's culture, but any form of technology, especially information technology, is not sensitive to cultural requirements.

Managers may try to fit the technology into their companies but it is generally within a framework provided by the physical domain. The objectives suitable for the technology do not always match existing cultural needs. To seek an explanation of the technological impact, therefore, we should no longer look at organizations in terms of departments and divisions. Any boundary established by such a definition may be rendered irrelevant. It is more sensible to consider an organization as a network of perceptual maps, dependent on an information network which is itself part of a wider network within the region, market, industry, and so on.

The need for such an outlook is underlined by the number of firms accessing information beyond their established functional boundaries. Internally, this involves different departments accessing a common pool from the company database; externally, employees gain entrance to public databases such as Prestel. It is increasingly difficult to understand these organizations as physically controllable entities. The problem, however, extends beyond management. If it is accepted that our models of organization are also too limiting because of their inability to highlight the dichotomy between the perceptual and the physical, then we must develop new models, which is one of the major proposals of the book. In order to do this we must first establish an appropriate methodology. The analysis which must be pursued is wide-ranging. It extends beyond the convenient boundaries that traditional theory has established. The tidy logic of an organization reaches only into the physical domain, beyond that is a vast perceptual arena which can be understood only as a network of relationships.

The Dynamic Element

Before its presentation, however, there are other factors which must be addressed. The point has already been made that an organization is a fluid and ever-changing entity. The components so far discussed form the framework of the organization but they are no more than boxes in an analyst's model. Other forces exist which breathe life into these concepts. They can be termed as the dynamics of an organization. People are the organization, and as such their perceptions, aspirations, alliances and conflicts form an important dynamic. It suggests that the outcome for any organization is not through a rational process, although that may seem to be apparent within the physical domain, but rather as a consequence of perceptual interaction between individuals or groups. These can be dysfunctional as well as functional.

For managers the issue is how such diverse forces can be controlled. They can only directly access the physical domain and therefore have to attempt to manipulate this in some way to have any impact upon the perceptual domain. One area, however, which allows a controllable linkage between two domains is the information network. The quality, quantity and content information amongst other factors such as historicity, will determine individual or group perception. On the other hand, the network itself can be inpysically manipulated thus affecting the quality, quantity and content of information. Its control is therefore of considerable importance to management.

Its particular emphasis is on the use of computer technology to generate information. Other forms of generated information through manual methods can also be controlled as information management, but because of the computer's ability to generate so much information other important forces come into play which are not present in a manual system.

The ways in which employees regard the characteristics of their information will determine in part the nature of their information network and ultimately the organization structure itself. Management must be aware of this and develop strategies through training and computer technology implementation which are sensitive to this. Information, however, is only part of the process. On its own it is not particularly a dynamic of the organization Individuals may receive information and do nothing with it. A firm, therefore, does not change because of information. Information must be used. Action or behaviour is the consequence of information being used in the physical domain. In the perceptual domain, information being used is manifest through the decision process. There are no actions without decisions, no matter how minor or simple they may be, so that an organization, which can be analysed in terms of its actions, is driven by its decision processes.

In any context there is no such thing as an individual decision, even if the person involved is on a deserted island. Especially within a complex social process such as an organization, a decision is based upon a range of perceptual and physical influences. A person's experience coming to bear in a decision, for example, is the consequence of previous interactions with other people and institutions. Therefore one cannot fully control the decision process by Controlling those individuals who are seen to own it. Their actions might be constrained but the source of their decisions is to be found in the perceptual domain. This is particularly important when such processes are affected by computer technology. Managers tend to develop mechanisms around the physical aspects of the technology and ignore the wider perceptual impact. It then places these ideas in the context of the other major components of a firm, in particular the information network, by highlighting the close relationship between a decision and information.

We have so far developed the framework of an organizational structure dominated by two domains: the physical and the perceptual. In a similar fashion to matter and anti-matter, their forces to Conflict and contradict one another. Management must maintain the narrow ground between the two, because it is only here that long-term stability is established. At this point the forces of both domains are in equilibrium, which for the purposes of the model has been termed balance. The achievement of such a state is one of the key outcomes to be identified.

The domination of one domain over another could lead to long-term instability, the degree of which depends upon a range of factors unique to specific organizations. For example, if there is no balance and an organization is dominated by its physical domain, then its short-term survival, at least, will depend upon how effective that domain is in dealing with the firm's particular environment. In the longer term, however, all firms must achieve an equilibrium whether the dominant domain is in tune with the environment or not. This is because the cost of not achieving equilibrium will be manifest in the dysfunctional relationship between the two domains. Forces will come into play that will undermine stability. It shows a complex social entity driven by an abstract relationship between two sets of forces. Much of this arena exists within the minds of the employees, of course, but like other societal phenomena its logic extends beyond them.

The forces can exist independently of particular individuals in that they are perpetuated by culture, technology and training. Individuals may come and go, some people may contribute more than others, but the logic of the organization as a separate entity remains consistent. It is proposed that an, organization can pass a significant point, the virtuality point, whereby its survival does not depend upon a particular set of individuals. This is a different world from the one portrayed by established theory. It comprises many of the same elements, such as structure and technology, recognized by conventional wisdom, but it is the perspective, the way in which those elements are arranged, that is different.

The emphasis is upon a force field relationship rather than the aspects of one domain or another. By having this different framework, we can also analyse the effects of change in other ways. In particular, the impact of information technology is shown to have a far wider effect upon organizations than the traditional models may lead us to suppose. Much of it is common sense, gleaned from the working environment and from those in it. Nevertheless, the model is placed before all management as a challenge: to use the ideas this book presents as a basis for analysing the worth of their information technology.

INFORMATION TECHNOLOGY AND LIBRARIES

Information technology (IT) may be defined as 'a combination of computer and telecommunications techniques which makes possible new systems and products to help people at work, in education, and at home'. Information technology is thus all about the application of a wide variety of electronic technologies to the information-handling activities that are central to the operation of any organisation. (Stephen Flowers).

In the domain of library information service, by information technology is meant the use or application of various technologies such as computer, telecommunications, word processing, micrographics, reprographics, video recording and other electronic devices for the storage, retrieval, reproduction and dissemination of information in an office or library environment. While hardware and software, aspects of computer have been discussed in the previous chapters, this chapter reviews host of other technologies and equipment widely used in library operations, or have valid potentials in future.

WORD PROCESSING

Word Processing is a technique for electronically storing, editing, and manipulating text using an electronic keyboard, computer and printer. A dedicated word processors consist of a TV-link viewing screen alongwith a keyboard similar to that of a typewriter, a programmemable microcomputer and magnetic floppy disk, and finally a high unit printing unit. However hard disks, and other media such as magnetic tapes and cards are also used in some systems. Regardless of their design almost all word processors have these five components viz a processor (CPU) a keyboard, a display screen or panel removable external storage, and a printer. In fact it is a special purpose microconputer. However, a general purpose microcomputer can also be used for word-processing if it has'sufficient internal and external storage capacity and special word processing software. Mainframe can also serve in the same way.

With the use of simple commands, material typed via the computer keyboard, is stored directly into the computer's memory. Once stored, the information can be reformatted and printed easily via a printer hooked to the computer that receives instructions and then flawlessly types the desired number of copies etc. The equipment also enables users to move words, sentences, paragraphs or whole sections of text, thereby saving enormous amount of retyping times.

Libraries and information centres are greatly benefitted by this machine. The areas of applications are: library catalogues, order processing, periodicals acquisition, abstracting and indexing bulletins, on-line searching, union lists. In addition to this, they are also used for thesaurus construction, database searching, and current Awareness Bulletins etc.

According to James Rice a modern word processing package (whether it is a stand-alone system or is part of a microcomputer system or a time-sharing system has the following capabilities:

1. It is easier to learn the use and does not require technical knowledge.
2. It has many text-editing and formatting capabilities. These include the following:
   (a) Right and left margin and right and left indentions of a types of charts, tables, figures can be easily adjusted.
   (b) An automatic spelling checks with a large vocabulary provided.
   (c) Text input is highly flexible. It means users can continuously keyboard text without regard to carriage returns, paragraph indentions, spaces between lines etc.
   (d) The insertion, deletion, or replacement of letter words, sentences possible. Even paragraphs can be moved and rearranged.

(e) Page headings are input once and then automatically repeated on each page.

(f) Pages are numbered automatically.

(g) Line lengths, page lengths are easily formatted.

3. It has the ability to integrate other information from other files into the document being processed.
4. It has some statistical and computational abilities. It means statistical information might be processed into averages or percentages and then formatted into a chart or table for a specific purpose.
5. It has the ability to converse with the user through terminals.
6. It has the ability to index and retrieve documents that are stored.

These are just a few of the fundamental features of modern word processors. They are becoming friendly, easier to use, more flexible, and more powerful all the time. (J. Rice).

DOCUMENT STORAGE AND REPRODUCTION

Micrographics

Micrographics is that filed of information technology which concerns making use of microforms. Here copies are produced in a highly reduced formats called microforms such as microfilms, microcards, microfiche, roll films of 8mm, 16mm, and 35mm, micro-opaque, ultrafiche, film strips, insert cards and computer output microform (COM). There are large variety of microforms and reduction ratio ranges from 20:1 to 300:1 or even more are said to be available. Today it is possible to images of thousands of pages on a standard 6" x 4" high density ultrafiche.

Regardless of type, microforms are created in either of two ways. Computer-output microfilm (COM) permits the direct recording of computer processed, machine-readable data onto microfilm or microfiche without first creating paper documents; the second method of microform production called source document microfilming, uses specially designed cameras to film paper documents, recording them as microimages on film or fiche. In either case a COM recorder or microfilm camera produces invisible images which require special reading equipment to be made visible and usable. However latest microform reading equipment making it possible to handle variety of microforms using simple lens changer or adaptor. Roll films in 16mm, 35mm positive and negative microforms, now can be handled with the same reader printer equipment.

Micrographics has enabled libraries to acquire rare material, preserve collections, conserve shelf space, and provide other libraries with copies of scholarly material.

Reprographics

The term reprographics is used to identify that field of information processing which concerns with technologies and equipment for the reproduction of documents. Although micrographics can be considered a specialized facet of reprographics, the term is usually applied to copying and duplicating equipment which makes paper copies at or near full size.

While computer remains the nucleus of library automation, copiers and duplicators are historically the most important category of automated equipment in library application. The electrostatic process in its plain paper (xerographic) and coated paper (elictrofax) still remain the dominant copier technology. The latest plain paper copier Xerox-9500 can give two copies per second. This invention has increased the information transfer process and is regarded a boon in the area of information technology. Copying and duplicating machines continue to improve capabilities. Photostat machines are available for two-sided copying, reduction and enlarging copying and colour copying. Automatic paper feeding and sorting of multiple copies of multipage documents and automatic stapling of copy sets are widely used in libraries.

Recently computer technology has further influenced document reproduction system. Potentially most important development has been the introduction of so-called intelligent copier, a microprocessor-controlled device which can function as both a conventional copier and an output device for data prepared by computers and word-processing systems. Using a combination of lasers and xerography to generate paper copies, intelligent copiers are related to the high-speed nonimpact printers. These new devices can perform two-sided printing, automatic sorting and automatic stapling. An interesting feature of intelligent copiers is their ability to print characters in multiple type fonts, sizes and intensities. In addition to functioning as conventional copiers, or computer printers, intelligent copiers can create new documents by merging information from existing paper documents with machine readable data prepared by a computer or word-processing system. (Saffady).

Expert Systems

Expert systems represent one of the most advanced facets of information technology. Basically expert systems are software packages aimed at providing expert consultancy advice and assistance with problem solving in specialist fields of knowledge.

The British Computer Society's glossary defines an expert system as "a computer system containing organized knowledge so that it can perform some of the functions of an expert human consultant". Expert systems are in fact intelligent computer applications that use data, a knowledge base and a control mechanism to solve difficult problems which demand significant human expertise for their solution. They are the best known form of Artificial Intelligence. Expert systems differ from the conventional computer programmes in that they keep separate the knowledge needed to solve problems from the methodology for doing so. The control strategy is maintained at a level distinct from the knowledge base.

The direct application of expert systems to information work has been primarily in the area of online bibliographic database searching. It is predicted that in future the researchers will be able to conduct comprehensive and successful online literature searches without the help of a librarian or information specialists.

TECHNOLOGY OF ONLINE SERVICES

During the last 20 to 25 years several kind of data processing and telecommunications technologies have evolved.

They have made online information service fast, cheap and attractive. Computer and data processing industries provide the hardware whereas telecommunications industries provide the low-cost data communication links between the user and the computers. (Detail follows under the caption "Telecommunication Aspects") Landau, Wanger and Berger have identified the following major technologies that have contributed to the success of online information services:

1. Powerful time-sharing computers
2. Machine-readable databases
3. Fast-access disc storage devices
4. Interactive retrieval programmes
5. Fast, low-cost computer terminals
6. Telecommunications networks

Time-sharing Computers

The modern (fifth-generation) computers are highspeed, have high capacity, for great storage, and data processing capabilities than their earlier (first-generation) ancestors. They too have greatly increased time-sharing capabilities. It means more people can use their resources at the same time from remote terminals. (Detail follows)

Machine-readable Databases

Databases have been defined in number of ways. These are collections of related textual and/or numeric data in machine-readable form that are processed for computerized publishing and/or electronic dissemination. These databases can be "read" and "understood" by a computer only as they are in a binary form.

An online information service essentially acquires machine-readable databases from database producers or suppliers and converts the data to a format compatible with the retrieval system design. Design specifications are developed for the users to convert programmes to transfer information from the supplier's magnetic tapes onto magnetic discs in the prescribed retrieval format.

Interactive Retrieval Programmes

Interactive retrieval programmes provide the means for the online user to get the information on the discs through the computer. Batch searching is not interactive, because it is done on database tapes rather than on discs. The tapes are searched sequentially from beginning to end. Discs only have made interactive retrieval possible. Interactive retrieval requires an interactive programme which enables the user to actively communicate with the database. As each stage the search strategy is typed at the terminal and sent to the computer programme, the results are immediately displayed. Although online retrieval programme are "Conversational", the interaction is not quite simple. It is achieved by most retrieval programmes through a structured protocol of user commands which the programme interprets as instructions to the computer to perform certain operations on the data. And the users have to pay for it.

Fast-access Disc Storage Devices

As discussed in the chapter 4, machine-readable data are stored in several ways such as: punched card, punched paper tape, magnetic tape, drums, discs and in the magnetic core of the central processing unit. Magnetic tape and discs are the most commonly used methods of storage. Floppy disc CD-ROM and erasable disc etc., with unbelievable storage capacity have made online service fast and cheap.

Low-cost Computer Terminals

The availability of high-speed, low-cost modern computer terminal has made online search service a success. At present a large variety of reliable, lightweight and inexpensive computer terminals is available.

Modern terminals have a typewriter-like keyboard, and typically one of two types of output or display-printing or cathode ray tube (CRT) screen. CRT terminals display output on a television-like screen and are usually used with an attached printer for paper copy.

Telecommunications Networks

Telecommunications networks are designed to handle digital machine-readable data and use telephone and lines, microwaves and communications satellites to transmit data. Networks such as Tymnet and Telenet provide communications links for online services, which in the early days had to rely on standard telephone lines designed for voice, not digital data. These networks rely on small switching computers (nodes) in key cities which permit most users to dial a local telephone number. The node computer then allows the user to access any dozens of online services. (Detail follows).

TELECOMMUNICATION ASPECTS

The purpose of telecommunications is 'to transmit representations of information (signals) between remote locations'. The signal carriers can be electrical, electromagnetic, or since the 1970s, light waves. Optical fibre cables are the medium for transmitting light waves.

The development of telecommunications has a great deal of kinship with that of computer science. In fact much of the equipment is common to both fields. Telephone, television, teletypewriters and terminals are just a few examples of engineering technology where improvements and developments are shared by both telecommunication and computing.

Telecommunications media transmit information in two ways: analog and digital. Analog transmission constitutes a jumble of frequencies which are in a continuous range (sound waves, light waves and temperature etc.) Digital transmission occurs in a stream of bits. The bits are binary digits which form a digital code. Not only can numbers, letters, and special symbols be converted into binary code, but sound, light waves, visuals and voice can also be converted. In fact any type of information can be transmitted in either analog or digital form. Some basic concepts are now briefly explained.

Simplex, Half-duplex and Full-duplex

The cables connecting terminals to a computer are generally of three types. Simplex cables permit transmission in one direction only. Half-duplex cables permit transmission in either direction but not at the same time. It means input must be received by the computer before output can be delivered. Many interactive computer system use full-duplex mode. It means data can travel either direction and simultaneously. In this system when information is input to a computer from a terminal, it is also printed at a terminal by a computer. The transmission both ways is so fast that the terminal prints what users input at virtually the same time it is typed on the keyboard.

Time-sharing Systems

The simultaneous interaction of two or more terminals with a computer system is called time-sharing. Many such systems employ a network of dedicated data grade cables. The OCLC network has thousands of terminals connected on dedicated cables.

Time-sharing is so powerful that more and more computer systems are designed for it. With time-sharing, the user inputs the programmeme on a terminal and gets virtually immediate feedback while still connected to the computer. Errors can be quickly edited and processing is much faster. Time-sharing is very much like a conversation. There is an interchange of information; questions and answers, back and forth. This system is often called interactive computing. It makes use of great deal of direct access storage, notably disk storage. This enables the computer to store and quickly retrieve information during processing.

Online *Vs.* Offline

When a terminal is communicating directly with a computer, it is said to be online. This term developed from telecommunications because, when a message was produced and sent in the same operation, the user was online. If the message was input via punched cards or paper tape, and then sent all at once, it would be off-line.

Online processing is often called real time processing. Here the user is working on the problem with the direct access to the computer system.

Terminals

Almost any device that is capable of transmitting or receiving information is regarded as a terminal. Terminals can be remote (from the main computer installation) and a batch or interactive.

Batch terminals allow large amount of batch processing. A simple remote batch terminal might consist of a card reader and a line printer coordinated by a control unit. Or it might contain a paper tape reader, paper tape punch, line printer and card reader etc.

Interactive terminals are now more common, and permit the keying in of data, the transmission of data to the control computer and within seconds, a computer response to the data received. A typical interactive terminal comprises either a VDU and its keyboard, and/or a printer.

Intelligent terminals do more than merely transmitting and receiving information. It has been programmemed to make logical decisions about the data that it handles. It can usually, examine, edit or validate the data, flag errors etc. It handles routine processing tasks without calling upon the main computer.

Transmission Media

The media that may be used for transmitting data are numerous. Twisted copper wires are used for normal telephone line. Coaxial cable is used in some telephone systems and for radio and TV transmission. Coaxial cables might be used for high quality bulk transmission at high speed. Optical fibres, which carry light waves, representing electrical impulses provide a very wide bandwidth and thus high transmission. It is identified that fibre cables have a bandwidth hundreds of times that of equivalent copper cables. One cable has been used that can transmit over one billion bits per second of information. It is estimated that fibre optics can transmit the entire contents of 30-volume encyclopaedia in one second, which may otherwise take several days using conventional transmission means.

Fibre optics is a technology which is to stay permanently. It has also found its way into computer engineering, reprography and a variety of other applications.

Cable Television

Cable television (CATV) appears to be a popular and cheap method of transmission of information even to home. Cable TV Companies (US) are literally wiring the community using coaxial cables that are capable of transmitting digital data as well as video, voice and facsimile. An extraordinary opportunity is emerging as more home computers are acquired, so, that the transmission capability of Cable Television, home computer, and Television receivers can be tied together. Since the Television Companies are required to make at least one channel available for public services, the library has an opportunity to interrelate with this new information service facility.

The potential applications to library and information of Cable Television (CATV) are therefore vast. It is stated that CATV offers public libraries the opportunity to expand two of their traditional services-children work and adult education.

Practically CATV takes the form of a TV camera used in the library to transmit a picture of a page of a reference book, illustration or other material over the cable network. Any user who telephones the library with an enquiry but has CATV facility can be shown material relating to their enquiry on their own television screen at home. Thus the marriage of libraries and television is an exciting and promising.

TELECOMMUNICATION NETWORKS

A data network always consists of host computer systems and remote terminals linked by a number of telecommunications channels. (See Figure.)

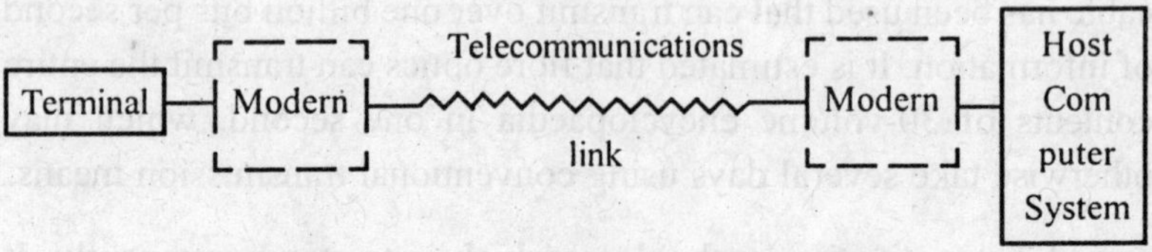

Fig. Linking a Terminal to a Computer System

These data networks have been developed to eliminate the public switched telephone network for carrying of digital information. The notable telecommunications networks are Telenet and Tymnet. These are predominantly North American, but have nodes in Europe, and other parts of the world. These two provides access to nearly all major American hosts. Access to Telenet and Tymnet from Europe is possible *via* agreements with the national Post, Telephone and Telegraph authorities (PTTs). In the United Kingdom, the International Packet Switch Stream (IPSS) enables searchers to access computers in North America. IPSS links to Tymnet, Telenet, Uninet and Autonet. Tymnet and Telenet now have many nodes all over the world. Many Arab countries too have access to Telenet, Tymnet, Uninet and Euronet.

Access to hosts in Europe is facilitated by Euronet Diane. A number of European hosts, including BLAISE, Infoline, DIMDI and Data-Star are accessible through Euronet. Euronet also provides links to other European networks. Hosts in Europe can also be contacted through the European part of IPSS network.

Other hosts also have their own networks. Dialog provides Dialnet as a link between California and London. SDC has a line from the USA to its computer in Working. ESA-IRS has Esanet which has a node in London. Most computers bureaux which host the factual databases have their own worldwide networks.

COMMUNICATIONS

To get into the national or international net-works a telephone link is used to access the closest node. Information is transmitted between the terminal and the host computer by direct-dialling or via PTTS in conjunction with datacommunications network or via a private leased telephone line. The data-bases available from the service suppliers are usually accessed over telecommunications network such as Tymnet or Telenet. Communications networks permit terminals to be connected to systems such as DIALOG, ORBIT or BLAISE by dialling the nearest node (*i.e.* an interchange point) of the network; this usually means a local telephone call to the network number. The user then pays as communication charge from the node to the host. Previously computer link-ups used cables designed to carry the spoken words; now packet-switching technology utilizes networks designed for the transmission of discrete packets of fast data signals via special high-grade paths between computers and terminals.

Information exchange is achieved over the communications network by the transmission of electrical signals in sound waves over the network distances between the user's terminal and the host computer. When the signals are transmitted, the computer's constant-

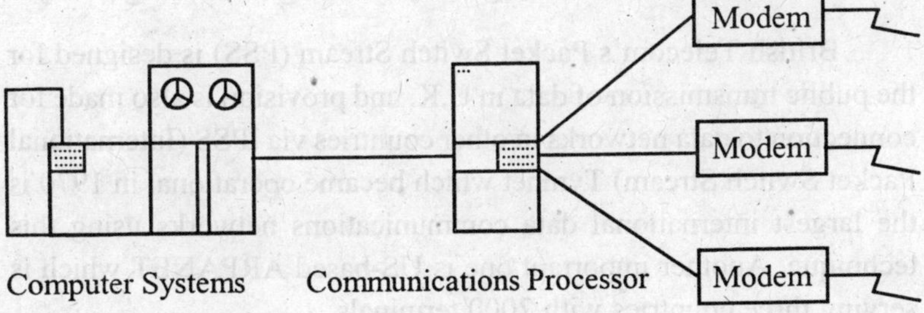

Fig. Communications Processor

level direct pulses are converted into signals suitable for transmission via telecommunications facilities. The reverse process is performed at the user's terminal. This process is called modulation and demodulation, and the device by which it is accomplished is the electrical coupler the modulator/demodulatior, or modem.

An acoustically coupled modem permits data to be transmitted via the receiver of the standard telephone. This coupler is connected to the terminal by a wired connection, and to the telephone network by an acoustic connection.

A modem is permanently Wired and converts digital messages *i.e.* bits which the terminal and computer understand, into analog messages *i.e.* sound waves, capable of being transmitted down to telephone lines. There is a special type of modem called acoustic couplers which are not permanently wired. These are often used in libraries.

Packet-switching Technique

As stated before, packet-switching system is now widely used. The technique of packet switching consists of breaking up each message in small packets and then switching each and every packet along the quickest communications path available at any instant. A minicomputer takes a thousand-word message and breaks it up into little packets, putting an electronic address on their fronts and another on their tails, as identification mark for each packet. The packets travel down different paths. They all stop at a mini-computer at the other end where the little packets are reassembled on the basis of their identification marks to generate the original message.

British Telecom's Packet Switch Stream (PSS) is designed for the public transmission of data in U.K. and provision is also made for connection to data networks in other countries via IPSS (International Packet Switch Stream) Tymnet which became operational in 1970 is the largest international data communications networks using this technique. Another important one is US-based ARPANET which is serving three countries with 2000 terminals.

LAN

A Local Area Network (LAN) is relatively new type of network which is used to link terminals and computer systems within one building or one local area. Due to close locations high speeds of data transmission are possible. LANs offer great potential use for the libraries.

Videotex and Teletext

Videotext and teletext were developed as a means of using existing equipment, that is to say, telephones, computers, microcomputers, and television receivers for additional information purposes. But the term 'videotex' was originally suggested by the Comite Consultatif International Telegraphique et Telephonique (CCITT) which is part of the International Telecommunications Union (ITU) responsible for standardization and tariff structures in telephony, telegraphy and data transmission.

Videotex

Videotex is used for a whole class of electronic systems which use a modified television set or a VDU to present computer-based information in a user-accessible visual form. As stated, videotex systems which use telephone lines, or other channels of communications that provide a two-way link, are known as interactive videotex or viewdata systems, whereas videotex systems in which information is broadcast to the terminals, are known as broadcast videotex or teletext systems.

In videotext technology a number of innovative approaches involving various combination of transmission technologies like telephone cable, TV cable, satellite, optical fibres have been recommended for videotext delivery. Personal Computers may become one kind of home terminal device used to approach videotext system. The users could store and interact with the information inexpensively through their home computers. They could get hard copy by using home facsimile or printing devices.

Teletext

Teletext services are broadcast information services which may be accessed in a non-interactive mode. These services may be accessed with a television and a telephone line but tend to be limited in the quantity of information that they can carry. In these systems a sequence of numbered information pages, or screensful of information, is broadcast cyclically over a television channel. The user Keys in the number of the required pages and that page is captured the next time it is transmitted and 'frozen' on the screen.

Videotext Services

Britain is credited for generating videotext services (formerly known as viewdata). There are in operation in Britain three videotext services; *(i)* CEEFAX (BBC), *(ii)* ORACLE (ITV), and *(iii)* the PRESTEL. The BBC service is known as CEEFAX and the ITV service is known as ORACLE. All the three services have been developed in Britain as a means of disseminating current information with the help of television equipment with special devices incorporated or attached.

Ceefax and Oracle are quite similar in nature. They involve selection of information by the user, using buttons on the decoder. Each is intended to offer about 200 pages of information—a page being the amount which can be shown on a television screen (920 characters) Colours are used, as are graphic displays. All the information for all the pages is sent by the same channel as is used for the television programmemes and simultaneously with them. It is transmitted continuously.

The PRESTEL service is different from CEEFAX and ORACLE services in that its signal is carried from the British Post Office to the User's television set via telephone line; and selection of particular pages of information is made by using the buttons on a push-button telephone.

In PRESTEL, by contrast to CEEFAX or ORACLE, only the information demanded by the individual user is transmitted, and it is transmitted only to him and only for the time he wants. Selection is carried out by computer at the transmission end. In sum, the PRESTEL service system is interactive *i.e.,* the subscriber cannot only receive data from the centre, but also respond to it with replies. But CEEFAX and ORACLE are not interactive services.

The other videotext services worth mentioning are West Law and LEXIS in USA for legal information, the application of CATV (USA) the Florida experiment of USA's Knight Ridder newspaper group, French P&PTIS viewdata terminal for home users replacing telephone directories.

Teleprinter

The teleprinter is to written word what the telephone is to the spoken word. It is a machine on which information is typed, the text is reproduced at a distance on a similar machine. The sending and receiving machines are connected by a telegraph cable or radio. A competent operator can transmit 35 to 40 words a minute. On some machines, the message to be transmitted can be coded on perforated paper tape and then transmitted automatically at 70 words a minute. Incoming messages can also be received in the form of perforated tape for subsequent decoding into printed form.

A teleprinter connected with the telex network may be left switched on but unattended throughout the day and night. Incoming messages are received and printed automatically - a service of particular importance for international communication between different time zones.

Teleprinters can also be purchased and installed internally for the purpose of communication between departments. They are ubiquitous in big libraries or information centres in industrialized countries and used to transmit reference information quickly and accurately.

Telefacsimile

Started in 1948 facsimile transmission is widely used in the libraries of U.S. and elsewhere. This is a system for transmitting visual images by scanning them at a transmitting station, sending them over a communication channel, and reconstructing them at a receiving station.

There are both analog and digital facsimile mechines and facsimile can be sent via cable, telephone lines, microwave and other means. Usually they are sent over telephone lines because it is economical. It takes from a few seconds to a few minutes per page to deliver facsimile documents.

David Heron has emphasized that the telefacsimile should be preferred due to its being faster, less expensive to operate rather than teletype writer manual system. Telefacsimile also known as facsimile or fax could be used for document delivery. Such a system will provide a copy of a page of text or graphics at a remote location using terrestrial or satellite links. There are a number of national and international organizations beginning to offer fax services.

Microfacsimile

It refers to the transmission of images on microforms to remotely located places electronically, where they may be received in the form of displays on screen, printed on paper or even in microforms. Thus it links two technologies *i.e.* facsimile transmission and micrographics to provide one of the useful information transmission systems. One of the recent developments is 'Telefiche' which consists of four integrated components:

1. A transmitter, called the Telefiche Image Processor, is both a microfiche storage and retrieval unit and a micro-image scanner capable of operating at a maximum resolution of 200 lines per inch. Micro-images are displayed on a rear-projection screen for operation verification prior to scanning. The Telefiche Image Processor's output is a compressed digital signal representing the information content of successive picture elements in the scanned image.

2. A choice of receiving terminals is available. For low volume printing requirements, a Rapifax 100 transreceiver will reconstruct microimage frames as enlarged paper prints at speed ranging from 25 to 90 seconds per frame. For high volume printing requirements, the Telefiche Digital Image Printer operates at a speed of 10 seconds per page (frame).

3. Where hard copy is not desired, a CRT terminal permits the high-speed, full-size display of alphanumeric or graphic images at remote locations.

4. The Telefiche system is designed for use with digital communication facilities.

Teleconferencing

Teleconferencing is a sort of network capability that uses the telephone as a medium for voice transmission, the television for video, and the computer for data transmission service. Data terminals are connected together via the telephone network. Three or more persons working on the same project can communicate with one another through terminals. One participant sends a message to many other participants for comments. Individual responses are appended to the original message and can be reviewed by other participants. These in turn may provoke responses which are themselves made available for review and comment. The result is a recorded dialogue which can be reviewed by all the authorized persons.

Teleconferencing removes barriers of time and geography and allows individuals to participate at their own pace. Donald D. Spencer reports that more than 20 million business meetings are held everyday in the U.S. Those firms which are equipped with proper teleconferencing equipment save travel time and money enormously.

Computerized Teleconferencing

Teleconferencing using audio and video-equipment, as indicated above, requires all the participants to be online at the same time. This more often poses problems. The device computerized teleconferencing permits the participants to attend meetings at their convenience. This is possible because the conference dialogue can be stored in computers.

A computer conference can be seen as something halfway between a conventional conference and a rapidly published newsletters. The system can be used by hundreds of people at diverse geographical locations. Each participant must have an access to a computer terminal connected to the conference network. One can sit at the terminal at a convenient time during the day call up any message and respond to them.

The system has a database containing a large number of text messages. The computer maintains a permanent history of all conference discussion. It remembers which message each user has already seen. When a terminal is switched on by a user, it displays all the entries which have not been seen. The user can directly write his own comments and messages which will be stored in the conference database.

Balagurusamy enumerates a number of advantages offered by computerized Teleconferencing as follow:

1. A person can take part in many ongoing conferences using much less time than for face-to-face meetings.
2. User can read and write at a time suitable to himself or herself.
3. Messages are well prepared.
4. Messages of less importance can be skipped.
5. User need not wait for a scheduled time to take up a problem. He can communicate on any day or as and when a problem comes up.
6. An issue or a problem could be addressed to a large group of people for their comments and suggestions. It is possible to consolidate the suggestions within a day or two.

7. People with different mother-tongues find it easier to understand written messages than spoken ones. They can take their time to read.

8. Since it does not involve any travel and stay, it not only saves money but also encourages even less interested people to participate.

Confravision

The British General Post Office is rendering another service known as CONFRAVISION. It enables meetings and conferences to be held by groups of people sitting in their own offices in various parts of the country. This service indicates the revolutionary changes that communication technology is brining about in all walks of life.

❐

2

Computer Architecture

Computing by mechanical means dates back to ancient time. The abacus has been used for thousands of years in China and Japan. This device satisfied most calculating requirements until the development of western societies which required assistance in managing large volumes of calculations. This led to the introduction of logarithms. These were developed by John Napier who published his first long tables in 1614. These devices provided methods by which multiplication and division could be achieved through addition and subtraction. In the 1620s William Oughtred developed the slide-rule based on the concept of logarithms. Both these inventions were widely used until the development of small electronic calculators in the late 1960s. Two further significant development took place in the seventeenth century. The first was the production of a mechanical calculator by Blaise Pascal in 1647. The second was a more effective calculator produced by Gottried Leibnitz in 1694 which performed multiplication and division. Although both the machines produced correct results, there were considerable problems still unsolved.

The work done by Charles Babbage in the nineteenth century is considered the next major development in the history of computer design. Babbage in 1821 designed his 'Difference Engine' and in 1832 his 'Analytical Engine', which is generally recognized as the milestone signifying the start of the computer age. Babbage's plans called for the machine to work from a set of instructions. These operating instructings would be stored in an appropriate sequence on punched cards. The Analytical Engine would also store information inside the machine so that the complex processing of numbers could be performed. From this perspective, it is clear that the ideas of internal memory, central processing, and storage of information on punched cards were actually conceived far ahead of their time. (Rowntree)

In the late 1800s, the idea of storing data on punched card was introduced in a tabulating machine. Herman Hollerith had developed this machine in 1883. Demographic data were stored on these cards and processed by the machine. This device was used in United States in 1890 census. (J. Rice) By the end of nineteenth century two key engineering concepts: a machine operated by set of instructions and data represented in code on cards had been established. Babbage's devices were purely mechanical whereas Hollerith's tabulator used electric power. In 1911 Hollerith's Tabulating Machine Company, which was founded in 1896, merged with two other companies, and in 1924 they became the International Business Machine Corporation (IBM).

In 1937, Howard Aiken, a Harvard graduate student in physics developed plans for an automatic digital calculator called Mark 1. Later IBM helped him making a large Automatic Sequence Controlled Calculator. It was a electromechanical device which performed automatically from stored instructions. During the coming years, scientists designed more powerful and more reliable computers. This involved a trend away from mechanical designs towards electronic designs. In 1946, a computer using vacuum tubes was built at the University of Pennsylvania named ENIAC. It is often called the first fully automatic electronic digital computer. One might not believe that the first computer weighted 30 tons, contained 18000 vacuum tubes, 70,000 resisters, 10,000 capacitors and 600 switches and cost amounted to U.S.$ 500,000. Still it was not considered reliable and would fail frequently. Research in the field of computing accelerated tremendously in the next four decades. Major advances however occurred in the following areas:

1. The ability to store greater amounts of information in the computer itself.

2. Speed of processing.
3. Miniaturization.
4. The ability to use instructions based on natural language.
5. The ability of the computer to interact with a variety of input/output remote terminals.
6. Auxiliary storage media such as floppy disk or CD-Rom Disk etc.
7. Marriage of computer with telecommunication and satellite communication.

Historically, the evolution of computers is divided into five generations. These are reviewed here in some detail.

First Generation of Computers

The first truly. electronic computer was the Electronic Numerical Integrator and calculator (ENIAC). It was completed in 1946 by Mauchly and Eckert at the University of Pennsylvania. It used high speed vacuum tube switching devices and had very small memory. It was basically designed to calculate the trajectories of missiles.

Commercial production of stored programme electronic computers began in the early 1950s. One of the early computers of this type was UNIVAC I. built by Univac division of Remington Rand. This computer also used vacuum tubes. As vacuum tubes used filaments as a source of electrons, they had a limited life.

During this period, computer programming was mainly done in machine language. Assembly language was invented in the early fifties. The initial applications was in the field of science and engineering.

The Second Generation

A big revolution in electronics took place with the advent of transistors by Bardeen, Brattain and Shockley in 1946. The first generation of computer had been characterized by the use of vacuum tubes in the electric circuity. This second generation used transistors instead of vacuum tubes. Transistors made of germanium semi-conductor material were highly reliable compared to tubes since transistors had no filament to burn. They occupied less space and used only a tenth of power required by tubes, and were ten times faster and cheaper than those using tubes.

During this period magnetic cores were invented. They were used to construct large random access memories. Magnetic disk storage was also developed during this period. High level languages such as Fortran, Cobol, Algol and Snobol were also developed during this generation.

The Third Generation

The third generation began in 1965. The germanium transistors were replaced by silicon transistors. This generation is characterized as "Integrated Circuits" computers. Integrated circuits, circuits consisting of transistors, registers, and capacitors grown on a single chip of silicon eliminating wired interconnection between components emerged on scene.

Significants improvements were brought about in the design of magnetic core memories, and magnetic disk technology. The combined effect of high memory, powerful CPU and large disk memories led to the development of time shared operating systems. Many important online systems became feasible. Airline reservation, interactive query systems were developed. Integrated data base management systems emerged.

High level languages improved. Fortran IV and optimizing Fortran compilers were developed. COBOL 68 was standardized. PL/I of IBM emerged and was a powerful language. The improvements in this period (1965-75) were substantial. This generation probably ended by 1975.

The Fourth Generation

The fourth generation of computer, in which we live is identified by the advent of the microprocessor chip. A large and a

Very Large Scale Integrated circuits (VLSI) packing about 50000 transistors in a chip is featured. Magnetic core memories have been replaced by semiconductor memories. The emergence of the microprocessor has led to two directions in computer development. One is the emergence of powerful personal computers. Computer cost has come down tremendously enabling anyone to buy it. Floppy disk provides a low cost high capacity back up peripheral memory.

The other direction of development is the decentralisation of computer organization. Individual microprocessor controls for terminals and peripheral devices have allowed the CPU to concentrate on processing the main programme. Networks of computers and distributed computer systems have been developed. Disk memories have become very large—CD-ROM being the latest invention. A significant development in software is the development of concurrent programming languages. Such languages are important to programme distributed systems and real time systems. Another important development is interactive graphic devices and language interfaces to graphic systems. Finally this generation has seen the coming of age of time shared interactive systems.

The Fifth Generation

What the fifth generation will contribute, is still unclear. In Japan research is making assault to develop artificial intelligence capable of accommodating functions such as intelligent conversation and inference functions employing knowledge bases. It would be a sublime achievement in the realm of computation research.

Expert systems are part of the broader science of Artificial Intelligence Systems, *i.e.* the fifth generation computer research programme as stated above. By Expert system means the computers that perform tasks that are usually performed by experts. These expert systems are quite new, highly sophisticated taking the users far beyond the limited functions of data processing storage or retrieval into the most exciting new area of decision making in the specific field of application. Although restricted in the type of tasks they can perform, demonstrate expertise in solving suitable problems. For instance robots are widely used in industrial sector. They keep the wheels of industry moving at all times. Once he is given programmemed instructions, the robot's mechanical arms do the work which normally require several pairs of human hands. The new robots (about 8000 are employed in the world) are not a simple mechanical arms, but intelligent, thinking devices that can 'see' what they are doing. Today robots can only 'see' but tomorrow they might 'hear' and then further develop the senses of touch and taste.

COMPUTER ARCHITECTURE

Hardware Aspects

The term hardware refers to the physical equipment of a computing system. In the early days the term hardware was used to denote mechanical devices such as analytical engine devised in 1833 to perform calculatings automatically using punched cards. In the 1940s the first electronic computer *i.e.* ENIAC, came into being. The equipment is known as hardware.

A computer system consists of three major groups of components. These are: hardware or equipment, software or the programmes, and the data or information which the hardware and software processes, stores, retrieves or manipulate. From hardware viewpoint a computer system may consist of several hundred thousand to several million electronic components. For a simplified description, a computer hardware components are generally divided into two broad groups:

(i) The computer itself. It is also called the central processor, the central processing unit (CPU) or graphically the mainframe.

(ii) The peripheral (input/output) devices. Peripheral means the devices which are associated with the CPU. They may be located around it; but are not a part of it. If a given peripheral is connected to the central processing unit it is said to be operating online, if not connected, it is called offline. (For diagram of a total computer system see figure 1).

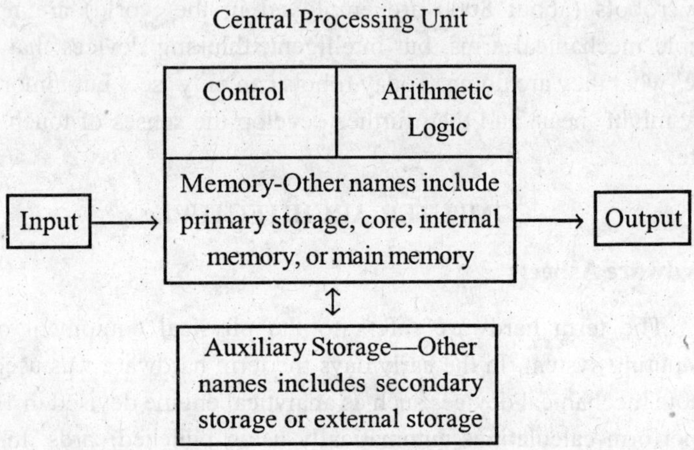

Fig. 1: A Total Computer System

This categorization is applicable almost to other types of information processing equipment including word processing systems, micrographic systems, and facsimile transmission systems. The various peripheral devices are design to perform one or more of the specialized information processing tasks such as input, output and storage.

Central Processing Unit (CPU)

Central Processing Unit is the central and the main unit of the computer. All manipulation and arrangements, arithmetic and logic operations or processing of data is performed in this unit. Sometimes CPU is referred to as the computer itself. It normally works under the control of a programme supplied to it by the computer programmemer. And a programme is a set of instructions which explains the complete logic of processing and direct the CPU to function. (See Figure 2).

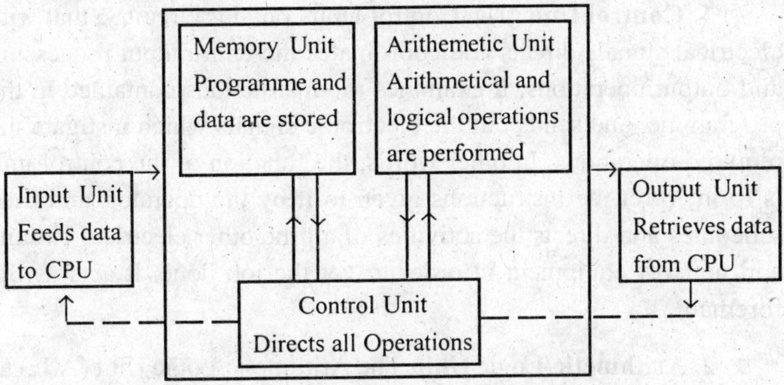

Fig. 2 : Central Processing Unit (CPU)

Functions of CPU Unit

The CPU performs at least the following six operations:

1. Provides, through the system, clock and controller all timing and control operations for the entire computer.
2. Fatches programmeme instructions and data from internal and external memories.
3. Transfers data to and from input and output devices.
4. Decodes instruction by assigning input code values to corresponding binary register values.
5. Manipulate data.
6. Alters the flow of instruction execution from signals generated by input and output devices.

The CPU contains the following three sub-units:

1. Control Unit.
2. Arithmetic/Logic Unit
3. Storage Unit

1. Control Unit. The Control Unit contains circuitry, that with electrical signals directs and coordinates the entire input processing and output operations. It examines the instructions contained in the programme, and sends out the electronic signals which instigate the required operations. In other words, the function of the control unit is to interpret the instructions given to it by the operator, and then schedules and directs the activities of all the other electrical circuits and units of equipment in order to get the job done. It acts as the foreman.

2. Arithmetic/Logic Unit. The Arithmetic/Logic Unit (A.L.U.) contains the electronic circuitry that controls all arithmetic and logical operations. It functions as the mill or processor which, under the leadership of the control unit, operates on the information given to it and perform all of the logical testing and processing required. It can perform arithmetic operations such as addition and multiplication as well as many logical operations such as comparisons, and the extractions of selected portions of a string of number or characters.

3. Storage Unit. The store or main memory of the computer holds items of information for as long as they are needed. The main store is used to store information currently being processed. The information may take the form of instructions constituting a programme to be executed, or data in which that programme is to operate.

The storage of a computer is not unlimited; it holds some maximum quantity of data. These data may be in the form of characters—usually, the digits 0 to 9, letter A to Z, and a number of special characters, such as *,.- + 0 $ @ # and %. The capacity of these memories is often used as a measure of the power of the computer. Storage devices are also rated by the speed with which data cim be withdrawn from them.

In early computer systems magnetic cores or rings were used, but now silicon chips are used which are much cheaper. The most common such memory can be written as well as read. There are four types of main memories, namely ROM, PROM, EPROM, and RAM.

A ROM or "Read Only Memory" refers to the memory composed of a chip with specific circuits designed to contain programmes and data that are permanently recorded into the memory and cannot be changed by the user. If the programme requires changes then the entire chip must be replaced and redesigned.

A PROM or "Programmemable Read Only Memory" is also used for specific application but does not need to be manipulated in large quantities. Rather simple chips may be programmemed by breaking connects between circuits holding the common value of all "Os" or all "IS".

EPROM or "Electronically Programmemable Read Only Memory" is constructed not by breaking circuits between values. It may be programmemed over an over again without being replaced. It is most expensive of all the memory types.

A RAM or "Random Access Memory" is a general purpose memory used by the Central Processing Unit (CPU) to store data and programmes. Random Access memory means that in order to know a value contained in the middle of the chip, there is no need to examine each circuit starting at the beginning and going forward one circuit at a time. Rather, the locations for the specific circuit values may be calculated and accessed randomly *i.e.* directly.

The individual units performing the above three functions are the sub-units of the CPU. They may be housed in a single physical unit or in more than one physical units. Generally, the Arithmetic/ Logic Unit, the Control Unit and some basic memory or primary storage are located in a single physical unit. Additional memory or auxiliary storage is attached to it in modules in additional physical units.

Backing Store

The information that is not currently being processed is kept on some form of backing storage device. This store actually provides the filing system for the computer and consists of magnetic tape reels. But in most mainframe computers backing stores magnetic disc is used. The input, output and backing store units together are called peripherals *i.e.* those which are outside and not part of main equipment.

Analog *vs.* Digital Computers

Analog computer accepts information for processing in physical form in terms of weight, volume, electric current etc. It can translate temperature, flow, speed altitude, voltage and other physical variable into related electrical quantities, and for this purpose it uses electrical equivalent circuits. It performs calculations on the incoming information according to a pre-determined pattern which is usually represented by mechanical, electro-mechanical or electronic units. The computer is usually built to satisfy a particular requirement and is mostly used for scientitic work. They are not suitable for library purpose.

Digital computer accepts information in a unitary form, *i.e.* letter, symbols and numbers. These may represent anything the computer user wants. All calculations or processing of the incoming data is done on the digital form, and the results are printed-out in conventional letters, symbols or numbers. It operates at a terrific high speed. The digital computers are general purpose computers suitable for information processing and are particularly suited to libraries.

METHODS OF PROCESSING

Three methods are identitied by which information can be processed by a computer system. These are:

(1) Batch Processing (offline)

(2) Real-Time Processing (online)

(3) Remote Job Entry Processing.

1. Batch Processing. The terms "batch processing" and real-time processing are commonly used to describe modes of data processing. Batch processing is a method of processing data in blocks or batches and prepared for computer input as a single unit. This means that one programme is finished before another is started and programmes are placed in a queue, or batched ready to be processed. Batch processing present problems for a librarian. First there will be a time delay before the results of a programme are obtained and secondly direct access to the computer is out of question. Therefore interaction with the programme or data file is not possible. Batch processing is one of the oldest and least costly mode of running programmes. Stephen Flowers outlines features of batch processing as follows:

1. Information held in batch-processing files is always out of date, silice it is only as recent as the last time a batch of transactions was submitted for processing. This may not be important for some applications.

2. Batch processing lends itself to the processing of large numbers of similar transactions which require careful checking.

3. It is easy to schedule processing at set times and therefore easier to organise work on a large computer with many competing users.

4. It is easier to control the input and processing of data with batch processing than with the on-line or distributed methods.

5. Transactions are passed to the computer centre for processing by specialist computer staff, with output being returned to the user to be stored or used at will.

6. Batch processing has been declining in use as on-line and distributed or remote job entry processing have been installed for applications requiring up-to-date information or decentralised computing facilities.

2. Real-Time Processing. Online processing is often called real time processing. In this system the terminals have a direct connection (or online) with the computer in such a way that data can be fed to the processor directly. The term 'real-time' means 'as they accur'. In this system, there is no need to present data in machine readable media such as punched cards or paper tape or magnetic tape because intake data are processed on arrival at the computer system and summarised instantaneously on the display screen as output.

Real-time processing derives from the fact that the computer can deliver the necessary output at the sametime the actual transaction is completed. In real-time processing many remote stations may be connected directly by the high-speed communication system with the central processor, and several stations may be operating at a time. In libraries a real-time circulation system has instant up-to-date circulation information available and is ready to complete the next transaction at once. Flowers features online processing as follows:

Features of On-line Processing

1. No delay in the processing of information, so that output can be received back as soon as processing is complete.

2. Associated with fairly low volumes of input and output from many separate locations combining to produce a high level of processing at the central computer.

3. Master files will always be up-to-date and reflect the current state of the business.

4. It is harder to control the quality of data input, since non-specialist users may be entering the data.

5. Increasingly used—it has been estimated that perhaps 75% of all processing may be done on-line by 1990.

6. The system will usually enable on-line enquiries to be made to the master file, requesting information on customer account balances etc.

3. Remote Job Entry. When batch and online processing is linked through an online terminal or typewriter like machine in order to enter a programme into the queue of programmes to be batch processed by the computer, this is called Remote Job Entry. When the computer has completed the programme the resultant tiles may be interrogated online from the terminal. (Tedd).

Bits, Bytes and Words

Binary digit or Bit is the basic unit of information storage used in all digital computer systems. In simple words computer memories use binary symbols (0. and 1) due to the nature of electronic circuits used in them. A bit is expressed by a high or low electrical voltage. Letters, numbers, punctuation marks, special symbols, etc. are represented by a specific combination or binary symbols for use with computers. The information (or input) to a computer consists only of symbols. Some of these symbols represent instrctions and the rest is data.

Bits can be group together to form a byte and a byte normally consists of 8 bits. A byte is often used to represent a character. And a "Character" is any letter, numeral, punctuation, mark or other symbol found in data. Byte being a unit of information consisting of a fixed number of bits, is treated as an entty for encoding a single letter, number or symbol. A number of coding schemes have been developed. For example the American Standard Code for Information Interchange (ASCII) uses 01100001 for the letter 'a' EBCDIC which stands for Extended Binary Code Decimal Interchange Code is another example. It is established by IBM and used extensively in the IBM 360/370 models as well as in the 4300 model series. This scheme of coding uses eight bits to represent a single character. The letter A for instance is represented by 110000l.

A computer's capacity that of both primary memory and secondary storage devices-is measured in bytes and expressed as a number followed by the symbol K or KB. 1KB stands for 1024 bytes. A computer having 128K of main memory can store 128 times 1024 bytes or characters.

While Byte is used to express the memory or storage capacity of CPU, the computer capacity is described in "words", a measure that denotes the number of bites the control unit can retrieve from the primary memory at one time. For example, an 8-bit word computer, can access 8 bits or one byte (one character) at a time. The word lengths of available computing devices range from 8 to 64-bits, although most of the machines installed in libraries have 8-or 16-bit word-length capacity. A word is thus a string of binary digits, which is treated as a single unit of data by a computer.

A computer's word can be used either for storing information or for storing instructions. A basic instruction is made up of two parts; firstly the operation code which describes what operation is to be performed and secondly the address (or addresses) of the data word (or words) which would be used for operation.

CLASSIFICATION OF COMPUTERS

Depending upon physical size, processing power, intended application and price, computers are generally categorized as mainframes, minicomputers and microcomputers. The differences among the three categories are ill-defined since the minis have become as fast and powerful as many mainframes and micros are challenging the minis. However the general range of their capabilities can be identified.

Mainframe

Mainframe or full-sized computers are very powerful and special-purpose equipment. They are designed for scientific or other research applications requiring extremely rapid execution of high volume of complex calculations. This type of computer is typically acquired by an organization such as university, research and industrial establishment to provide them a centralized service for a wide variety of purposes. Mainframes have a lot of storage facilities, enable the information to be input and output in a variety of ways. They can support a large number of terminals, provide a range of special features for the programmemer and so on. They are available in different sizes. At the low end of this product group, the small full-size computers are virtually, in some cases less powerful than the largest minicomputers. Their main memory capacities range from

512K to several megabytes. They access 32-bit words and their operation speeds are typically measured in microseconds (millionths of a second). On the other end of the full size computer group are so-called Supercomputers, very Powerful, special-purpose machines designed for scientific or other research applications requiring the very fast execution of a high volume of complex calculations. Their word size is 64 bits; their operating speeds are measured in fractions of a nanosecond (a billionth of a second). They provide main memory capacity for millions of characters.

Between these two extremes, most full-size computers are properly identified as medium or large-scale devices designed to perform the most commonly done scientific and data processing tasks. Medium-scale computers are generally faster and support a wide range of peripheral devices than the small full-size computers. They access 64-bits words, offer several megabytes of main memory and operating speed is measured in nanoseconds. Examples of mainframe computers include the Amdhal 470 series, Honeywell 6000 series, CDC 7600 series, IBM 370 series, etc.

Full-size computers are used in U.S. by bibliographic utilities, online search services and other organizations providing automated reference and technical services to libraries (Saffady).

Mini-computers

Produced in the late 1950s using the then technology of integrated circuits were called mini-computers. They are also available in a wide range of sizes and speeds. "Super-minis" are more powerful than some smaller full-sized computers. These are 32 bit word length machines; operating speed *i.e.* CPU speeds is measured in microseconds or even nanoseconds.

A typical mini-computers are with word length as 12 to 16 bits; operating speed measured in microseconds and main memory capacities of 512K to several megabytes etc.

American firm Digital Equipment Corporation has developed a variety of minicomputer such as PDP-II, DEC-10 and the VAX series. Minicomputers are acquired by individual departments such as a library or information unit and may be linked to a mainframe for the provision of extra processing requirements. Sometimes several minicomputers are linked together in order to provide a centralized computing resource within an organization.

Minicomputers are often incorporated in the turnkey systems developed for library applications: They are sometimes used to control all the input from, and output to, terminals linked to a mainframe computer. In general the speed, storage capacity, software facilities are not as great on minicomputer systems as on mainframe computers.

Microcomputer

The mini is being increasingly challenged by microcomputer on various reasons. Microcomputers appeared in the late 1970s when microprocessors were linked with appropriate storage and input and output devices to provide a computing system. They are now capable of storing a fair amount of information and provide a variety of programming possibilities. The first microcomputers were based on microprocessors with a word length of 8 bits. Examples of 8 bit microcomputers are Apple-II and Apple-III. More recent microcomputers are based on microprocessors with a word length of 16 bits and 32 bits thus providing faster processing speeds and increased storage facilities. 16-bit and 32-bit microprocessors support longer instruction; a larger, more versatile instruction set; and large memory configurations. Among 32 bit microcomputer the IBM Personal System/2 Model 80 is most suitable for library application.

Multi-user, multi-task microcomputers hold great promise for libralies on the ground that they can accommodate several terminals and can do several jobs concurrently.

Microcomputers have also become popular for individual computer use. They are identified as "Personal Computer", or more recently as "Professional Computer" and can be used by one person. The simplest personal computers incorporate a microprocessor, random access memory circuits and a Keyboard in a single unit designed to be attached to a television monitor. But personal computers are never recommended for use in libraries.

Saffady has pointed out that relatively few libraries and library systems have their own mainframe or full-sized computers. Many libraries have only access to full-sized computers operated by an institutional or corporate data processing centre. Although mainframe computers provide a centralized data processing facilities, a number of libraries have expressed dissatisfaction with such arrangements mainly because of un-responsive attitude of computer centre personnel and demand direct control over computing resources. Development in electronics technology, advent of silicon chip resulting in drastic low cost, availability of microcomputers and turnkey systems etc. have further increased libraries desire to have their own computer systems.

General Characteristics of Computer

A computer can be better understood from the various functions it can perform. But still the latest equipment lacks human intelligence and acts with its inherent limitations. Some of the interesting features of the computer are reviewed as follow:

1. Computers are built to carry out a small variety of instructions. It is not necessary to have more than about 100 distinct instructions even for a very powerful equipment.
2. Instructions are extremely simple *e.g.* add, subtract, read a character, write a character, compare number.
3. Instructions are carried out obediently with no question asked.
4. Most instructions are carried out in less than millionth of a second.
5. Instructions are carried out without any mistake.

Computer is like a servant who would carry out instructions obediently, uncritically at a very high speed, and without expressing any emotions. It must be understood that computers are machines which can be programmemed to follow instructions; they don't have their own priorities and judgments.

INPUT/OUTPUT CONCEPTS AND DEVICES

As discussed in the previous chapter the primary storage or internal storage of a computer is located within its central processing unit (CPU). Sometimes this unit itself is called computer. This chapter elucidates the variety of devices which work with the CPU to produce a complete computing task. These input/out auxiliary or seconday storage devices are often called peripherals because they communicate with the computer from outside the CPU.

In the early day of computers, practically all input was done by using punched cards and punched paper tape. Even output was on punched cards or paper tape which was then fed into machines like telex printers or tabulator printers.

As computer systems have developed crossing their four generations from off-line batch processing through multi-access and time-sharing systems to online, real-time systems, so input and output devices have improved and developed a lot in parallel. Fig. 3 projects input/output devices.

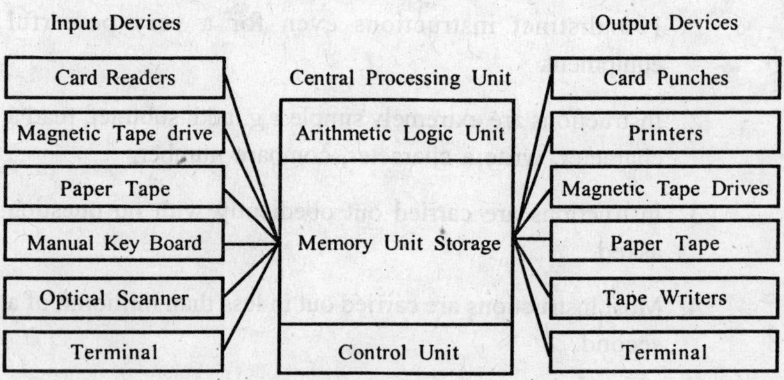

Fig. 3 Input/output Devices And CPU

Input Peripherals

The function of input peripherals is to convert human-readable information to machine-readable form required by the central processing unit. From amongst the available input peripherals, two types of equipment are commonly identified as being widely used. These are: Keyboard-oriented devices and optical recognition equipment. The Keyboard oriented devices feature a typewriter-like Keyboard on which the data are typed character by character. On the other hand optical recognition also called electronic scanning uses reflected light to determine the content of material. Once identified, the data are encoded and recorded on magnetic media or transmitted directly to a computer Fig 3. illustrates all methods of Input.

Keyboard Input

1. Punched Cards. The first generation of keyboard-oriented input equipment recorded data in machine-readable form on paper media such as cards or tape generally identified as Punched cards and Punched Paper Tape. The Key-punch machine converts individually typed characters to a specified pattern of holes punched in successive columns of a specially designed card. A card is divided into rows and columns. Each column usually encodes one character which also appears in its usual readable form at the top of the card. The most widely used cards are 80 columns with row numbered 0-9. They can store eight characters of information per card. The cards are subsequently read by a machine called a card reader. Some read the cards mechanically and some read the cards photo-electrically *i.e.* by passing light through the holes to detect the code.

Punched cards can also be output by a computer on device called a card punch. Other punched card devices include sorters, which require a deck of cards; reproducers which duplicate copies of punched cards, and verifiers which check the data on a card for accuracy.

Although keypunching cards is a slow process, the punched cards can be read at a rate of several thousand per minute.

A card is usually used to store a single record such as a user's name and address, the title and other data about a serial, or a publisher's name and address etc. Because of this, punched cards are often called unit records and their associated devices as unit record equipment.

2. Punched Paper Tape. Using keyboard, data are encoded on tape much the same way they are on punched cards. The tape is divided into columns (usually eight space wide) which run along the width. Information is encoded by punching the appropriate pattern of holes in each column.

Paper tape punches can be attached to typewriters, calculators, cash registers and other equipment so that information can be economically stored in computer-readable form. The computer record can therefore be produced at the same time as the actual typed document. (J.Rice).

3. Magnetic Tape. The typical key-to-tape unit is a microprocessor-controlled device which consists of a Keyboard, a cathode-ray tube (CRT) screen and a magnetic tape recorder. Character typed at the keyboard are displayed on the CRT screen and recorded on magnetic tape. The keyboard being electronic can accept keystrokes as fast as the operator can enter them. The typical key-to-tape machine produces a reel or cassette of magnetic tape which must then be taken to a tape reader for input to computer.

Magnetic tape is inexpensive and durable and stores a great-deal of heavily packed information. The computer can read tape much faster than it can read cards: several hundred thousand character per second.

4. Magnetic Disks. Magnetic disks are probably most commonly used type of storage medium. It is replacing tape. The key-to disk equipment consists of a CRT display with keyboard which operates online to computer. Characters entered at the keyboard are transmitted directly to a magnetic disk where they are stored pending later processing. In many applications, the terminal displays a formatted screen with labelled areas designed to prompt and guide the operator in entering specific data. Some key-to-disk systems feature sophisticated microprocessor controlled "intelligent" terminal which can be programmemed to perform certain data validation procedures before transmission. (Saffady).

Disks have several advantages over other media. Thousands of characters can be stored on each disk and the access time is extremely fast. Information can be input at a rate of about 200,000 characters per second.

Optical Recognition Devices

Since more sophisticated and powerful computing equipment are occupying the market, the old-fashion keyboard oriented data entry devices are considered time-consuming, labour-intensive and expensive activity. The optical recognition technology attempts to minimize data entry labour by substituting electronic scanning for keystroking.

Broadly defined, optical recognition uses reflected light to determine the content of material. Once identified, the data is encoded and recorded on magnetic media or transmitted directly to computer. Several types of optical recognition devices are designed for special applications.

1. Mark-Sense. Mark-sense recognition relies on a specially designed input document with predesigned spaces to be filled in by pencil. Completed documents are then scanned by a machine which determines the meaning of individual marks by their location. This device is widely used in educational application involving standardized multiple-choice examination. (Saffady).

2. Bar Coding. Bar code recognition is well known in libraries and retail stores. This device uses a specially designed label consisting of closely spaced lines of varying width to encode a number identifier. The label may be affixed to a document or other object and is scanned by a pencil shaped wand or a laser. The bar-coded label recognition device is used in library circulation systems.

3. Optical Character Recognition (OCR). OCR is another type of optical recognition technology. It uses reflected light to identify the individual character content of input documents-letters, numbers, punctuation marks or special symbols. Since character vary in size and shape, each will reflect light differently. An input device called and OCR reader scans the material and identifies individual characters by comparing their light reflectance properties with definitions already stored in the computer. The identified characters are then encoded in machine-readable computer-processible form. Keystroking labour is eliminated.

OCR although looks attractive, has not successful due to the high cost of character equipment.

4. Image Digitizer. While OCR readers accept textual documents as input a special type of optical recognition device called an image digitizer is designed to convert photographs, drawings and other graphic documents to machine-readable computer-processible forms. An image digitizer divides input documents into a series of rectangular picture elements, or pixels, each of which is analysed and its tonal value encoded. At present, image digitizers are not used for library application. (Saffady).

A final input technique which is still in its infancy, is speech input systems. The problems of machine recognition of human speech have proved difficult but some input devices do exist. Generally the machine is taught to recognize individual words spoken and will then be able to recognize and generate the appropriate codes for the word when spoken by that speaker. (Tedd).

OUTPUT PERIPHERALS

The function of output peripherals is to convert machine-readable, computer-processed data to human readable form. All output devices present the results of computer processing to users. A variety of output devices is available but not all of them are useful in library application. Instead, library automation relies only on those output peripherals which print information onto paper, record it on microfilm, or display it on a screen.

Although "Paperless" information is now available on large scale, paper printers still remain a very important type of computer output device. Even these computer systems which are heavily oriented towards screen displays use paper output for backup.

Printers

Quite a number of printers are available in the market. They vary considerably in technology, output characteristics, operating speed and intended application. One could choose a particular printer depending on the office needs. The common types of printers available are categorized as follow:

1. Impact Printers

(i) Line printer

(ii) Dot matrix printer

(iii) Daisy wheel printer

2. Non-Impact Printer

(i) Ink-jet printer

(ii) Laser printer

Impact printers have been around for a number of years. They print by striking the type against the ribbon and paper (similar to a simple typewriter). Printers that can print only one character at a time are called "character printers" as against the line printers" which print an entire line at a time. They can produce carbon copies, if necessary.

Non-impact printers are practically noiseless and create images only one at a time. They require special paper and provide better quality output than impact printers.

Line Printers

Line printer which prints an entire line at a time rather than a character is the fastest printer. Its speed varies from 300 to 3,000 lines per minute. It has been used in data processing applications for many years. They normally have 132 print positions per line.

Line printers generally produce only upper case (capital) letters though some provide both upper and lower case letters. The quality of printing is poor in terms of style and density for office use. However, they are used for internal reports in big organizations.

Dot Matrix Printer

Dot matrix printer is an impact printer which prints one character at a time. The print head comprises a matrix of tiny needles, usually seven rows and five columns. These are electrical driven and punch characters in the form of patterns of tiny dots. The pattern of dots for each character is dictated by the information held electronically in the printer.

Dot matrix printers can produce capital as well as lower case letters. Some printers have a capability of producing compressed or expanded letters. Its speed varies in the range from 40 to 600 characters per second. The printing is poor for business letters. Nevertheless, they are used extensively in word processing for internal correspondence and rough drafts. Matrix printers are much cheaper than the line printers.

Daisy Wheel Printers

Daisy wheel printer is a character printer and derives it name from the shape of the print wheel. The daisy shaped wheel is made of metal or plastic and holds characters on its petals. The wheel rotates at high speed and when the required character is positioned over the ribbon, a tiny hammer strikes it against the ribbon thus transferring the character symbol to the paper.

Daisy wheels are interchangeable and therefore different sizes and shapes of letters can be used. These are slow printers. The speed ranges from 17 to 200 characters per second. These produce good quality printing and are extensively used in word processing applications.

Ink-jet Printers

These printers print characters by spraying electrically charged ink onto the paper. These are capable of producing a variety of character shapes and sizes. The speed is around 100 characters per second.

Laser Printers

These are high speed, high quality printers. A laser beam is used to burn character images onto a rotating drum and the heated surface area picks up toner which is then offset to paper. Laser printers can produce around 15,000 characters per second. Though these can produce good quality characters of different styles and sizes and print even logos for letter heads, but are very expensive and are therefore not popular with small organizations.

COMPUTER OUTPUT MICROFILM (COM)

COM is a variant form of nonimpact output technology in which data is recorded on micro film rather than printed onto paper. Actually, a computer output microtilmer, or COM recorder, is both a computer peripheral device and a high-speed micro filmer capable of recording document images at rates ranging from slightly less than 10,000 to more than 40,000 lines per minute. COM recorders are expensive.

Two recording methods are widely used: *(1)* in CRT photography, information displayed on a cathode ray tube contained with the recorder is microfilmed by a specially designed camera; and *(2)* in laser beam recording a laser writes alphanumeric character on thermally sensitive microfilm. With either method, document images are recorded in greatly reduced size on rolls of 16 or 35 mm microfilm or on sheets of 105 × 148 microfiche. The computer produces an index to locate the proper role and frame for a given output.

COM is often employed to create a back-up medium or to store historical data from a computer system.

Screen Display (Terminals)

Third category of output peripherals displays the result of computer processed data on a screen. There screen-oriented output devices are collectively called video display units (VDUs) and they are most often built with a keyboard to enable the VDUs to operate as interactive computer terminals. The basic functions of any terminal are those of data entry, data display and data communication.

Terminals are basically of two types-printer terminals or video display units (VDUs) , although one terminal may include both print and display, facilities. A printer terminal consists of a keyboard and a printer on which are recorded both the characters typed by the user and the charactets transmitted by the computer.

The second type of terminal *i.e.* VDU consists of a television-like screen, which is used to display characters, and a keyboard. Most VDUs display 24 lines each of 80 characters, although some can now have 132 characters in a line.. VDUs normally display information using a technique known as faster scanning, from a cathode Ray Tube (CRT).

Auxiliary Storage Media and Devices

Auxiliary or secondary storage devices are designed to retain information in machine-readable form while awaiting computer processing. They supplement the necessarily limited capacity of the CPU's primary or main memory which is reserved for the storage of programmes and the data that the computer is processing at a given moment. Earlier computer systems used paper media such as punched cards or punched tape for recording and storing machine-readable data, but now magnetic storage devices have become the most widely used means of auxiliary storage.

There are two types of auxiliary storage: sequential and direct access. Sequential storage is non-addressable, *i.e.* one cannot directly refer to he contents of a particular storage location. Using sequential auxiliary storage such as magnetic tape or cassette tape, entails going through the tape in sequence to locate the desired information. It is a searching by starting at the beginning and searching through all data records until the desired information is found. Direct storage also called random storage, allows users immediate access to information. Magnetic disks, floppy disks, wincheseter disks, magnetic drum, and video disks are all forms of direct access storage.

Magnetic Tape

Magnetic tape is a principal input/output device which provides a rapid way of entering data and recording processed data. Information is recorded on magnetic tape as magnetized spots called bits. The recording can be retained indefinitely or the information can be erased automatically and the tape reused many times.

As used in full sized and minicomputers systems, the typical magnetic tape measures one-half inch wide by 2400 feet long and is wound on a plastic reel. Regardless of its housing the tape is divided across its width into seven or more commonly, nine parallel tracks, each track being intended for the recording of one bit. The accumulation of six or eight parallel bits encodes a single character. Data are grouped in clusters called a logical record. Each record is physically separated from the next by a blank space called an interrecord gap (IRG).

The magnetic tape drive is the mechanism that pulls the magnetic tape into position past the read/write head. The read/write head converts the magnetized bits it senses on the tape into electrical pulses and transmits them to the central processing unit. When data are being written onto the tape, the read/write head magnetizes the appropriate areas and simultaneously erases any information previously stored in that location.

Magnetic tape is widely used as auxiliary storage. Upto 640,000 numerical characters per second can be read from or written onto a tape. While tape drives operate online *i.e.* connected to computer, the tapes themselves are typically stored online. It is widely used in library application for the sale or exchange of bibliographic data. Magnetic tape is not a suitable storage medium for interactive and computing application in which data must be accessed rapidly and in more or less random order with respect to its recorded sequence. Such applications must use the more expensive direct access storage devices.

Magnetic Disk

Magnetic disk is used in full-sized minicomputer system. The typical magnetic disk is rigid, magnetic coated platter on which data is stored character by character in a series of concentric tracks, and is divided into a number of storage sectors. The surface is used to hold magnetised information that is written on and retrieved from the disk by a disk drive. In most cases two or more disks are aligned into a common spindle in a configuration called a disk pack. The capacity of disk packs varies with the number of platters and the density of recording at the present time ranges from 10 million to over 300 million characters.

Disks have several advantages over some other media. Their storage capacity, speed of access, reusability and ability to be in direct communication with the computer merit preference to tape media.

Although records stored on magnetic disks are often sequentially organized and processed like tape records, the popularity of disk storage is largely due to their direct access capabilities.

Floppy Disk

Floppy disks also called diskettes and flexible disks are popular media for auxiliary storage. They are widely used in microcomputer minicomputer, data entry, and word processing systems, as well as in remote terminals. The floppy disk is a compact flexible, magneticoxide-coated mylar disk. They are individually contained in envelopes or jackets for protection. It comes in three popular diameters: 20 cm, 13 em, 9 cm. The last two are called mini-floppy and microfloppy disk respectively.

Information is recorded in digital fashion on the disk's magnetic surface which it is rotating. Entire disk is inserted into disk drive for reading or writing. Almost all micros now make use of floppies as the main secondary storage medium. They are comparatively inexpensive compact and easy to use.

Winchester Disk

Quite recently introduced winchester disk uses thin-film technology that permits bit densities of 12000 per inch. Winchester disks are sealed modules that contain both a disk and a read/write head mechanism. The sealed conditions provides protection against contamination, crash and losing data. For these reasons they are extremely reliable, and provide highest storage capacity.

Magnetic Drums

A less frequently employed form of direct-access storage is magnetic drum. It functions in much the same manner as disks. Data is recorded in tracks on magnetic-coated cylinder which rotates to position a specified sector of a given track under a read/write head. Although operate at somewhat faster reading and writing speed, they offer less storage capacity and are somewhat more expensive.

Optical Storage

Optical disks and video disks represent an important and rapidly growing technology. Both the CD-ROM (computer disk/read only memory) or simply known as the "compact disk" and video disk are types of optical storage made possible by laser optics. VIDEO DISKS can store both pictures and text in extremely high density and provide fast access to individual frames on a disk. The visual images such as pictures, graphics, charts or print can be retrieved in motion picture form (for a movie) or still pictures, and can be retrieved in slow motion or reverse. A video disk is about the size of a long-playing record and can hold several hours of television pictures and sound or the equivalence of more than 50,000 photographic slides.

The use of videodisks with the computer system is still in the early development stage. One drawback is that videodisks only have play-back capacity; they cannot have data written on them. Therefore most applications involve entertainment and the storage of information is not dynamic in nature.

An OPTICAL DISK is next of kin to a videodisk. Binary digits are stored on this medium optically (using laser light) rather than magnetically. Optical disks store information with much higher density than magnetic disks do, and they provide extremely rapid access. Nearly all optical disks now in use are in a form of read only memory device. This means it cannot be re-recorded (like videodisk) over an over like magnetic media. However, the recent advant of erasable disk has solved this problem. (J. Rice).

One advantage of the optical disk is that plastic material used in the disk is not expensive. Optical storage is also now being packaged in other forms besides disks. These include cartridges and cards.

CD-ROM is designed specifically for machine-readable, computer processible data. Its main feature is that it is a permanent form of storage and the data recorded cannot be altered. It is being used as a means of distributing large amounts of information in a compact form. With 550 megabytes of data CD-ROM is useful medium for database publishing. The majority of CD-ROM publications produced to date are reference and research data bases designed for the library market where they offer a potentially cost effective alternative or supplement to equivalent databases offered by online search services on a timeshearing basis. One CD-ROM can accommodate complete Encyclopaedia Britannica. CD-ROM can also replace computer output microfilm in certain types of micropublishing applications. The disks are read by relatively inexpensive drives (Saffady).

A typical CD-ROM can store about 300,000 book pages. The collection of Library of Congress Prints and Photographic Reading Room are on Videodisks, each of which holds about 54,000 separate pictures. (W.A.Katz).

Still another variety of compact disk is called COMPACT DISK-INTERACTIVE (CD-1). It is similar to CD-ROM, but has the advantage of storing not only text, but video and audio as well on a single medium.

Holographic Storage

Recently a new form of storage device using laser technology to store information on holographic film is seen. Three-dimensional images can be stored and then read by lightsensitive electronic equipment. This enables binary information to be stored optically yielding an extremely high capacity and yet very rapid access. (J. Rice)

Mass Storage Devices

Where very large (multibillion or trillion character) data storage capacity is required, several available mass storage systems employ magnetic-coated tubes or strips stored in specially designed data cells. These data cells provide a kind of online tertiary storage for information which is used relatively infrequently and would otherwise have to be removed offline, or "archived" to magnetic tape (Saffady). An example of such a device is the IBM Mass Storage System.

❒

3

Software Aspects

Computer are terrific problem solvers, but they can't do their work without assistance. All computer equipment including the central processing unit and all of its online and offline peripheral devices such as visual displays, magnetic disk drives, printers and data preparation devices are called hardware. This physical equipment won't work without programmes that instruct and guide the operations of each device. These programmes is called software; without them computer systems are as useless as a car without fuel. Tedd defines it as: "software is the general term used to describe the types of programmes, or lists of instructions which are needed to enable the computer system to carry out the necessary processing." (Spencer)

Unlike different car models which can run on the same types of fuel, computer hardware cannot be run on just one kind of software. Thus software is machine-specific-what runs on one machine may not run on another system and vice versa. Whether it is on disk, cassette, magnetic tape, or plug-in modules, software is designed specifically for one type of machine and is not compatible with other hardware.

Some computer manufacturers provide total hardware and software, or turnkey systems for library applications. But more often the hardware and software are supplied separately. Therefore, the librarians interested in acquiring any computer systems have to decide what software should be purchased as well as what hardware.

TYPES OF SOFTWARE

There are basically two types of software: system software and application software. Both are essential before any useful work can be obtained from computer systems. All computer software is made up of programmes.

System Software

System software means collection of those programmes which enable a computer to function and control its own operation. They are routines residing in the computer's memory that help the programmer to write, test, modify or execute an applications programme. This type of software makes computers easier to use because it facilitates communications between the machine and its operator or programmer. System software is further divided into three categories:

1. Operating Systems. Modern computer hardware is highly powerful and complicated which more often creates difficult situation for the users. The operating system serves as an interface between the user and the computer. In other words it acts as intermediary between the user and the computer accepting and responding to commands submitted in a special job control language (JCL). It is a programme that controls the operation of various computer resources. For example it determines which programme of instructions the central processing unit works on at each point time. It allocates primary storage space to programmes and data. It shifts progress and data from lower levels of storage to main storage and back again.

The Operating System (OS) is a large and complex programme that determines how a particular computer's CPU accepts incoming signals, transmits ongoing signals, allocates storage space to individual use and programme, control the various peripheral devices, permits access to various files of data and accomplishes other house keeping tasks. Thus the purpose of the operating system is to manage computer hardware so that it is used as efficiently as possible. For instance, a CPU operates much faster than lower levels of storage and other I/O devices. Because of this as resorts to multiprogramming and it interupts to keep the CPU busy. Multiprogramming has led to the use of virtual memory. The virtual storage system attempts to make internal storage appear larger than it really is through the use of an extremely fast auxiliazy storage device located close to the CPU. When virtual storage is used, portion of data files and programmes are moved-back and forth between it and internal storage by the operating system. Thus the operating system becomes an extremely dynamic manager of space, changing the contents of internal storage in response to the user's needs.

Operating systems are divided intô single user and multi-user as. Those operating systems designed for personal computer, handle one task only at a time, but now multitask as are available on PC. The operating systems designed for mainframe, minicomputer, and microcomputers are capable of multiprogramming—that is maintaining two or more programmes in main memory and executing two or more tasks simultaneously. The operating system is normally written by the computer manufacturer and provided with their equipment.

2. Utility Programme. Utility programmes are routine programmes of general nature which are often required to be used during the processing of the application systems and testing of the programmes. Examples of these programmes are file conversion programmes like copying a card file to a magnetic tape, magnetic tape to disk, print out of magnetic tape or disk, card to print, printing the contents of the CPU memory etc. Other common utility programmes are designed to sort data into a predefined sequence or to merge two or more sets of presorted data. Other programmes assist in the detection and correction of errors or "bugs" faced during programme testing.

Utility programmes may be obtained from computer equipment manufacturers or companies specializing in software development, or may be developed by local programmers.

3. Data Base Management Systems. The term database generally refers to a machine-readable file of bibliographic records, for example the MARC database. However in computer science the term is also used to refer to a more general shared collection of data which is used by several, often many, applications programmes. The software which handles all access to such a database is known as a database management system (DBMS). The system has become a popular way of handling large files of nonnumerical data, including bibliographic information. The formal definition of data base management systems is "a data base management system allows multiple independent users to have concurrent access to a central repository of information". Tedd with reference to Kvitsand describes the components of a DBMS as under:

(1) Provides a way of describing the structure of the data.

(2) Enables existing data to be incorporated into the new database.

(3) Provides facilities for the manipulation of data from application programmes.

(4) Enables the database to be maintained and updated as and when necessary.

A DBMS eliminates data redundancy. Each bibliographic record has to be entered only once as a DBMS permits access to the entire record through any of its fields. Before the development of DBMSs, one had to either create separate files for each required access approach—author, title, subject, call number ete;—or create multiple indexes to the bibliographic file at the time the data base was being developed. A DBMS provides the ability to modify and even restructure the database without affecting existing programmes or creating new file structure. This facility is known as data independence.

The design and architecture of almost all DBMS software packages permit multiple independent users to access common data. When the same data are accessed by independent users, data are said to be "shared". Again sharing means not only that the data base can be accessed by multiple independent users, but it can also be accessed by multiple users at the same time.

A DBMS is more important when several users are working with the data base at the same time than when data are accessed serially because concurrent users can more easily interfere with each other's use of the data base. A DBMS does require the use of considerable computer resources, but this can be justified by the benefits it provides. A DBMS is most useful in an online environment with large data bases and a need for concurrency.

DBMS software are available on mainframe and minicomputer systems. ADABAS is one example of such a DBMS. Data Retrieval System (DRS) is used in US and INFO is used in the UK by various libraries. One of the most sophisticated DBMS packages available on microcomputers is MDBS-microdatabase management system. Another popular DBMS package for microcomputers is Dbase II, III & IV developed by Ashton-Tate in the US and is used by many libraries. The advent of DBMS software on microcomputer has radically resolved library problems. A number of libraries and information units in US are using standard DBMS or DMS software, and adopting their data if necessary, rather than develop special purpose programmes.

The medium of communication with the computer is the computer language. Since all the computers understand the coded programmes, such programmes are known as the coded language. If the coded languages are machine-dependent, they are called lower level language. But there are now several machine-independent languages: they are known as higher-level language.

All computer programmes are written in programming languages. System software too is written in a programming language, but the term is most commonly used in connection with application software. Three other examples of system software, *i.e.* assemblers, compilers and interpreters are also discussed here because they function as "Translator" of programming languages.

TYPES OF PROGRAMMING LANGUAGES

Computers use different programming languages just as people in various parts of the world speak different languages. Programming is therefore key to successful computer use. As stated earlier, it involves writing a set of instructions in a sequence that produces a desired result when the sequence is executed by the computer. There are many different levels of programming languages levels of coding) but they are generally organized into the following categories: *(1)* Machine Language, *(2)* Assembly Language, *(3)* Higher-level Language.

All programming languages except machine language are symbolic and must be translated into machine language instructions. Symbolic coding involves programming a computer to recognize instructions in a language more easily understood by the user and then translating these expressions into machine language.

1. Machine Language. Machine language is the common language of a particular computer and does not require further modification before use. A programme written in machine language is a sequence of binary numbers (I's and O's) Once the problem is identified, the programmer codes the operation using codes the computer can interpret. Basic instructions to a computer consists of operations such as add, subtract, multiply, divide, store, read, write etc.

As stated above, a machine language comprises numeric symbols and is designed for use by a computer directly without translation. Machine language consists of the total set or stock of operations instructions the machine can perform. For instance a hundred different instructions including input/out as well as arithmetical operations for handling numeric data and logical operations for handling alphanumeric data. A decimal number is converted into the corresponding binary number when the instruction is read into the CPU.

The translation of data from alphanumeric symbols to binary codes and back is done by the computer itself. The computer programmers normally write their instructions using either assembler language or a higher level language.

2. Assembly Language.. Assembly language is similar to machine language but it has been designed to facilitate human understanding. Symbols and abbreviations are used in assembly language instead of I's and O's (bits) used in machine language. Writing programmes using mnemonic commands in place of binary codes has made software development process more efficient. In assembly language, it is common to use mnemonic codes in programming such as ADD, MOV (move) and STO (Store). These commands are much easier for a programmer to remember than the machine-level counterparts. Frequently used instruction sequences can be combined into a single mnemonic code.

Although easier to write, the individual instructions comprising assembly language programmes are then translated into the binary-coded machine language that the computer requires. This translation is performed automatically by the computer using a special programme called is assembler. The assembly routine reads the symbolic programme from input such as punched cards, translates the mnemonic operation codes to machine operation codes and assigns memory locations for storing instruction and data. The assembler outputs a machine- language programme.

The advantage of the symbolic coding and assembly programme compared with coding directly in machine coding are as follow:

1. Coding is easier, since the programmer can use easy-to-remember mnemonic and symbolic address tags.
2. If a programme is changed later on or if two programmes are combined, machine language programming would require extensive checking to prevent incompatible memory location use. Programmes written in symbolic code are merely reassembled to provide a reassignment of memory locations.
3. The assembly routine provides diagnostic routines to detect errors.

Since assembly language is akin to machine language, it is most often used in those situations where the programmer requires very close control over the internal operation of CPU. Although it is suitable for writing applications programmes, assembly language is relatively slow to use from the standpoint of the programmer. While they differ in ease of use, machine language and assembly language are collectively called lowerlevel languages. As a result, applications software is now usually written in one of the so-called higher-level programming languages such as COBOL FORTRAN etc.

3. Higher-level Languages. In contrast to machine and assembly languages which are machine-dependent, higher-level languages are relatively machine-independent. Higher level languages are closer to natural language. Many higher-level language allow the use of English-language commands. Higher language programmes are easier, faster and less expensive to develop than those written in machine or assembly language. The higher level languages are often called application languages. A variety of such languages has been developed: the most popular are FORTRAN, COBOL PL/l, BASIC and Pascal.

Examples of Higher-Level Languages:

1. Algol 60. Algol 60 was designed by an international Committee in 1960 for the solution of scientific problems, but has been used for some library applications. It has influenced the design of nearly all more modern language (Tedd).

2. Basic. Basic, or Beginner's all-purpose symbolic instruction code, was designed by J. Kemeny and T.E. Kurtz of Dartmouth College, New Jersey to be an easy to-learn language suitable for beginners. Nearly all microcomputers have facilities for writing Basic programmes and although it is a fairly simple language it has been used for a number of library applications.

3. Comit. Comit has string manipulation facility like SNOBOL. Being a higher-level language, it is relatively easy to learn. It is a special purpose language and can work in a limited field. COMIT is basically designed for use in studies of mechanical translation of human language. SNOBOL IV and COMIT-the string processing programme languages are used only where highly complex bibliographic records are to be manipulated.

4. Cobol. Cobol stands for Common Business Oriented Language and was desigped in the late 1950s. Most library applications have more in common with business than science and so COBOL has been used for programming many library systems.

5. Fortran. Fortran stands for Formula Translator and was designed, mainly by people working at IBM, in the US in the mid-1950s. There have been several versions of the language accepted as standard by the American National Standards Institute (ANSI). During the early 1970s the standard was known as Fortran IV and the current standard is known as Fortran 77. Fortran has been used for many library applications programmes.

6. PL/l. This stands for Programming Language One, which was designed in the mid-1960s to combine the file-handling properties of Cobol, the numerical features of Fortran and the Structure of Algol 60. (Tedd).

7. Pascal. This was designed by Nicklaus Wirth, in Zurich, in the early 1970s. It is gaining favour amongst some as a better language for beginners than Basic. It is available on many microcomputer systems.

8. Snobol. Stands for string-oriented symbolic language. This programme language has string-manipulation facility as in PL/l. It is the unique programme language that provides complete facilities for the manipulation of strings of characters and capability in programme compilation and generation of symbolic operations. The revised version of SNOBOL is SNOBOL IV. It can perform general data processing functions.

Higher-Ievel languages are either procedure-oriented or problem oriented. Most are procedure-oriented, designed for writing logical sequences of instructions. COBOL is typical example. Problem-oriented languages are designed for solving specific types of problems.

Higher-level languages offer some advantages such as: *(1)* require fewer instructions to accomplish a task than assembler languages, *(2)* provide instructions specifically oriented towards the problem at hand, and *(3)* tend to be relatively "portable" meaning that a programme written in PASCAL for an IBM mainframe computer is likely to work on a DEC minicomputer (assuming that both have PASCAL compilers) and with only minor changes may also work on an Apple microcomputer.

Compilers And Interpreters

All the higher level languages are finally translated into the machine language which is processed by the computer. The translation of higher level languages is accomplished by two kinds of software: *Compilers* and *Interpreters*. Compilers translate the complete programme, written in a high-level language called a "source language" into the equivalent machine level programme before the programme is actually executed by the computer. An interpreter, on the other hand, translates each instructions separately as the computer needs it in order to process a given task. It means the interpreter must go back and forth from the programme many a time for complete execution. In this process erroneous instructions are quickly detected and eliminated. However interpreters execute programmes more slowly than those executed by compilers. Like assemblers, both compilers and interpreters are system software and, as such are typically obtained from computer equipment manufacturers.

Command Language

Many programmes, written to accomplish tasks contain keywords that make the programmes perform certain functions. For example a simple programme may include five commands: Search, Edit, Delete, Save and Merge ete. These are operation instructions which enable the users to learn and use software more easily. With these instructions, a user of the programme can perform all of the functions of maintaining the user file. These instructions might be called the command language of the programme.

Most modern computing systems of all types have an operating language which is contained within the programme and which enables untrained users to perform system functions. Although the software itself is written in high-level language and is translated by a compiler into machine language, the user of the system never comes into contract with any of these levels of the software. The only instructions the user needs to know to perform the function of the system is the command language itself. In this sense one can refer the command languages as the highest level of software (J. Rice).

Command languages are also part of any sharing system, computer network, or online search service. These languages are developed carefully to be learned by users who have no knowledge of programming (J. Rice)

APPLICATION SOFTWARE

A computer application software is a user programme. It is a set of instructions which tells the computer how to execute a specific task on the particular set of data provided. Application software for libraries contains a sequence of instructions designed to perform tasks such as preparing list of defaulters, list of outstanding book order, list of journals received and numerous other specific tasks done in library operation. Application software can be categorized in number of ways. These can be broadly presented as follow:

1. Organizational information processing (data processing and MIS)
2. Mathematical, statistical and modeling.
3. Information retrieval.
4. computer-assisted instructions.
5. Data Communication.
6. Process control.

The basic approach to develop and execute application software is very much similar for all types of computer application. The programme is developed on a sequence of operations technically referred to as an algorithm. (Fig. 1 illustrates steps for programming.) An algorithm may be defined as a finite sequence of instructions to solve a problem. It is like a formula or recipe, in that its application will always produce an identical result if it is followed precisely. An algorithm is always developed by the programmer to solve a specific problem at hand and that in turn is used for developing a computer programme. Much time is spent in inventing, refining and perfecting algorithms to solve specific problems. It is common to express an algorithm in the form of a flow chart, using boxes of various shapes to denote various functions. (Figure 2 is an example of a typical task oriented flowchart illustrating the algorithm.)

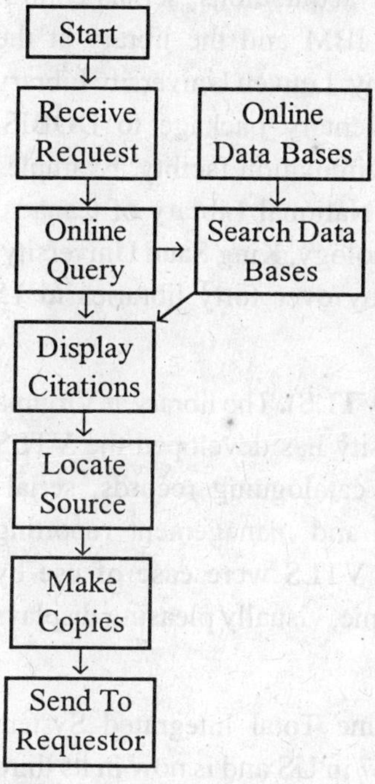

Fig. 2: Task Oriented Flowchart

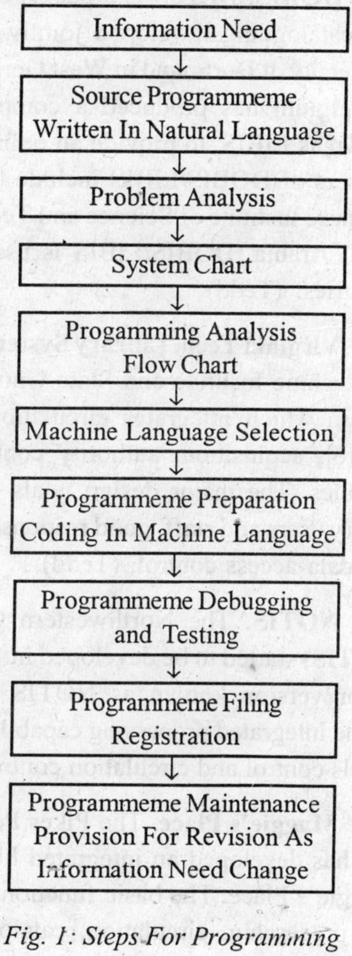

Fig. 1: Steps For Programming

As stated above developing application software is the user's responsibility. In general it is not supplied by the computer manufacturer. It is developed in-house or obtained from some other supplier. But writing in-house software is expensive and time-consuming. Instead the users prefer to purchase. packaged or prewritten software. Some of the well known packages developed as integrated library systems are discussed here briefly.

Packaged Library Application Software

DOBIS. DOBIS is a package for acquisitions, serials control and cataloguing developed jointly by IBM and the library at the University of Dortmund in West Germany. Leuven University Library in Belgium has produced a complementary package to DOBIS, known as LIBIS, to provide an online circulation facility. Examples of users of DOBIS/LIBIS include the National Library of Canada, Japanese Institute of Science and Technology, King Saud University, Saudi Arabia. DOBIS/LIBIS is used by over forty libraries in 15 countries. (Tedd).

Virginia Tech. Library System (VTLS). The library at Virginia Polytechnic Institute and State University has developed the VTLS system which integrates circulations, cataloguing records, serials control, acquisition, authority control and management reporting modules. The major design goals for VTLS were ease of use by library users and staff, good response time, visually pleasing displays and data access control. (Tedd).

NOTIS. The Northwestern Online Total Integrated System (NOTIS) started to be developed in 1967 in US and is now in its third major version known as NOTIS III. It provides comprehensive online integrated processing capabilities for cataloguing, acquisition, serials control and circulation control.

Maggie's Place. The Pikes Peak Library District in Colorado, US, has developed an integrated library system which is known as Maggie's Place. The basic functions supported include acquisitions, and processing, circulation, catalogue access, serials control and management. The community information file is also processed by the package.

The five longest turnkey (system) vendors are: CLSI, CTI, Library systems Inc., Data-Phase Systems, Geac Canada Ltd. and Universal Library Systems Ltd. The supply of application software, in these cases is a part and parcel of hardware.

Pak Book Library Package

In Pakistan Pak Book Corporation has developed a user friendly software package (by using PCS Micro-Computers) to automatic library activities such as:

1. Inventory control.
2. Ordering and acquisition.
3. Cataloguing.
4. Circulation.
5. Serials control.
6. Information retrieval.

It is a first standard software package developed by a Pakistani firm to operate outline. It may be preferred to in-house stand-alone system which is always expensive for small libraries.

The package has been developed under Foxbase Version 2.1 (Which is the fastest database manager available in the market). It has been designed to run on IBM or IBM compatible Computers-XT or AT with colour monitors (Screens) and DOS Operating Systems. However it can be used on monochrome (single colour) screens.

SOFTWARE DOCUMENTATION

Documentation is the set of materials which actually describe the purpose, operation, use and structure of computer programmes. When a prewritten software is obtained, it is necessary for the purchaser to be well trained for ongoing software maintenance and use. Documentation therefore comprises detailed written information about the development of the software and the various aspects of the system. During the development of a computer programme, documentation of how the programme was designed is essential so that all people involved in a project will know what has been done and pass on this information to others. The system analysts and programmeers involved in a given software development effort are normally responsible for preparing appropriate documentation.

Davis and Rush, as quoted by Tedd, state that a complete software documentation package should include the following elements:

1. A statement of the problem to be solved.
2. A detailed description of the functions the software is to perform, and the functions that it permits the user to perform.
3. Definition of file structures to be used by the software.
4. Definition of the data structure to be used.
5. Overall software design including algorithms to be used.
6. Computer system resources which the software will need for successful execution.
7. Definition of the data contents acceptable in these data structures.
8. Other resources requirements (Personnel, equipment, materials).
9. Specification of the test data and procedures to be used to determine correct performance of the software once written.

After the programmes have been written and tested:

1. Test results and software evaluation.
2. Execution cost estimates.

3. Detailed description of how the software works.
4. User manual.
5. Operations manual.

James Rice adds that the best documentation also includes self-teaching material (tutorials) to train users how to use the package. Because higher level languages are much closer to material language, it is understandable that their documentation would also be much easier to develop and much easier to understand.

ELECTRONIC SERVICES

Library management systems are but a segment of a world of information technology and elsewhere there are a variety of systems which are designed primarily to present the customer with information which they can use directly, but in electronic form. In the last survey hyperbole was necessary to describe the impact that the CD Rom had made on public libraries. LIke the compact disc in the audio market, the CD Rom has been the high flier of the late 1980s and will continue to change the way that we operate as librarians (and listeners) well into the 90s. Just to remind you, before looking more closely at the data from the present survey, in 1987 two libraries indicated that they were considering using CD Rom while in 1989, 49 were actually in the thick of it.

In four years the number has gone up 50 times, since 1989 it has more than doubled. Any way you look at it, CD Rom is a popular delivery system for information and is likely to continue its sweep through public libraries. The data are pretty self-evident, there are increases everywhere. Northern Ireland scores a full house while all other authorities show a rapid take-up. Only Scotland and the Non-Mets lag behind the 60% and over which is seen elsewhere. I commented last time that the size of these two exceptions might create barriers to buying the system and that still seems to be the case; although the relative cheapness of the hardware and the real savings and benefits of using Bookbank, for example, continue to raise question marks about these discrepancies. There are in the end only two possibilities. Either the scale of operations in these two types of authority is such that resources cannot be found for what elsewhere is spreading like wild-fire or, the nature of demand means that other priorities must take precedence. Looking closely it is not clear that all authorities are using Bookbank, although the vast majority are. Indeed it may well be that those who did not report its use felt that it was not worth mentioning! The data also show, however, that a wide range of databases are now in use, ranging from those of local relevance, such as the Northern Echo (affectionately known as Panda), to national newspapers, official publications, British Standards and the odd encyclopedia. Selection tools remain a popular sue for the CD Rom equipment and alongside Bookbank we now find Bookfind (from Bookdata), American Books in Print, BNB and the British Library Catalogue. Respondents were asked to indicate whether the systems were staff only or made available directly to the public, without staff intervention. Of the 101 total, 66 indicated that their systems were staff only while nine report direct use by the public. That leaves 26 who said nothing about access. From the databases the 26 'question marks' are using I am pretty sure that they are not providing public access, which means that only about one tenth of CD Romers are allowing customers to get their hands on the technology. Of the nine allowing public access, a fair smattering (five actually) are providing it to the Northern Echo, evidently a strong catalyst to encourage public access. This balance of 10% public access to 90% of authorities using staff as intermediaries is in marked constrast to the developments taking place in university and polytechnic libraries where CD Rom networks (clusters of terminals linked to a jukebox of CD Roms) are seen as an essential means of giving the customers what they want. For a whole variety of reasons we in public libraries are taking a different approach. The case for CD Roms as selection/ bibliographic aids is won, the case for purchasing databases to support reference and information services looks set to be a victory, but, perhaps because of the diversity and differing levels of customer ability in public libraries, direct access is not yet seen as the highest priority. We certainly hope that we are not, since it is costly to provide one PC and CD rom drive per database and, if there are fewer PCs than databases, switching disks in and out all the time is a pain. The evidence from the academic sector in that the task is labour intensive and leads to disks 'disappearing'. With the jukebox well out of harm's way and a menu of databases to choose from at the terminal the process is much simplified. We are confident that the benefits of direct public access and the provision of networks will appear in the returns when this survey is undertaken again. The breakthrough will come when three criteria can be met. First, that jukeboxes can be readily connected to the big networks supported by library management systems so that the richness of CD Rom databases can be exploited at terminals far and wide. So far, experiments have hit a number of problems of software compatibility and lack of intelligence on the networks and these problems have kept the breakthrough from coming, but come it must. Second, search software can provide a standard query language which is applicable to all CD Rom databases so that the user once trained can sue any system, and finally, that reasonable pricing structures can be negotiated with CD Rom publishers for networking agreements.

Online access to remote database hosts has been around for a long time. It must have been in use outside esoteric research labs for twenty years and many public libraries have been providing online access for upwards of ten. In some ways the potential of online access is not unlike that of CD ROM-providing the ability to search very large stores of data-with the added advantage that the information can be as up to date as today. The risks of incurring high costs through long searches has damped any enthusiasm for providing direct public access to hosts, but online access remains an important tool to those librarians involved in the provision of information services. Pricing structures which do not discourage the occasional user and the wide availability of microcomputers have seen a steady increase in use over recent years. What used to be a hit-and-miss affair using dedicated terminals and devices called acoustic couplers has become a simple and reliable matter of hitting 'a few keys. However, we suspect that a continuing subjective feeling that searching online is expensive and complicated has created some barriers and the growing availability of databases on CD Rom which incur no cost at point of use has influenced decisions on whether or not to use online searching. There is no conclusive evidence that the two methods overlap significantly, however subjective evidence suggests that an important use of CD Rom is the formulation of search strategies which can then be used during an online search. Also, it would appear from a recent report on the 1991 International Online Information Meeting that demand for online hosts continues to grow despite the popularity of CD Rom databases.

Turning to the data from this current survey, there are now 107 authorities using online searching. That is a 10% increase over the figure in 1989, which was 97. Looking at the percentage changes since 1985, we can see that there has been a slowing down in the increase-the change between 1985 and 1987 was 30% up, and 1987 to 1989, 13%. This suggests that the majority of those libraries who see online searching as an asset to their services have already begun using the technique and that the increases seen in the past are tending to plateau. Whether the remaining 60 authorities suffer a financial barrier, a psychological one or simply do not believe that online searching is relevant to their services cannot be evinced from the data available. However, as we shall see below, the nature of the databases most used implies use by libraries who prioritise bibliographic and business information as important. Perhaps the non-users have set other priorities for their services.

The fact that only 25% of Scottish authorities use the technique influences significantly the overall total. Non-mets are also at 25% but they are only four in number, yet Scotland, with the largest number of authorities, lags far behind. We cannot claim an in-depth knowledge of Scottish library services, however elsewhere in this review we will see that they tend to plough a separate furrow in their use of IT. The other data show manly steady increases and no decreases, from which we may conclude that once adopted, online searching has lasting value to service delivery.

A trend which previously proved of interest is the method of access used to search online hosts. Trend is an important word in this context since, on occasion, the replies received from the questionnaire needed some interpretation. When compared with 1985, the data from the current survey reinforce patterns which were noted in 1989. The fairly even mix of dedicated terminal, Prestel and microcomputer which existed in 1985 has been routed by the micro which now stands head, shoulders and keyboard above all other access methods. Not really very surprising when you come to think about it since the micro has been widely adopted as the access medium for those who operate outside our world. Modem boards can be fitted into machines and there is bags of cheap software around to be played with. Insofar as online searching can be a suer-friendly business, the micro can facilitate it since it is possible to set up dialling and log-in codes for rapid access, and the micro can still be used for so many other things. The other significant feature of the data is the steady increase in the number of authorities using the circulation system as the medium of access. While five is a very small figure when compared with the micros, there are some interesting implications in the decision to use the library management system for online searching. First, most of the new systems allow you to do so, and have done for some time. There is nothing particularly fancy about it, but for very good reasons most libraries have shied away from doing so. While in principle it should be a good thing to provide online access in a variety of locations, where the information is really needed, it requires trained staff to use the systems effectively and untrained staff can run up some hefty bills in no time at all. Use can be limited to defined terminals, but the strategy which has been to focus online searching to key locations where specialist staff, capable of knowing for certain when online should be used, are on hand. Without doubt, the use of the library management system as a delivery medium holds great potential and we will be very surprised if more libraries do not take the plunge (or the risk?). Certainly if the complexities which remain in host interfaces can be reduced so that infrequent users have a chance of getting in and out more quickly, there is every incentive to widen the network, and that is precisely the value of the library management system 0 it has a wide network of terminals.

The truth of these comments becomes more clear when the total terminal population is considered, rather than the use of the medium alone. What we have been looking at so far is the number of authorities using each method, rather than the number of terminals used by each.

	1989	1991
Dedicated terminal	45	68
Circulation system	35	61
Microcomputer	121	263
Prestel, etc.	4	2

The above table provides a comparison only between 1989 and 1991 since the information is not available for 1985 or 1987. Of course, there can be no certainty about the freedom which is allowed for all of the library management system terminals to be used for on line searching, but the potential is clear. Other points to note from these data are that although the number of dedicated terminal users has risen by only one in two years, there has been a 50% increase in the terminals in use; suggesting that while this route may not be the one chosen now by new entries, for those already using the method, it is of sufficient value to encourage wider availability. Finally on hardware, there are now a great many micros being used for online searching; the total more than doubling while the number of authorities has only increased by 14%.

Next we must look at the purposes for which online searching is being used-the hosts being accessed. Just as with the CD Rom world, we are facing more diversity all the time. While 'umbrella' hosts can give access to a wide range of databases, sometimes duplicating other hosts, there are also individual database providers who are being used by public libraries. The two obvious examples are laser's Viscount interlending service and Volnet, which is a database of importance to the voluntary sector. In reality, rather than this diversity being reflected in the data from libraries, the range reported is very similar to 1989. This tends to suggest that the markets being served by online searching are quite clearly defined and are common to most users.

If these data are considered in conjunction with the 'other' category, the trend in the use of online searching is quite apparent. Blaise is still an important source of bibliographic information, but with a growing range of CD rom-based products it may become less used. The major use for online searching is clearly business information. Added together these business-orientated databases dominate Blaise by a factor of more than three to one. The only joker to be found is Acompline, which is unique in providing current information on local authority affairs and which is still quite popular. The fact that access to this database, which is provided by the London Research Centre, is free may have something to do with this continuing popularity.

The last two aspects of online searching which can be considered here relate not to the technology or the range of services available, but how they are delivered to users. The first factor is the costs which are passed on to users and the second is the management of the service-staff skilled in the techniques and how it has changed traditional provision.

Charging policies ought to tell us a great deal about the priorities of libraries and their responses to changes especially those outside their control, whether from competition or from the comments of the Minister for the Arts! Back in 1989 made some observations about the reasons for the high level of certain replies. Discretion, for example, could be an excuse for saying one thing and doing another-telling everyone that certain categories of user are charged, or charges are levied when a search is requested, while not bothering because of the hassle of recovering the money. No comment, on the other hand could be an excuse for doing almost anything; anything that is except charge. The use of online searching has grown up in a tradition where it is the exception to levy a fee for a service at point of use.

"The management of the service includes the organisation of specialist staff and the changes which have resulted from the development of online searching. There is just as much need to have highly trained staff undertaking searches as there has ever been. Despite developments in the design of user-friendly interfaces, online searching remains a special skill, both in the knowledge of command languages and in the formulation of suitable search strategies. It is likely to be a long time before access is provided to customers without the need for a trained intermediary, since cost rises and effectiveness falls if the searcher is not properly trained. Libraries were asked to indicate numbers of locations of trained staff and 86 provided replies, as opposed to 78 in 1989. As with all questions demanding more than a yes or no reply, we must be cautious about making too many assumptions from the data. The evidence provided in the replies shows that all but a very few authorities focus their online services (and staff) in key locations-usually reference libraries, business information centres and the like. The average number of trained staff in each authority is something over four, a slight increase on 1989, but remains fairly stable. It seems that whatever changes may face public libraries in the next few years, this is at least one service which will continue to require 'gatekeepers' to make it fully effective.

Changes in the form of other services resulting from the use of online searching was the last question asked on this subject. Again, since the data re textual rather than precise responses, only general conclusions may be drawn. Despite that, the replies add some detail to the overall picture of online searching in public libraries. Fifty seven authorities commented, compared with the 39 who did so in 1989. Of those 28 implied in their reply that cnline searching had enriched the range of services available. Eight libraries reported that printed sources had been cancelled and ten that there had been no significant change; either because online had been used for so long that no-one could remember what life was like before, or online was such a new acquisition that there had not been time to see any impact.

While online searching involves only a few staff and demands small amounts of the budget, it is an important and emotive topic. The trend which has emerged over the past four or five years is for the databases to form part of services to business and now, for those services to be viewed in many places as 'suitable cases for charging'. The CD rom/online searching duopoly should be a key focus for our attention over the next few years and will, I am sure, be the subject of further research. Indeed, a recent report from the Centre for Communication and Information Studies at the Polytechnic of Central London reports research which looked in much more detail at the actual pattern of database use by analyzing bills from a range of authorities, and interviewing a sample of users in great detail. The general trends reported above are echoed in the research results and the report is well worth reading to gain a clearer picture of what the future may hold.

We cannot end this section without saying something about LANet since Email is just a special sort of online searching. We suggested that is most public libraries used LANet regularly, it might be used as a medium to distribute the results of this survey. There are now more on the network, but so far as I can ascertain, it has not become an important element in the pattern of our communications. What is puzzling is the fact that the academic network JANET is widely used by university and polytechnic libraries and librarians to talk to each other. Quite why this difference should exist is not easily explained, yet the result is that once again you are reading the results in hardcopy.

Videotext/Teletext

By and large, through this survey until now we have seen a mixture of steady growth in some applications, dramatic growth in others. Turning now to videotex and teletext we are in the realm of technologies which have been around for some years, have become well established, to the point where we are beginning to see them superseded. We can remember a time when there was much talk about Prestel (videotex) as a major medium of information delivery.

Organisations were clamouring to be a part of a readily accessible and widely spread public network. Today Prestel is still around, but many new systems have arrived which are Prestel-like in their utility, but have much more power to exploit data resources. Such systems are now used in private viewdata networks, closed user group systems providing information using the format of Prestel, but managed by some local information provider. Teletext, an information system available on broadcast television networks such as Ceefax and Oracle has never been a critical element in publicly provided information services since the data cannot be manipulated locally and is usually of momentary interest-news, racing results, etc. Moreover, it is common for home use television sets to be sold with Ceefax and Oracle decoders as standard.

The trends for teletext and videotex show a situation which has matured to the point where use has levelled off and appears at present to be falling slightly. We have already indicated possible reasons for this above. Private viewdata, on the other hand, is growing steadily in popularity as a medium for the delivery of information tailored to the local community. In six years there has been an almost threefold increase in the systems in use and we may expect this to continue since often these systems are developed as corporate information systems, sometimes managed by the library service, sometimes not and while libraries may find themselves low down on the corporate IT programmeme private viewdata systems may not. Analysing use at the level of the authrity provides only a general picture of developments and that to establish more clearly the impact made it is necessary to consider the penetration of systems within individual authorities. Respondents were asked to report the numbers of terminals used on each of these systems and, in addition, to show whether their use was seldom, steady or constant. These data support earlier points about the fall in the popularity of videotex and teletext as information systems in libraries. Not only has there been a fall in the number of authorities using the systems, but the number of terminals provided has also dropped—videotex almost to the level of 1985, teletext below it. Of course, mean numbers are just that, and the actual distribution shows that in a few authorities there are relatively large populations of terminals. Wiltshire, for example, reports 38 for videotex. In contrast, not only has the total number of authorities using private viewdata risen, but the mean number of terminals shows a 23.5% rise. Not surprising since if private viewdata is the means of delivering community information, as it usually is, then terminals should be as widely available as possible.

Having descended from the level of total use to penetration within a library system, we can finally consider how much the systems are used. The questionnaire invited comment on whether the use of each of the three system was seldom, steady or constant. We must exercise some caution. One person's steady is another's constant and we can only draw limited information from these data. Also, use is likely to vary from terminal to terminal so the single comment may not reflect reality where more than one is in use. Steady is the most frequently cited option, except for videotex where seldom is top. We do not think there is much value in a detailed analysis of these data since their objectivity is questionable, but we can give a personal opinion. Videotex is not used much since alternative sources of information may provide speedier access (and you have to pay to use Prestel). The cost of teletext is unaffected by use since it is broadcast with the TV signals. Leaving terminals lying about for people to play with, therefore carries no risk of large bills. Save for the customer to come in and tinker with. Moreover, many customers will now know more about the resources available on teletext than the managers providing it they will have it at home. We see in private viewdata systems a locally tailored system more likely to meet customer information needs and it should be no surprise that respondents reported many more steady and constants (83% of the total) than its cousin videotex (45% of the total), and even more than teletext (75% of the total) which is free of use cost [private viewdata has a cost in use since remote terminals will be connected by a telephone line or wide area network].

Community Information

The automation of community information highlights one of the paradoxes of information technology. It is very easy to start-just buy a micro and printer, some database software and off you go-but it can be very hard to keep the data comprehensive and up to date. Anyone who has had much to do with computers knows that the data are the most valuable commodity, much more valuable than the hardware or software that can be replaced at the corner shop. Creating any database takes time, maintaining it takes time, and time is money. Community information has always been an attractive product to automate since so much of it is in the form that can readily be fitted into database software products. Clubs, societies, business organisations and the like are the lifeblood of the community information database and are maintained in some form or other by the vast majority of libraries. Indeed, comprehensive community systems are something unique to libraries; you certainly can't buy them at Smiths.

Not surprisingly then the number of libraries automating community information continues to grow. 1987 and 1989 has been matched in the past two years by a total increase of just over 19%. the rend which was apparent between 1985 and 1987, use of the micro and Wordprocessor, has now changed. This time the micro, still the most popular medium, remains unchanged at 38 while use of the library management system shows the most significant growth, up by 75%. It is also not unexpected that private viewdata continues to increase since we have already noted in this chapter that the number of authorities providing the medium continues to rise. One question which comes immediately to mind, however, is if 40 authorities reported use of the system under the videotex/teletext section above, but only 18 report using it for community information, what are the other 22 doing? Just the same question had to be asked in the last survey and suggested that the problem was one of interpretation-that the authorities might not be managing the private viewdata system and therefore thought that it should not be reported under the community information banner. Whether that is true one cannot say. Certainly the prime purpose of private viewdata networks is to deliver information of relevance to the community. Finally, while considering the method of processing, it should be noted that a further five libraries indicated that they were actively investigating the automation on their community information files, and by now they may have done just that.

Micros and wordprocessors have been around for so many years, have at least 40% of the libraries in the country not started to automate the community information files which they certainly must have. With common sense, transferring manual files to a micro can save time and make the product much more useful. Mail merge makes remainders easier and with multiple indexing possible, more variety of presentation is not a problem. A micro/printer set up is not pricey and there are so many examples of applications that not to try seems swimming against the stream. To see whether there was any pattern to this reticence we looked a bit more closely at the 66 libraries without automated community information. An interesting fact emerged that nearly half of the 66 were authorities of the same type. Twenty seven of the 41 Scottish authorities (66%) have yet to do anything about automating their community information; only one of the four Welsh Non-Mets has done so and none of the Northern Ireland libraries has started. Elsewhere, the most likely authority type to find automated systems is the English county where 85% have automated their community information. London, the Mets and the Welsh counties range from 74% uptake down to 63%. You will remember that Scottish authorities were also behind on the library management system front and one can only repeat that perhaps they have set different priorities or lack of resources places severe restrictions on the acquisition of technology. Conversely, English counties are large organisations with disparate service points and the benefits of using IT for community information has clearly been recognised. Lastly, the questionnaire sought details of how the information is actually made available to customers. There are three possibilities-online, hardcopy and a mixture of both-online in some places, or for staff use, hardcopy elsewhere, or for the customers.

Online as the only means of delivery has increased by more than a third and online/hardcopy has also edged up. On the other hand hardcopy has fallen by something over 10%, having remained unchanged for the two years before. It is a pity that ten libraries did not give any indication of dissemination format since, had they, the data might have looked different. Nevertheless, from what we have it seems that progress towards direct public access for customers continues. Hardcopy should not be dismissed as an anachronism just yet since there are many occasions when it is useful to send the customer away with a list to browse through-doing that online in the library has implications for the number of terminals provided. The benefits of online access include the freedom of the customer to search in their own way to search the database from the comfort of the office or the front room.

VARIOUS NETWORKS

Computer networks can be categorized along several dimensions and by differing criteria; however, there is no single set of exclusive categories into which all types can be fitted, and networks which are similar in some ways will display contrasting characteristics in others. A network consists essentially of two kinds of elements:

- — the network nodes which are the actual computing end systems, for example larger computer systems, personal workstations, terminals etc;
- — the connections between these along which data transmissions travel.

Network nodes can have a greater or lesser degree of autonomy in local processing power and ability to control the communication process. The connections can be implemented in various media, but in some way serve to switch data flows between these network nodes, to pass information from a source to a destination in the most appropriate way. As a first stage, networks can usefully be categorized by the type of switching which is used.

There are three basic types of switching:

(1) Circuit switching occurs when a physical link is made between the two network nodes for the duration of a session, along which the data can flow under the control of the end systems. The connection must be set up before the information exchange can begin, and released once the session is completed; in the interim, the circuit is only available to the two participants even though the channel may have spare capacity which is unused.

(2) Message switching does not establish a physical connection, but relies on the network to deliver a message successfully once sent. The network is used as an intermediary: the source end system delivers the message to the network and then has no further involvement; the network will carry the message to its destination as a discrete process. The source end system is not aware of the details of this process, and does not work interactively with the destination end system. The network may use a broadcast technique to convey the message; or may route it through a series of intermediate staging posts, each of which receives the message, stores it, and forwards it on to the next step when possible.

(3) Packet switching techniques take a more structured approach, dividing an individual message into separate 'packets', each of which can travel independently through the network. The network is responsible for the safe delivery of these packets, creating them from the message dispatched from the source end system at the point of entry to the network, and re-assembling them into the original message at the point of exit for the destination end system. Since the network is dealing with smaller standard size packets in a predetermined way, a faster transmission rate can be achieved. The network is able to make its own decisions on routing, and can change these dynamically as traffic conditions change, with no apparent difference to the end user.

A second characteristic of network types concerns the geographical extent of coverage, and the size in terms of the total number of network nodes which can be feasibly connected. A general classification is to describe networks as either:

— local area networks, which are limited to a single site or building, interconnecting nodes within a single organization;

— wide area networks, which are not geographically limited in scope, and are capable of national- and global-level interconnections.

This distinction arises from the very different technologies from which each of these approaches have grown; however, these categories are beginning to break down, as local area networks become more powerful and can themselves be interlinked to form larger entities. An intermediate category is now emerging, which can potentially provide a link between the first two:

(a) metropolitan area networks, which exploit the new transmission

(b) media such as fibre optic cable, to build city-wide capabilities.

Wide area networks can be usefully seen in two groups, distinguishing public and private systems:

(a) public telecommunications networks are international in scope, and accessible as a publicly available service;

(b) private data networks may also be on a national or international scale, but are intended for a distinct user group and not for general public access, although they are likely to make use of services offered by public telecommunications operators.

Each of these network types uses networking technologies which are most appropriate for their purposes. These may be quite unlike each other, employing different techniques, principles and protocols which are not easily compatible. Stemming from these different technologies, there are consequent differences in maximum data transmission rates, number of possible network connections, response times and overloading factors etc.

Network Control

The degree of control which is placed within the network, and the location of this control also arises from these differences in approach. This may be characterized along a continuum, which offers at the extremes:

— a centralized network, with a single main switch to which all nodes are connected, and through which they communicate with each other;

— a decentralised peer-to-peer network, in which each node possesses the same status as any other, and can communicate with any other of its peers on an equal basis.

For large-and small-scale networks, there are various compromise points along this continuum where they can be placed; an inter-network can also be constructed using various different topological arrangements which are interconnected at specific gateways-links from one type to the other type.

Terminal Networks

Terminal networks are perhaps the simplest form of computer network, consisting of a number of relatively unintelligent terminals, each of which is linked to the central computer system and not directly to other terminals. These two elements work in a masterslave relationship to each other, in that the central system has much more extensive control of the process than the terminal, even though this may in fact be a more powerful machine, such as a personal computer emulating a terminal. In such centralized systems, the connections between terminals and central computer are arranged in a star topology, with communications routed through the central switch; if this should fail the main communication channel is cut off.

Terminal networks are very commonly used in large organizations that wish to pursue a centralized information policy, holding data and information systems at a single main point and providing widespread access to this. There may be a high level of communication requirements for this arrangement, however, where speed of response is important; for example a lending desk terminal in a branch public library may be required to transmit loan information to a central database and check appropriate records in a very few seconds.

Micro-mainframe Connections

The growth in use of desktop and personal computers has had a significant influence on the development of centralized systems, swaying the balance of control more towards the end user. This has led to attempts at creating a greater integration and cohesion between information systems at an organisational level, linking the departmental/ office information into the corporate database level.

Terminal emulation packages allow the end user to utilize a familiar desktop PC as a central terminal without the need to switch equipment, and increasingly to use the computing power of the PC to improve screen presentation rather than simply emulating a dumb terminal. This provides the user with a more familiar and 'friendly' workspace environment. Developments in software compatibility are integrating the standard software packages in use on both central and local systems for mainstream applications such as databases.

Local Area Networks

A local area network is a means of linking together a collection of computer-based devices, within a limited geographical area, on a more or less equal basis. This equality makes the local area network (LAN) radically different from a terminal-based network, because each of the computer systems connected is an independent self-governing entity working in a co-operative relationship. Local area networks fall principally into two types:

— proprietary networks which are used to interconnect a number of computers and their peripherals of the same type, for example a network of IBMPC or Macintosh personal computers;

— standards-based networks which can interlink computer systems and devices whatever their type and specification, through the use of common network technology.

For both types of LAN, every device connected to the network must communicate through a uniform hardware interface and software protocol to achieve compatibility. Standardization of the communication process is therefore very important to the concept of local area networks. Since no one method of operation would be suitable for all possible needs, a number of alternative 'standards exist, reflected in the different types of LAN available. A local area network will typically be provided to support:

(a) resource sharing of expensive hardware resources, for example a colour printer, a high-speed modem, or a CDROM drive accessible to all nodes on the network;

(b) resource sharing of software and access to specialized facilities;

(c) file transfer and access to support the sharing of information between different users, and to provide wider access to central information while ensuring consistency by maintaining a single copy of the data;

(d) messaging and conferencing to enhance organizational communications and co-operative working;

The most commonly found use of proprietary local area networks is to interconnect IBM-PCs within a single site or building. There are broadly two types of PC-based local area network, distinguished by the operating system by which they are managed.

1. In peer-to-peer PC networks all the network nodes interrelate as equals, able to call on the services of other nodes and to offer their own at all times. This is an intuitively natural way of sharing resources, and is cheap and effective to implement for small workgroups.

2. In server-based PC networks, one or more network nodes act as a provider of services for the other client nodes. Clients can only call on the services of a server node, which is dedicated to this purpose; there are three main types of server: a file server dispenses data and programme files across the network, either in whole or in part; a print server drives the printing devices and manages the print queues; and a communications server controls external links, such as facsimile machines, or modems.

Standards-based LANs

There are two industry wide standards for more broadly based local area networks, known as Ethernet and Token Ring.

Ethernet is the most widely installed local area network at the current time. This describes a specification for a LAN rather than an actual product; there are many implementations of Ethernet from a range of suppliers.

Ethernet aims to provide a high-speed network which gives all nodes stable and equal access to the network, in such a way as to prevent individual stations interfering with each other; and allowing a transmission to be addressed to individual nodes, a group of nodes, or the whole network community. The intention is that all Ethernet installations are compatible with each other, since they use the same set of protocols. The stations on an Ethernet are each linked directly to a main transmission channel in a bus topology. Stations may not transmit at the same time, but must wait for the channel to be free before sending. Transmissions are broadcast to all nodes on the network, but only utilized by those stations to which the message is addressed.

There is a mechanism for the detection of collisions when stations broadcast together, which requires a station to rebroadcast after a random interval. Thus, all stations are in contention for the channel and cannot be guaranteed a fixed rate of access. This method works well for small to medium size networks, where traffic is in irregular short bursts rather than at regular intervals.

Ethernet therefore suits the typical office environment where user activity follows this pattern. It has a relatively high data rate of up to 10 Megabits per second (Mbps) and is able to support large data file transfers without undue disruption to the user. It does not, however, support voice and video transmission, because the nature of the access medium cannot guarantee the continuity necessary for voice or moving image. There are technical limitations to the size of Ethernet networks, both in length of cabling and in the amount of data traffic which can be supported.

The Token Ring network takes a different approach and as the form chosen by IBM for its own local area network has become more popular. The nodes are connected in a ring configuration, with each node receiving information from its 'upstream' neighbour and re-transmitting it to its nearest 'downstream' neighhour Each node, either originates its own transmission, passes on the data exactly as is received, or removes the data which is addressed to itself.

To control transmission collisions, each node has the opportunity to transmit in turn, governed by the passing of an electronic 'token' around the ring. The Token Ring thus provides for both an egalitarian 'round robin' access, and multiple priority levels for urgent messages. The method is self-governing to quite a high degree, and able to react dynamically to changing conditions.

IEEE Standards

International standards development for local area networks has been co-ordinated by the Institute of Electrical and Electronic Engineers (IEEE) in the United States. This work is intended to develop a framework within which the major types of LAN can be encompassed rather than to specify one single standard for all requirements.

The standards are known by numerical, rather than product names, and cover both Ethernet and Token Ring style networks.

1. The 802.3 standard defines a broadcast bus-based network, which is effectively the same as the Ethernet type.

2. The 802.5 standard defines a token passing ring network similar to the IBM Token Ring local area network.
3. The 802.4 standard describes a token passing bus network, which combines features of the first two types.
4. The 802.6 standard defines a high-speed broadband network, better known as a metropolitan area network.

LANs Interconnections

As the local area network grows in size and complexity the amount of traffic increases, overloading the network and degrading response time and reliability. A number of devices have emerged to support both the partitioning of over-large LANs and the desirable interlinking of others.

1. A repeater carries messages between two sections of a single network, allowing it to be extended beyond the maximum cable limit.
2. A bridge is a station which is connected to two networks, through which the two LANs can exchange data frames. The networks must be using the same protocols so that they look like one logical network, but only traffic destined for nodes on the other network will pass over.
3. A router is a device for sending data frames between two dissimilar LANs, since the router can deal with both network types.
4. A gateway links a local area network to a different networking environment altogether, such as a wide area network.

The development of standards for local area networks is continuing with the emergence of newer technology and physical media. In particular, the use of fibre optics is having a substantial impact, potentially opening up the geographic and bandwidth limitations in this field to such an extent that distinctions between local and wide area networks are becoming less meaningful.

Wide Area Networks

In the wide area environment, the communications process is seen as a multi-stage process. Networks are constructed from point-to-point links between different nodes on a store and forward basis. Data transmission are passed from one node to the next, *en route,* with each node making its own routing decision based on matching the information which it holds in a routing table with the destination address on the data packet, and in the context of current network traffic conditions.

Control and management of the network is therefore distributed throughout, and not located in any single central point. The network can be extended by adding new connections between nodes and making appropriate updates to routing tables. There are likely to be alternative routes between nodes which can be used at different times. The relaying of data between nodes in this way requires the use of protocols to ensure correct delivery and protect against the corruption of transmissions *en route.*

The protocols normally operate both within the end systems and within the network relay nodes themselves. There are several alternative protocols suites which may be in use; however, all nodes on the network must be running the same protocols to communicate successfully, since this is the glue which binds the disparate systems together.

As an indication, *some common wide area protocols are:*

- the X.25 protocols which have been developed for public telecommunications, and ensure international compatibility in this area; these have also been adopted in some private networks;
- the TCP/IP protocol suite, widely used in private networks and in the academic and research world.

Private Data Networks

Private data networks can be constructed from a number of different elements, as appropriate to requirements and conditions. They, may be national or international in scope, and involve the co-ordination of several different network operators and administrations, using elements from:

— public telecommunications operators, in the form of leased data lines or use of the public data network;

— private network operators, including commercial long-haul network operators and satellite communications suppliers with independent local or wider scale data lines directly owned.

The Leasing Telecommunication Lines

The leasing of dedicated digital data lines is an alternative to use of the public data network. These are private circuits, provided as a carrier by the telecommunications authority, but under the control of the organisation which is renting the line.

Leased lines are point to point connections, permanently linking one site with another, rather than dynamically switchable channels. Since they are leased at a fixed annual rate, the greater the use made of the line the more efficient it becomes.

Multiple rented private circuits are used by large organizations to create private networks, linking remote sites together on a point-to-point basis, or providing a high-speed network backbone for a high volume of traffic between main sites. In the United Kingdom BT provide a range of leased circuits with varying data carrying capacities:

— *Kilostream* and Kilostream N lines provide bulk data transmission at rates from 64 Kbps up to about 1 Megabit per second (Mbps);

— *Megastream* lines provide higher speeds of up to 2 Mbps;

— *Satstream* utilizes satellite capacity to offer point-to-multipoint connections over a wide geographical area.

The use of leased lines is a more secure and flexible option for the larger organization, which is able to deploy the systems and protocols which it finds most suitable, rather than having to conform to those used in public systems.

Telecommunications Networks

There are three types of telecommunications networks presently available for use for computer-based information networking; each of these represents a phase of the developmental efforts to improve services over several decades, using quite different technology and approaches.

Public Switched Telephone Networks

This is an extensive network of cabling reaching into almost all inhabited parts of developed countries, and providing international connections worldwide. This made it attractive as an immediately available option for computer networking in its early stages. The PSTN network is designed for voice communication, and therefore requires the use of an interfacing data communication device, usually a modem, to be used.

The network makes use of circuit switching technology for the same reason, and is a rather noisy and unreliable channel, prone to errors and misconnection. It is poorly suited to fast and reliable data transfer and depends on the end systems alone to maintain quality through the use of suitable protocols.

The PSTN makes inefficient use of the available carrying capacity because the circuit is idle when neither end system is transmitting but cannot be used by waiting nodes. Since a switched phone line is charged on a time and distance basis, regardless of the amount of traffic, it is not ideal for inter-computer communication over long distances.

Public Data Networks

The public data networks have been constructed specifically for the transmission of computer information, and cannot be used for voice conversations. They provide fast and reliable data transfer, more flexibility and international communications at a reasonable cost, since they are charged for by the amount of data transferred.

The *advantages of packet switching* are the following:

— there is no need for a direct physical connection between sender and receiver;

— information from different calls can then be interleaved on the network channels to make maximum use of the available bandwidth; the user, therefore, pays only for information actually transmitted, rather than for elapsed time regardless of the transfer activity;

— standard use of communication protocols facilitates the inter-connection of equipment from different manufacturers, operating at different data rates.

The X.25 protocol set is the standard for public packet switched networks. This is an open standard which is available for end systems as well as internally to the network.

Public data networks are mostly managed on a national basis with international connections between them, and so X.25 forms something approaching a global standard in this area. There are, however, two versions of the X.25 protocol; the latest 1988 version is not used by all public telecommunications operators. The public data network is essentially a store and forward network which operates at speeds fast enough to give the impression of a direct connection to the end user:

The network can be considered as an opaque entity—a 'cloud'—by the end systems which need only to specify an address for the remote end system which is being called, having no concern with the details of routing. The network 'cloud'- consists of a collection of packet switching exchanges (PSEs) which forward packets through the high-speed network from the local exchange to the destination PSE.

Integrated Services Digital Networks

The development of public data networks for digital communications led to the existence of different networks for different purposes-one for voice, one for data-and requiring organizations using these systems to connect to both. A duplication of networks is undesirable, and also works against the integration of information types, for instance the co-ordination of voice, data, and image, which is increasingly needed to support multimedia information networking. Two *development programmemes in the telecommunications infrastructure* provided the platform for the development of integrated services digital networks:

1. The digitization of the trunk network lines, the main arteries used by the network operator.
2. The replacement of electro-mechanical local telephone exchanges by digital switches, such as System X and System Y.

The ISDN aims to build a public network providing end-to-end digital connectivity which is capable of supporting a range of digital devices and services, both voice and non-voice, on the same basis. This allows users to send and receive data, text and image from computer systems as well as offering an enhanced telephone service. This is achieved over a single ISDN connection, so that one network may be used for all applications, at the same time as providing higher transmission speeds. The ISDN approach is to enable the existing local telephone circuitry-the 'local loop-to carry digital signals through the use of specialized equipment and adapters, rather than a wholesale and long-term replacement programmeme.

This requires the installation of suitable network connections in the customer premises, which acts as the interface to the digital network. Despite this fully digital transmission system it is still not possible to connect all computer equipment directly to the network, unless the equipment is designed or adapted to work-with the ISDN system. Access to the ISDN network is available at two different capacity rates, known as basic rate and primary rate.

The access rate refers to the number of logical channels which are available on a single ISDN connection. Each of these channels constitutes a circuit which is independently usable by different information media, and can be switched to different destination points.

The Basic Access Rate provides two *bearer* channels and one *data* channel, and for this reason is otherwise known as 213 + D. Each of the bearer channels can simultaneously carry a separate information stream, at a transfer rate of 64 Kbps—for example, one for a voice call and the other for data.

The Primary Access Rate gives a higher number of bearer channels, although the exact number is variable between countries-the United Kingdom, Europe and Australia supply 30 bearer channels to the user in one ISDN connection (known as SOB + D); in the United States, Japan and South East Asia 23 channels are used. SOB + D gives an overall data rate of some 2 Mbps (the equivalent to a BT Megastream leased line) and necessitates the use of extra equipment at the subscriber premises to manage the multiple channels.

Potential benefits from the use of ISDN are the following:

(a) all 30 ISDN connections can be switched to different locations; clearer calls and more reliable data transfers, with less line noise;

(b) the ability to send two information streams to the same locations, to support remote co-operative working; for example, two users might discuss over the phone the contents of a computer screen which can be transferred between their terminals;

(c) enabling domestic services, such as home shopping and banking, online database access, security, and control services for the home; feasible desktop videoconferencing;

(d) providing a better infrastructure for teleworking, for example by providing a gateway to an office LAN for home-based workers.

Frame Relay Networks

Frame relay networks technologies are in development which may threaten to overwhelm ISDN before its full potential is reached. These involve the use of high-speed packet switching on high bandwidth networks which will offer much greater information transmission capabilities than the present public data networks. Frame relay networks are made possible by use of less noisy transmission media, such as fibre optic cable, in the network infrastructure, exploiting this greater reliability to simplify the protocols necessary and thus speed up the transmission process.

Integrated Broadband Networks

Integrated broadband networks are sometimes referred to as broadband ISDN (B-ISDN) systems and will also exploit the advantages of fibre optic to offer a dramatically enhanced communication facility, far more powerful than exists at present and able to deliver a wider range of services more effectively.

The intention of developing integrated broadband communications systems is to provide a single network for all services, which can be flexibly and dynamically configured according to individual circumstances and priorities. Digital networks allow both data, voice and image to be sent along the same connection, but these information types have different desirable transmission characteristics.

Data and text require a high degree of accuracy, since the quality of the received information is more easily affected by corruption, but are more tolerant of short transmission delays. Voice and the moving image, on the other hand, are more tolerant of errors since these can be interpreted by human interpretation, but are more susceptible to variations in transmission delays. Existing or narrowband ISDN circuits do not have a high degree of flexibility in adjusting to these varying demands: for instance, a voice call does not use the full capacity of a 64 Kbps channel, but the spare cannot be freed up for use by others during a session.

Broadband networks aim to overcome such problems by using a universal fast packet switching technique for all information streams, and allocating 'bandwidth on demand' rather than relying on fixed bandwidth channels. Two rates have been proposed for B-ISDN: a basic rate service with a digital access rate of 155 Mbps, and a primary rate service at 622 Mbps, although the full specifications for these have yet to be defined.

A technique known as the Asynchronous Transfer Mode (ATM) is used to transfer the data. This divides the data stream into cells, which are smaller than X.25 packets in size, and can travel through the network at a faster rate. Since the channel is more reliable, quality control is performed at each end of the link and not by each intermediate network switch as well. This ATM approach is particularly suitable for information activity which is inherently 'bursty' in nature.

For example, a service would be able to ensure fast delivery of high definition images, and then free the channel for other use during the reading and thinking time in which the user is not generating any network activity. This will allow the development of true multimedia information services.

Developments in the wider networking field are increasing aiming to deliver faster data transfer rates, on integrated networks which make no distinction between information types.

As the amount of electronic information available across networks grows exponentially, and the sophistication of end-user computing equipment encourages the sharing of information in more intensive forms, network infrastructures respond with the ability to communicate sophisticated forms fast enough to make actual use of the network transparent to the user. At the organizational level, local area networks are also undergoing technical developments which increase their speed and potential for the delivery of more sophisticated and high-powered information applications.

A situation in which these applications can make use of the network 'on demand' in a flexible manner which can respond to changes in circumstance is foreseeable. There is, however, much effort required to make this a reality; the current situation reflects a confusing picture of many alternative networking options which conflict and compete with each other, and which are poorly suited to widespread interconnection between different types of network. The concept of connectivity stresses the importance of this ability to interconnect networks and information networking applications in a reliable and effective manner, and without the need for equipment which is difficult to obtain, install, and use, and soon becomes redundant.

❐

4

Technical Services

Since the late 1960s early 1970s participatory management has been in vogue in libraries. Staff are interested in participating on committees in order to have input in the way the library is run. There are several dangers here: that committee reports will be *(1)* endorsed, but operations will continue as usual; *(2)* accepted and implemented without serious administrative consideration; and *(3)* filed away without further comment. All three situations pose problems.

The type of decisions made at the administrative level should be policy decisions; the decisions made at the departmental level should be procedural decisions on how to implement established policy. You as the technical services manager should work with department heads to determine what specific policies are desirable from a departmental viewpoint. You as technical services manager will want to take advantage of a variety of ways to make decisions.

Certainly, for some things there is not enough time for, the topic is not worth taking the time for, and! or you do not wish to receive, input. For other the process of getting it. When obtaining input, it is necessary for staff to understand that you will make the decision after carefully weighing the input. It may be helpful for staff to structure their input in terms of scenarios or alternatives. You should be willing to explain why you choose the alternative you do.

You might find it helpful to follow an established pattern, such as the following, when making a decision.

1. First, describe the problem. What is it? What are its political implications? What factors are involved that you cannot change?

2. Choose what you deem to be the best alternative given all the factors of which you are aware.

3. Next, describe the alternatives. You might find it useful to develop a scenario for each alternative, if different alternatives involve different cash outlays, project the cost for each. Develop Gantt charts, flowcharts, or PERT charts as appropriate. Gather information and seek input as appropriate. Gather information and seek input as appropriate-in individual conversations, from a special meeting, from the literature through and ad hoc committee.

4. Implement that alternative by identifying those who are to carry it out, describing to them both the problem and its solution, providing a way for them to buy into the idea so they are willing to make it work, having them reiterate to you what they think you expect them to do, having them give you an action plan with anticipated completion dates, and repeatedly checking back with them to make sure that what you think is happening is truly happening.

5. Evaluate the results. Decide who will evaluate the solution and determine the process of evaluation. For example, agree that on a certain date you and a department head will discuss the choice and its impact. Or, identify certain staff members to submit a report evaluating the solution at a certain time. Mark your calendar and make sure that the appropriate evaluation is done ,lt the specified time.

If the evaluation indicates that the decision was a poor one, reconsider the initial alternatives and describe new ones. When it is clear that another alternative or even the original solution would be better, do not hesitate to recognize the situation and change what is. happening by implementing the better choice. To function well, a committee needs a dearly defined charge, a specific timeframe for action, a chairman who knows how to run a meeting effectively, and members who are willing to work.

Review each standing committee on a regular basis (*e.g.*, annually) to determine whether its charge needs to be revised and whether its membership should change. In order to involve people who are interested in serving and in order to give everyone an opportunity to express interest, you might ask for nominations and volunteers for new committees or committee vacancies. Remember, you can always nominate additional people if you wish. Before each meeting the committee chair should formulate an agenda, even if a formal agenda is not distributed. He should have clearly in mind what topics are to be discussed, what kinds of decisions are to be made, what assignments are necessary, and how long those assignments should take.

At the beginning of the meeting, he should outline the topics to be addressed and ask if anyone wishes to add others. He should give some indication of how long the meeting is to last and then stick to that timeframe. If a committee member "takes over", the chair should regain control by rephrasing what has been said, adding information or asking someone else a question. The chair should outline at the end of the meeting just what has been decided, what assignments have been made, and when the next meeting is to take place. The chair should occasionally touch base with the person who created the committee charge to make slire that what is being done is germane to the charge. Committee members should come prepared to address the committee's topics. They should have completed assignments in hand, with copies of relevant materials for an committee members as appropriate. They should voice their opinions without dominating the conversation or promoting disharmony among the committee. If committee direction is unclear, they should ask for clarification or suggest actions. Decisions may be reached by consensus. If it is unclear that there is a consensus, the chair may wish to call for a vote, which may be by secret ballot.

If serious exception is taken on a major issue, both the minority and majority opinions should be reflected in the committee's report. If weightings are used as a mechanism for arriving at a decision, the rankings determined by the weightings should be reviewed and discussed by the committee to ascertain whether all are indeed comfortable with the results. Committee members should then be allowed to offer justification for reordering. A decision reached by consensus will best reflect the opinion of all members.

Planning

A healthy library organization has a set of documents which describe where it is, where it wants to go (its objective), and how it plans to get there (its goals). Most libraries periodically produce the first document in the form of an annual report. Some libraries have the second as a general mission statement. Few libraries have a concrete process for achieving the third document: a description of departmental goals that can be directly tied to the individual goals of each staff member. It is not critical that these documents, which structure a planning cycle, exist in published form. What is critical is that library managers review on a regular basis (semiannual or annual) where they are and how they plan to get to where they want to go, and that they communicate their ideas to library staff so that staff activities match administrative expectations. It is helpful to include staff input in the process. Existing working groups, such as a department heads group and a general representative staff board or council which can provide a cross-section of perspectives, may be called upon to meet in a retreat setting for 6 or 8 hours to begin the process. "Retreat" here means "getting away from the telephones," so the actual meeting may be in a nearby building or somewhere away from the institutional setting. By alternatively dividing into discussion groups and working all together, the group can address such topics as: what we have accomplished in the last 6 months; which of these things we did that we have not expected to. do and why; what new environmental factors exist which we had not expected 6 months ago; what do we plan to do ill the next 6 months; and, being realistic, what can we really expect to accomplish in the next 6 months. Each discussion group should have a recorder and someone who reports to the larger group. These individuals may be appointed by the retreat facilitator or by the discussion group members. A specific topic (*e.g.*, what do you expect to do in the next 6 months) and a timeframe (*e.g.*, 45 minutes should be established Encourage brainstorming, with the understood ground rule that no judgmental comment may be made on anything suggested. Do not overload anyone group with an out-sized proportion of administrators and/or, department heads. Encourage everyone to participate. On the first go round, staff may find it awkward to participate. Some may forget the ground rule of no criticism; others may be hesitant to participate-especially if their department heads are nearby. The process is good for several reasons. If the library staff numbers more than a dozen, it is unlikely that anyone participating was aware of all of the library's accomplishments prior to the exercise of listing them. Many ideas arise that could not possibly have been thought of by the administration and/or department heads alone. Some natural leaders appear who were not obvious before. You may think that your library does not provide an environment in which such planning sessions can work. Even if they cannot be planned for the entire library, you can certainly institute them for techniCal services. If you have no staff board or council, you might have staff in each department elect representatives for the planning session. The record of goals for the next 6 months may be copied and distributed to all staff, who then on a department or unit basis decide what they really expect to do in the next 6 months. These goals should be reviewed by the administration to make sure they are in keeping with the overall library goals.

In establishing goals, staff may become immersed in defining their normal business and ignore anticipated special projects, or vice versa. To overcome this, it is best to ask for both kinds of goals: *(1)* the maintenance goals, or "daily business function" goals; and *(2)* the developmental goals, or special project goals (*e.g.*, retrospective conversion of the "Ds"). Each goal should be measurable and the measure should be defined. Individuals who will be involved in accomplishing the goal should be listed. Ideally, the annual goals established in this planning cycle should be tied to the individual goals established annually in the evaluation cycle. At least, you and the technical services department heads should check to make sure that each individual goal falls within a unit or departmental goal. It is important to realize that the planning cycle is a means to the end of a well run library. As with the evaluation process, library staff should not become so immersed in the planning process that they lose sight of or time for their actual functions.

Budgetary Considerations

The scope of the hbrary's fiscal responsibility is determined by the institution. Some library directors are able to move monies around between salary and nonsalary budget lines. Some are able to reallocate monies accrued from vacant positions or revenues generated from book fines and copy facilities to other budget lines. Most fortunate are the directors who have the latitude to use salary savings for temporary positions or as supplements for any nonsalary budge lines. Likewise, the scope of your fiscal responsibility as a technical services manager is defined by your local situation. Generally, technical services managers deal primarily with the library materials budget. Some are responsible for the management of all the financial resources that support technical services operations. They may or may not participate in budget formulation for the entire library. It is helpful to think of a budget as the fiscal approach to planning that provides a series of snapshots of the library's financial status. The proposed budget for the next fiscal year explains where you expect to allocate anticipated financial resources for the next year. It should mesh with the planning cycle so that it provides financial support for all new planning thrusts as well as for continuing services. The financial statement is a picture of just where the library is fiscally at a given point in time. In provides the opportunity to reevaluate the fiscal situation and make adjustments as necessary. It also provides a tracking system that explains what happens to every dollar allocated. No matter what your span of fiscal control is, it is important for you to analyze each financial statement in terms of annual percentages: What portion of the annual allocation for each category has been encumbered or expended? Is this appropriate? Should the pace of encumbering/expending be decreased or increased? Should any funds moved from one category to another? Do the encumbrances and expenditures for budget in line "look right?" For example, is the book budget balance higher than what you thought it would be? Check it out; is the accounting current or are some recent purchase orders or processed invoices not reflected? Do what your span of fiscal control allows to ensure that the money is spent (but not overspent) by year's end. If you see severe problems in areas of the budget outside of your control, ask questions of those responsible to see if they are aware of additional factors which explain the situation. Make suggestions as appropriate. Those technical services managers who do have fiscal management of all budgets related to their operations may have the advantage of being able to move monies from one budget line *e.g.*, telecommunications) to another (*e.g.*, book budget). This allows some latitude, but division territoriality resulting from such a situation may hamper the opportunity to reallocate monies throughout the entire library budget. Unexpected expenditures are more difficult to handle within one division than they are if the entire budget is considered as a single entity. In such a situation it is important for the technical services manager to develop a relationship of mutual trust with the other individuals who are responsible for budget segments. Making realistic budget projections (rather than padding anticipated costs in order to get a larger budget share) and cooperating to coordinate the entire budget (rather than clinging to budget territories) are crucial factors for sound budget management.

Budget Fluctuations

Both budget cuts and budget supplements can be traumatic, for a change in the amount of financial resources automatically causes a change in the entire library plan. Cut result in some curtailment in library operations and unexpected additional funds cause immediate, often temporary and sometimes frenetic, increased activity. Budget fluctuations require that managers reassess the total library operations package and consider reallocations of human resources in tandem with the financial changes. Take into account the influence of budget alterations on staff. If cuts are expected, some new staff may be seriously concerned that their jobs are in jeopardy. Managers may allay some fears by citing previous institutional experience (*e.g.*, "in the past we have never been forced to release people due to budget cuts, although we have lost positions through attrition"). With the help of department heads, the technical services manager must rethink departmental goals when facing the frozen or lost positions. The manager, along with collection management and acquisitions staffs, must chart an altered course for acquiring monographs and serials if the library materials budget is slashed.

Supplements may be dumped into the library budget during the fiscal year to help compensate for previous cuts (usually to the materials budget) or to support a special projed (*e.g.*, automation). Dramatic budget increases toward the end of the year are not unusual because libraries can quickly dispose of institutional surplus funds by prepaying for ongoing services such as serials subscriptions, approval plans, and services of bibliographic utilities. The technical services manager's challenge is to spend any additional funds within his purview sensibly in the amount of time allowed. Set out an action plan. Make certain that each staff member involved is aware of his role in the special expenditure push and follow through to be certain that the plan is actually being executed. When dealing with library budgets remember that the value orientation for libraries is different from that of business. The bottom line for libraries is service, not profit. Even so, your job is not solely to provide vision and justification to explain what you would do if only you has a bigger budget, it is also to wisely allocate, monitor, and expend ,what you do have. As a technical services manager, you should strive to deal with staff fairly, consistently, and in as open a manner as is possible for you. You can go to endless management training courses and learn about the different leadership styles and McGregor's theories X and Y and quality groups and on and on, but if you are not comfortable with a certain approach, attempting to use it will not help. One of the best rules of thumb is to treat staff the way you would like to be treated.

Hiring

The local hiring procedure may be conduded by the immediate supervisor and department head alone or it may involve a personnel office outside the library, a personnel staff within the library, or a search committee. Be aware of the regulations involved and make sure that the entire procedure incorporates the steps described here.

Evaluate the Vacancy

When a vacancy occurs, important questions to answer include, Did the previous incumbant have unique talents or deficiencies that caused us to shape his job differently than we would with him? Should the new position be classified in a different job category or at a level different from the one held by the previous incumbent? Once you have determined just what you are hoping to do, develop a set of job specifications that describes what knowledge, skills, and abilities you expect the new incumbent to have, rather than reiterating those the previous incumbent had. If there is someone on the staff who might be appropriate for the job, analyze why you consider this to be true. Remember that a person who performs well in one job may not do at all well in another. Do you think this person would be good due to the knowledge, skills, and abilities he exhibits in connection with his present job or in connection with those sought for the vacant position? Remember, the best cataloger does not necessarily make the best head of cataloguing. When encouraging a current staff member to apply for a vacancy, make clear that his application will be considered along with all others received. Depending upon the strengths of the pool for the position, he mayor may not be interviewed. In your job advertisement clearly delineate which qualifications are mandatory (everyone you consider must fulfill these) and which are preferred. If you may fill the position at more than one rank, say so in your advertisement so that you will not have to readvertise before offering the job at a higher or lower classification.

Interviews should be conducted for all levels of applicants; even if they are transferring within the library. Naturally, institution regulations govern the procedures for hiring, and the procedures for hiring, and the procedures may be different for different levels of staff. Ideally, the department head conducts the interview for support staff, having the candidates talk as appropriate with other staff whose work relates directly to the work of the position that is open.

Interviews for librarians should be longer and more rigorous. If you are fortunate enough to have a large pool of viable applicants, you may find it helpful to interview five or six of them by telephone in order to determine which candidates to bring in for on-site interviews. The length of the interview for professional positions will vary with the requirements and the customs of the library and its institution. When interviewing people who are coming in from out of town, you mayor may not arrange to have them met upon arrival and transported to the hotel where they will be staying. (Indeed, the candidate's ability to show up at the right place at the right time may be the first "test" of the interview.) Formulate your interview questions in advance. Consider- the mix of questions. Make the beginning questions relatively easy so the candidate has a chance of "warm up" to the interview situation. Intersperse difficult questions with easier ones. Federal regulations dictate that hiring decisions may not be based on attributes of the candidate that are not relevant to professional performance. Consequently, certain topics may not be covered by interview questions: topics dealing wIth race, color, religion, sex, national origin, age, handicap, applicant is pregnant, marital status, or veteran's status.

Unfortunately, no interview has been designed that helps' predict how an applicant, if hired, will perform. Some people are more interested in playing attention to detail, it is reasonable to explore thoroughly what previous experiences the candidate may have had that indicate interest in and attention to detail. In addition, ask the applicant if he is interested in detail arid to give examples of how he has handled an array of details in the past. The ability to solve problems is also an asset in technical services work. Asking several "what if" questions may give the interviewer an idea about the way a candidate might approach a problem. For example: What would you do if you are lost in a town in which you do not speak the local language? How would you find your lodging for the night? Another quality technical services managers normally seek in staff is good judgment. This, again, is impossible to measure in an interview, but the candidate may be asked to cite examples of instances in which he has exercised good judgment. If risk-taking is important to the job at hand, ask for an example in which the candidate took a risk that was successful and an example in which the risk. was unsuccessful. A good question to ask support staff is to discuss the most complex set of tasks he was ever asked to do. When interviewing someone for a supervisory position, ask: What is the hardest decision you ever had to make? Have you ever fired someone? Do you think you could carry out the process to fire someone? It is helpful to include as many settings as possible for the candidate during the interview. Variety can be provided by having him meet and/or talk with the different groups with which he will work, by having him give a brief presentation to staff, by having coffee with a specific group, and by varying the direction of questioning. It is helpful for one or two staff members to see the candidate in as many segments of the interviews situation as possible, to see how he conducts himself in and reacts to different settings. Each group should repeat the same format for questioning for each person interviewed for the same position. The candidate should not be permitted to "take over" by asking the questions rather than answering them. One person in each interview group should be designated to redirect the situation should this occur.

In setting up an interview schedule, remember to leave time for rest breaks and have water available every time the candidate is required to talk for a while. Leave time for him to see the library, to tour at least part of the institution and to look at the city and possible housing if he is from out of town. Remember that you are trying to recruit. You expect the candidate to sell himself, but you should also be selling your institution. Emphasize the assets, and be honest about the disadvantages. Realize that people with families want to know about local schools and arrange for them to talk with someone who has current information. Address the applicant's professional expectations. Describe travel support and the opportunities for salary increases and promotion.

Check References

It is most important to check out references for all levels of staff-even if they have been working elsewhere within the library or the institution. If this is not done before the interview to help select who will be interviewed, it must be done before an offer is made. Good questions to ask (in addition to the normal ones about past experience, strengths/weaknesses, and career goals) include: How would you describe this person's interaction with other staff members-support staff, librarians, administration? Would you hire this person again? Would you like to work for this person? Are you aware of any procedures initiated to fire or otherwise release this person from a job? Bland or non-committal references frequently are omitting more than they are including. It is more worthwhile to talk with the reference than to simply receive that individual's comments in writing. When talking with a reference, respect his pauses in conversation and wait for him to say more. Try to draw him out by saying "Why do you say that?" Or "Can you give me an example?"

If you still do not have a good feel for the applicant after talking with the references, consider asking for more. If, for example, you never end up talking with a working peer or supervisor who has been directly aware of the applicant's recent work, it is legitimate to ask for the name of someone who can give you that type of information.

Carefully explore any gaps in career history. What was that person doing during that time? Also, ask detailed question about reasons for moving from job to job if a candidate has a history of never staying long in anyone place. The interview cycle can take months, especially in academic institutions. Remember to keep applicants informed during the different stages of the process.

Acknowledge receipt of the initial application and request additional paperwork, if any is needed. After narrowing the pool, contact those who have been eliminated to let them know they are no longer being considered. However, do not eliminate viable candidates who will still be considered if those interviewed do not receiver or accept an offer. As soon as the candidate of your choice has formally accepted your offer, contact those remaining in the pool to let them know that the position has been filled. If your library has a personnel officer or a staff development officer, procedures may already exist for keeping in touch with the new employee before his arrival and for formal orientation once he is on board. If these mechanisms are not on place, set up something yourself. Send maps and newspapers to a new staff member who will be coming from out of town. Offer assistance in putting him in touch with relators or apartment rental agents. Encourage him to call as questions arise in connection with the move. Once he has arrived, make. sure that he is introduced to other staff.

You may find it valuable to hold entrance and exit interviews with each new technical services member. Through an entrance interview you can find out something about the individual where he went to school, what he majored in, what his primary outside interests are, where he has lived before—so you can better talk with that individual in informal situations later and most importantly, so you can remember his name. You may take this opportunity to explain a particular aspect of the library organization and to ask if the new staff member has any questions about the library in general. If you do not know a specific answer, ask the person who does and get back to the new staff member as Soon as possible. Make sure that each new staff member is told what general library policies exist and how he may gain access to them.

Evaluation

It is important to let staff know how they are doing their job. It is good for people who are doing well to know just how well they are doing. It is necessary to have evaluations that support merit and promotion recommendations. Also it is imperative, if you ever hope to improve the situation, that people who are not doing well are told, and that you have documentation to prove that they have been told in case they file a grievance or a lawsuit. Evaluations should occur on a regular basis. Ideally, a staff member should receive feedback whenever he is not performing as expected. Unfortunately, giving such feedback is not an enjoyable task and supervisors tend to postpone potentially uncomfortable meetings. Therefore, it is best to set up an evaluation cycle which includes quarterly of semi-annual discussions as well as written documentation annually. The annual evaluation should include both an evaluation instrument (form) and a meeting of the supervisor and employee in which the written evaluation is discussed. No matter what evaluation form is used-and no matter how often it is reworked-people will not be satisfied with it. The process is a difficult one and it is a process with which people naturally have great concern. The clearest means of comparing evaluations is by scoring or rating them in some fashion. If a rating scale is used on the form, it should have an odd number of categories, so an individual may be rated at the midpoint as "acceptable" or "entirely satisfactory." The rating categories need not be defined, although the top and bottom of the scale have to be clearly delineated. The characteristics being evaluated should be defined. The scale should be applied as evenly as possible throughout the library. To ensure this consistency, an administrative review of the ratings before they are given is appropriate.

Supervisors should agree that the "score" for each staff member places that individual in an appropriate position compared to their other staff. If a supervisor is having particular difficulty in differentiating among ratings for several staff members, have him list all of his staff in order of their importance to the department and then ask for the reasoning behind this ranking. The establishment of production norms is helpful to justify an employee's ranking in certain categories. Being able to say what quantity of a certain task is acceptable within a certain time period, what quantity is unacceptable, and what quantity is exceptional requires a series of time studies involving multiple staff members who agree that the results are reasonable. Over a period of several years norms can be established for a variety of tasks, but norms cannot be established to quantify all areas that are ranked. Performance evaluation is basically a subjective process. Consequently, a written narrative should be included to explain any evaluation that rates an employee higher or lower than the midpoint.

You may find it useful to approach the evaluation period not only to evaluate staff, but also as a time to step back with the department heads and look at their areas. How satisfied does each staff member appear to be with his job? Who is likely to be leaving the library within the next year? If a certain person left, how would you be inclined to restructure the department? The individual who fails to contribute his share of work causes a morale problem. Even if they do not verbalize it, fellow employees wonder how he can get away with so little work, such long coffee breaks, such long conversations about non-library matters, and so much time on the phone. As the technical services manager, you should make sure that an establish procedure is followed when dealing with such a problem. If there is no library or institutional procedure, you should make sure that the immediate supervisor begins documenting a problem situation as soon as a pattern develops. Documentation can be as simple as daily notes jotted on a desk calendar or on scraps of paper that are dated and gathered together in a file folder. If necessary, these notes can then be organized into a chronological description of the problem. Ideally, the supervisor should immediately bring to the employee's attention the fact that there is a problem and just how it should be corrected. This initial contact should be informal, may be oral, and should be done in private. The supervisor should include in his documentation the date and length of this conversation. You should evaluate the supervisor's documentation after this initial meeting. Does the employee appear to be a problem due to a shortcoming within the library, or due to a personal shortcoming? Consider these questions:

* Initially, was the person trained properly?
* Are ongoing training and documentation (*e.g.*, manuals) sufficient?
* Is there a problem with the facilities or the equipment? Is the supervisor inadequate?
* What is, his track record? Was he a productive employee before this particular situation or has his performance bordered on unacceptable in the past?

* Does the employee appear to have a learning disability?
* Has the employee gained or lost a considerable amount of weight for no apparent reason?
* Is there a way to restructure the employees duties satisfactorily for both the library and the employee?

Inform both the library personnel officer and your supervisor of the situation. If the problem appears to be one caused by factors not of the employee's making or if it appears that he needs professional help, determine an appropriate course of action apart from the procedures described here. If you work within a union environment, be sure to follow required procedures. Continue to work with the supervisor to document the situation. Problems associated with time are the easiest to document. It is a clear-cut process to establish when an employee fails to report for work, comes in tardy, leaves early, takes extended coffee breaks or lunch hours, or cannot account for time away from the work station. Production problems may be harder to document, but can be handled by establishing norms for the tasks involved. These norms can be determined in-house and verified by library directors or technical services managers in several other libraries of similar size and purpose. Then a daily account can be taken of the individual's work production with an assessment of "acceptable" or "unacceptable". If an individual has a job that requires judgment, examples of lack of judgment should be documented. If the individual's problem relates to his interpersonal skills, examples of the problem should be documented. It is preferable that the supervisor has first-hand knowledge of these examples, but examples reported to the supervisor by others in the department and by other supervisors may be recorded to demonstrate a pattern.

If the problem continues, the supervisor should arrange a formal meeting with the employee preferably within a month of the informal contact. The supervisor should outline the problem, state that it has continued even after the informal oral request that it be corrected, outline specifically what must be done within a specific timeframe, and state the consequences (*e.g.*, meeting with department division head. written reprimand, evaluation of "unsatisfactory") if the problem is not corrected within that timeframe. This formal meeting should be outlined in a memorandum from the supervisor to the employee with copies for appropriate individuals (*e.g.*, department head, division head, personnel officer, union representative). Prior to the meeting, you should discuss the situation with the library director to determine just what consequences the library administration can support. The goal of this process is to correct the problem and end up with a more productive employee. If the problem is corrected, such correction should be noted in a positive manner either orally or in written form, depending on the gravity of the problem at the next performance evaluation. If the problem still exists at the pre-established deadline, the consequence that had been outlined in the formal meeting should occur, It, too, should be formally documented. If the problem is not corrected by yet another established deadline, a more serious consequence should be established. In subsequent conferences it may be helpful to have an additional person present to corroborate the discussion. This individual, who may be the unit head, the department head, or you as the technical services manager, should immediately write his summary of what occurred during the meeting: This process should continue, with formal documentation at each point, until the employee is terminated or until the library administration or the institution determines another alternative.

Dealing consistently with a problem employee is a very time-consuming process. All too often, the effort does not correct the situation. However, the supervisor should not give up on the situation. Even if the environment does not provide the opportunity for the employee to be dismissed, it is important to continue to document the process. If other employees realize that the problem employee is being called to task, the situation may not be an energy drain on the entire department. Also, if documentcltion continues to mount, the organizational environment may change so that the employee may be moved or terminated; or, the problem employee may become so weary of the repeated attention to the problem that he may leave. In many organizations employees have an opportunity to voice a complaint through an established grievance procedure. Be sure that you are thoroughly acquainted with your institution's procedure. Inform an employee who appears to have a complaint that there is a formal procedure through which he may make that complaint. Give him a copy of the procedure. The grievance process usually calls for the employee to describe his complaint in writing and then to meet with those who may be helpful in resolving the problem-either those within the supervisory hierarchy of the organization or a review panel which presents its findings to a member of the administration.

If there is no grievance procedure or if the employee who has grieved is not satisfied with the outcome, the employee may bring legal action against the library's documentation may be used and to know how best to describe the situation during legal proceedings. Frequently technical services managers especially after they have been around a few years and there fore worked with a number of people are asked to serve as references for library staff members or. for colleagues with whom they have worked in other professional capacities.

Potential employers seeking references or present employers seeking comments in connection withy a colleague's eligibility for promotion often ask specific questions about that individual or outline specific areas on which they would like comment. If you have worked directly with the individual for whom you are serving as a reference, it is relatively straightforward to respond to such requests. However, if the person for whom you are a reference has not worked with you directly (say, for example, he has reported to someone who reported to you or is someone from another institution with whom you have worked in a committee situation oniy), then giving a reference is not as simple. Giving recommendations is one of your professional responsibilities. What you write is important, for it stands as a record of your integrity. The following points may be helpful in writing references.

1. If the person is a member of the library staff, state the dates of the individual's employment in the library and the duties involved in the position(s) he has held.

2. If the person held different positions within the library, explain why he asked to move from one to another (*e.g.*, assumed more responsibility).
3. State the time span during which you have known the person and in what capacity. If you never worked directly with him, make that clear by explaining the reporting hierarchy (if the individual is on the library staff) or by describing just what your professional relationship has been (*e.g.*, worked with him on a certain library association committee, have communicated with him frequently as a fellow technical services manager, have coauthored papers with him).
4. Address as many of the questions asked or points raised by the employer or potential employer as possible.
5. If the person has held other positions since leaving the library staff, suggest that references be sought from subsequent employers.
6. If you are asked to comment in a specific area in which you have not had an opportunity to evaluate the individual's capabilities, so state. For example, if you are asked to evaluate the individual's supervisory abilities and he never held any supervesory position while you worked with him, explain, that. Also, if the individual's working relationships with other library staff were very good, you can make that observation and say that, on the basis of that observation, the individual may have the potential to become a good supervisor.
7. If you are making your comments from more than one vantage point (*e.g.*, as a fellow staff member, a professional colleague, a scholar, an author, an active participant in a professional organization), make that clear.
8. Offer to answer any further questions and provide your telephone number.

Occasionally you will be asked to give a reference for an individual who did not work out well in the position in which you knew him. Frequently you will have some reservations about the individual for whom you are a reference. Three suggestions may be helpful here.

1. If you have serious reservations about the individual, let him know your specific concerns and explain to him in what areas you can make positive comments and in what areas, if asked, you cannot make positive comments.

2. Be aware of the federal/state/institution regulations that affect the reference process. Some institutions require that the person for whom you are giving a reference has given permission for you serve as a reference.

3. Remember that an individual who has not worked out well in one situation may work out very well in another. For example, a person who has not met the high pressure requirements in a publish-or-perish environment in a research library may do very well in a public library or in an academic institution in which there is no pressure to publish. Or someone who did not cope well with a position supervising 20 people may do a fine job in a position in which there is no supervisory responsibility. When giving the reference, point out the individual's strengths which would be advantageous in the new position. However, do not fail to mention problems which would most likely effect any job situation adversely.

The most important thing to remember in giving a reference is to be truthful. Make a strong evaluation mean something. Reserve "recommendations without reservation" to a very small percentage of your references. Give the kind of reference you would like to receive when asking for a reference for a potential employee.

Exit Interview

The exit interview should begin with questions about the staff member's future plans: when they are going, what the new job will be like. It may be helpful for you to briefly reiterate the specific responsibilities the staff member has had in the library and ask him to elaborate on them. You may find these four questions most useful: *(1)* What did you like best about your work in the library? *(2)* What did you like least about your work in the library? *(3)* While you have been here have you felt that you received as much information as you needed about what is going on other places in the library? And *(4)* What suggestions do you have for the library administration? They may all be answered on many levels and you may pursue the answers as you wish by saying "Can you give me an example?" Or "Can you explain that a little more?" As with any interview, it is important to sit through pauses even though you may be tempted to go on to another question or fill in the silence with words of your own. Often the staff member is formulating thoughts and if given a chance will say quite a bit more. Exit interviews can be particularly helpful in finding out about the working atmosphere in the department an individual is leaving. Keep in mind, however, that once a person has made a decision to go elsewhere, he may feel the need to justify it by condemning the place he has been. Weigh carefully just what might be sour grapes and what might be a legitimate complaint.

Employee observations about morale are difficult to address, probably because this subject is rarely mentioned in a positive light. When one hears over a span of years that morale is at an all-time low, one wonders how it is possible to have gotten worse when we were at bottom quite some time ago. The following may help.

1. Different staff members have different vantage points. Those commenting negatively on morale may not have an administrative perspective.

2. Morale stems from a feeling, a perception, that things are all right or all wrong. Suggest to the key complainants that they approach things in a positive manner and work to reverse the viewpoint.

3. Give staff something else to think about. For example, have them pull together on a special project.

4. Recognize staff members who do approach things in a positive manner and who do their jobs well (*e.g.*, annual staff award or staff member of the month).
5. Ask the vociferous individual who continues to perceive that morale is low why he thinks this is so. If the factors cited are not within your power to adjust, or if they are and you do not choose to adjust them, consider suggesting that this person seek employment in an arena that he perceives has more positive morale factors.

The ways in which you make decisions and manage change- and even the manner in which you arrange your office—contribute to the image others have of you as a manager. When making decisions, you will never know all the pieces and most of the time you will be dealing with very incomplete information. As a manager coming from a technical services orientation of exacting detail, learning to deal with ambiguity can be a difficult task. To develop your ability to deal with various problems, intentionally place yourself in new personal situations. Take a different route home from work occasionally. Shop in a different grocery store. Force yourself to find a particular place with exact directions.

If you are an ardent note-taker, are you really referring to your notes? If so, what portion? Filing. notes so you will be able to retrieve them later takes time. To what extent can you eliminate your note-dependence? Begin taking briefer notes. Once you are successful, target a session for which it is not necessary that you know every detail. Do not take notes at all; try to memorize the key points covered. Write down these key points when the session is over. Vary the degree of notes you take to match the amount of information you really need later. In large organizations departmental staff may feel that their opinions or concerns are not heard. To overcome the idea that you as an administrator never pay atten.tion to the low man on the totem pole, you may espouse an "open door policy"-a willingness to talk with any staff member at any time. This should at least be controlled to the extent that these meetings are primarily by appointment.

From your department heads' viewpoints, the problem with such a policy is that staff can "go around" them and discuss issues on which they have no input. Whenever a staff member talks with you to express an idea or concern related to technical services work, it is important to inform the department head of the meeting. Procedural concerns can usually be handled in a straightforward manner. Personality conflicts, however, can be very "sticky wickets"-especially if the staff member's concern is the manner in which the department head is handling things. There are always as many sides to a story as there are personal interactions, so you should hear what the department head or others involved have to say. If there is a repeated pattern of staff members in a department complaining about a department head, a problem exists. It is up to you, in consultation with the personnel librarian (if there is one) and fellow administrators, to work with the department head to correct the problem. If that is unsuccessful, the department head should be moved to another assignment.

Communication

Frequently, what is meant by the speaker or writer is not what is heard or red by the listener or reader. For this reason, it is important to have staff discuss what eye are doing or attempting to do when given a specific charge. One of the important tenets of management is "follow through; follow through; follow through." After asking that a certain letter be sent, if that letter is at all necessary, check to make sure that it has gone out. After initiating the directions for a special project, check to see how it is being implemented and, as it is going along, check to see what is happening. As the technical services department and unit heads, and other staff. It helps if these meetings occur on a regular basis. Providing routine meeting times is a sensible practice, for it allows all parties involved to know there will soon be a forum for certain concerns. Ideally, the administrative group should meet regularly to exchange information and establish policy. This works well if (and these are big if) the library director is comfortable in such an open environment and if the administrative group works well as a team. If no regular meetings are established for the administrative group, set them up to the extent that it is within your authority to do so. Suggest specific topics for discussion. If the administrative group does not work well together, you may find it necessary to have a preliminary talk with each one, explaining the topic, determining his opinions on it and how it affects his area of responsibility. You should meet with each department head on a weekly basis. At this meeting both you and the department head will have various topics collected during the week that you wish to address and you should have an idea of the importance of each topic so low priority items can be deferred it there is a lot to discuss.

It is not necessary to have a formal agenda, but you should be the individual determining the direction that the meeting takes. If the technical services division is large enough to have organizational units within its departments, you should also meet periodically with each unit head and his respective department head in order to discuss unit specifics and how any general technical services direction applies to the unit. These meetings may be on a "called" basis, but once their cycle is established they should occur at least once every quarter. You should take the lead in these meetings, going through the agenda you have established, asking the unit head for additional topics and, before the end of the meeting, asking the department head for additional points of discussion. If the library director meets with the entire library staff once or twice a year, it may not be necessary for you to call general meetings with the technical services staff. However, it may be necessary to assemble the technical services staff to explain a specific topic (*e.g.*, the time-table for a specific phase of automation). In all meetings or at lest several times a year you may call for general questions. This gives staff the opportunity to find out what is going on in an open forum. However, it also gives a staff member with a bone to pick an opportunity to do so publicly. It is important for you to respond to loaded questions with self-confidence. The answer to an unwelcome question may be given in generalities, possibly with an invitation to the questioner to discuss it after the meeting.

It is important to initiate the change process only in areas in which it is worth the time and effort to change. If something is working well, why alter it? Remember, staff have only so much time and energy and if they are involved in something of high priority, that project will be affected if they are expected to address additional change as well. It is important to approach change as a positive event—an opportunity. Some events automatically provide opportunities for change. Examples are the arrival of a new department head, the departure of an employee who was particularly hesitant or disruptive about a change, reorganization, moving into new space, and automation may provide the opportunity to reorganize a specific area that needed a leadership re-arrangement anyway. It is important to remember that change is a difficult thing for anyone. Even moving the furniture around can cause one to become disoriented for a while. Change provides disruption and an excellent opportunity tor a while. Change provides disruption and an excellent Opportunity for the grumblers to grumble and the rumor mill to overflow. It is important to orchestrate the change well. Carefully map out the order in which you will talk to fellow administrators, department heads, unit heads, those directly affected by the change, and other staff. Explain to those who will be affected why a certain change is coming about; tell them that you know change is disruptive and sometimes frightening; assure them that they will all still have jobs and that they will be doing most of the tasks they are already doing.

Your Office Location

Should your office be located "with the troops" in technical services or in the library administrative office complex? You may have no choice, for your office might be firmly established in one location. If there is a choice, consider the following: Where are the offices for the other division heads located? If some are in the administrative office complex, those individuals will automatically have access to more library-wide information than those located elsewhere. They will also have more perceived power because they are physically closer to the director. Having an office in the technical services area allows the manager to have a daily sense of what is happening within the division. Technical services staff will feel more comfortable by "just walking in" to talk or touch base. It is most helpful if this office is a totally private one, for if it is necessary to go elsewhere to have a private discussion, leaving the office for a meeting with someone in a private location gives a signal to the staff that something is going on. Insofar as space permits, providing a variety of seating arrangements in your office is a good idea. Where you sit and where others sit during a meeting often suggests hierarchy and can easily set the tone, making people comfortable or not. Sitting at a table implies that the participants are getting down to business. If there is no documentation to look at, the table can be perceived as a barrier and the situation can appear formidable especially to a staff member who serves at a lower organizational level. Having people sit in a circle with chairs equal spaces apart, possibly around a round table, implies equality. Having people sit on a couch and padded chairs provides an informal setting to put people at ease. Remaining in your desk chair while other sit in chairs in front of your desk keeps you in the seat of authority. If you remain standing or stand during the conversation, you are suggesting through body language that is time for the others to leave. It is helpful to choose a seating arrangement that will set the atmosphere you want. Plan this in advance, so that when the other participants arrive, an adequate number of seats are available and you can easily direct them where to sit.

Can you remember what you did while at work yesterday? Think through the entire day. With whom did you talk? In what meetings did you participate? What phone calls did you make or receive? How many times did you play telephone tag? What letters or messages did you send? Where you able to get through the incoming mail? Of those things that you had planned to do at the beginning of the day, how many were still left undone at the end? How many unfinished items could have effectively and logically been delegated, to someone else? While thinking back, can you account for all-hours of the day? The number of topics a technical services manager addresses within one day can be amazing, so it is' not surprising to be unable to piece together what you did Just 24 hours ago. If you feel that you are not quite in control when it comes to managing your work day, you may. find some of the following suggestions useful.

For a "typical" work day (meaning one when you are in the library and nothing highly unusual is scheduled in advance), jot down what is going on. Once or twice during the day and then again in the evening, think back on just how you have spent your time. Outline your activities in the order they happened. Indicate topic, amount of time spent, and people involved. Several days later, review your outline. How many activities were planned in advance? How many unplanned activities were unavoidable? Where there any new topics introduced for which you could have provided an immediate decision, rather than setting them aside to be addressed later? How many interruptions did you receive from staff who could have logically gotten their answers from someone else within technical services or the administrative office? You may find it helpful to outline your activities for a week. Examine the outline for obvious patterns. For example, one particular staff member may be interrupting you repeatedly for answers that could be reasonably provided by another staff member. If so, redirect them when you next receive their questions. If many people are reporting directly to you might consider establishing several functional units, each with a head who handles routine questions. If you never have time to address the stacks on your desk, consider closing your door and having messages held one hour each day so you have a set time to tackle the paperwork, such as schedules or timesheets, you might delegate those tasks to someone else.

Keep a Legible Desk Calendar

Record your appointments on a calendar (electronic or not) which both you and your secretary can understand. Make sure the entries are made in a routine format, so you can with a quick glance easily understand what is scheduled. At the end of your desk calendar, record in a logical fashion the appointments and conferences scheduled for the next calendar year. Set up a calendar for the subsequent year at least 8 weeks before the current calendar ends so you have ample time to transfer appropriate notes and begin entering additional commitments on the new calendar. If you have tasks that you plan to do later, but have no definite time set, provide a "tickler" system what will allow you to remember them. If you have a paper calendar, you might use self-sticking notes inserted at the beginning of the appropriate week or month. On these, list the people with whom you intend to make contact and the topics that need to be addressed. It is best to keep only one calendar. Carrying one and having another at the office may drive you crazy, because multiple calendars increase the possibilities of scheduling two things at once or forgetting to look at all things scheduled. Office software systems provide calendars that are designed to coordinate office meetings. These work well when everyone who is supposed to be entering schedule information actually does. But no -matter the format of your calendar, the most important thing is, remember to read it daily-at the beginning of the day!

The most economical way to address mail is to actually do something with each piece as you come to it, rather than simply reading it and leaving it somewhere on your desk. You might lightly jot down on the back of a letter or in its margins the steps needed to respond to it. If you are going to write back, outline all of the topics you plan to cover in the letter. If you are going to send copies to others, record that fact. If you need additional information, make a list of what you need and pull it yourself or ask someone to begin gathering it for you. If you can handle the item with one or two phone calls, go ahead and make them. Consider which pieces of mail you do not really need to keep. Throw away those ~avertisements you know are being mailed to the library In quantity. Read and then toss into the wastebasket whose items that have been sent to you for your information if a designated agent is retaining a copy for the record. Items that fall into this category are minutes or notes of meetings, institution newsletters, and routine materials (another copy of which office staff have already been instructed to save). Consider which pieces of mail you should route to others right away. You may wish to stipulate that the item be returned to you after everyone else has seen it, if you hope to read it later. Do not feel obligated to read every word of every piece of mail, especially when it comes to newsletters and journals. Scan the contents or the article titles and read only those that really interest you. You might divide future reading possibilities into categories, such as "Red Today," "Red Later" and "may be." Try to get through the "Red Today" within a week, the "Read Laters" by the end of the month, and stash the. "maybes" on a lower shelf so you can get back to them later if necessary.

If possible, use electronic mail at the library level, institution level, and beyond the-institution level. It will speed up your contact with whatever group of people you can reach through it. It will eliminate a great deal of telephone tag. It will allow you to reach more people. at one time. Its conventions permit short, informal messages. If you have no e-mail access, do what you can to get it. Meanwhile, use the phone. Telephone tag is cheaper than letter writing. If you cannot reach the person you are calling, leave a message that you would like the call returned. Include the times during which the chances of your being able to take the call are the greatest. If .there is a time zone difference, point it out to the person .who is taking the message. Using electronic mail can certainly change habits. It may keep you from walking around too much. Consider the side effects: you may want to walk through various work areas on a routine basis anyway, even though you do not need to actually go in to talk with a particular person; you may need to exercise more or eat less. As with the use of calendars, the prime suggestion is: remember to read your e-mail and respond to it regularly. The best way to encourage others to check their e-mail is to use it to annouhce meetings and to send necessary documents. However, remember to make copies of those things that need to be kept on file-especially messages which reflect policy decisions. The danger of staying in a job until one understands all of the aspects of it and even becomes comfortable in it is that the tasks become stale or the pressures too routine and haggling and the incumbent burns out. To prevent burnout, it is important to introduce for yourself some new challenges along the way, such as learning something new., assuming additional duties, or becoming involved in a different level of professional activities. If study leave, educational leave, or sabbatical leave are available at your institution; apply for leave when eligible or seek funding from an outside source (*e.g.*, council on Library Resources or an ALA award programme) and request leave without pay from your home institution. Expanding your horizons is important if you are to continue to be a productive technical services manager. If you find no channels to new horizons within your present position, seriously consider whether or not you will be happy in your current position for the rest of your professional career. If not, get another job.

It is important to stay abreast of what is happening in the library world especially in the technical services areas. Meet and stay in touch with other technical services managers. Join local, state, and national library groups. If you are in the United States, go to an American Library Association meeting. Plan your schedule carefully. Within the Association for Library Collections and Technical Services of the American Library Association you can find more than 80 Committees and discussion groups working on various technical services issues. Depending on the type of library you working groups within other divisions of ALA, such as the Association of College and Research Libraries, the Library Administration and Management Association, or the Public Library Association. Visit the exhibits. Find out what is going on. Talk with people. Find others who have the same current concerns you do and make arrangements to talk with them more. The most valuable part of any meeting is talking with others who have similar interests. Stay in touch with the library world and with librarians in your specific area of interest, for through this contact you can continue to receive new ideas and support. Read library publications relevant to your areas of interest.

❐

5

Computer in Library Management

The use of computers has been steadily increasing in Science and Technology since the Second World War. Most of the advanced countries of the world have made much advance in this respect but India has just made a start, especially in industry and business and there also these are witnessing stiff opposition from the employees and their trade because of the fear of retrenchment. However, their application is increasing day by day in science, technology, industry and business. Their recent conquest is railways. Libraries are no exception to them. As the Library Authorities and Librarians are becoming aware of their potential uses, these are being put to more use. So much so that not only some courses in computer applications are being arranged regularly by the private sector, but they are finding their pride place in Library science courses also. For example, the syllabus of the Master's Comrse in Library and Information Science: of Delhi University has included "Computer use in Libraries as a part of one of the papers. It is hoped that their use libraries would increase in the years to come in India, thought not at a rapid speed, especially because of our socio-economic conditions and the prohibitive of their installation and maintenance.

A computer is a device which is capable of accepting information/data automatically, applying a sequence of prescribed processes to the information/data and supplying the results of these processes. It usually of input and output devices, storage arithmetic and local units and a control unit.

Thought the first automatic general purpose digital computer, designed by the Havard university, was built in 1944 by the I.B.M. yet its technology dates back to 1833 when Charles Babbage devised an idea of a computer which was utilised by George R Stibitz of the bell telephone laboratories in 1930s for using telephone relays in the construction of a computing machine. Further, A. M. Turing gave the theory of computability in 1936 which provided a theoretical basis for designing a computing machine. However, the first electronic digital computer ENIAC was built in 1946 at the University of Pennsylvania under the over all guidance of John W. Mauchly and J. Presper Eckert. Similarly, the first EDVAC was built at the University of Pennsylvania under the guidance of John Von Neumann in mid-1940s and the first stored-programme machine EDSAC was designed at the Cambridge University, England in 1949.

There have been very rapid changes in computer technology. First generation computers developed during 1954-59 had vacuum tubes. These were replaced by pea-sized transistors in the Second Generation Computers developed during 1964. The Third Generation Computers developed after 1964 used tiny chips sized transistors. The forth generation computers which will make use of integrated circuits have been developed in 1970. There is a possibility of BIC to be replaced by 'GIC' *i.e.* Gigantic Integrated Circuits which will have the speed of more than one billion operation per second. These may have memory, equivalent to a million volumes of 500 pages each. These developments will have immense impact on the storage and retrieval of information in Libraries.

Dr. Jerome B. Wiesner, former Science Advisor to the late President Kennedy of USA rightly remarked that the Computer with its promise of million fold increase in man's capacity to handle information, will undoubtedly have the most far-teaching social consequences of any contemporary technical development. The potential for good in the computer and the danger inherent in its misuse exceed our ability to imagine.

The latest development in the field of computer technology is the reported Soviet-patented high capacity computer called Recursion

Computer which is capable of coping with sophisticated scientific and technological task, thousands of time quicker than the present Computers as the new computer is multi-processor. Soviet specialists according to Prof. Mikhail Ignatiev are now developing Computers capable of performing 12.5 million operations per second for serial productions.

Another development in computer technology is the production of handy computers which will cut down home and office drudgery. It performs daily household chores such as putting the lights off and on, protecting the homes, balancing the cheque books, reading one' pulse and helping in the preparation of breakfast. These mini-compute may be available even in pocket calculators or micro wave ovens sewing machines or automobiles. These microprocessors which ar low-cost computers capable of performing jobs equivalent to thos of room-size computers will change the whole picture. It is estimate that within less than 10 years, some limited use computers will cos between 5 and 10. Voice-computers are in the air. As such the new computers will help people to overcome the fear of big brothe computers. Similarly, special-purpose computers will cost betwee 100 and 1000.

The Computer can either purchased right away or in eas instalments or can be hired. No doubt, various computer manufacturin companies allure the prospective purchasers by stressing that th total cost of the computer can be realised in the form of savings ar the cost of service for which additional staff has to be pressed in service. However, in view of the fast-changing computer technolog and the increasing manufacture of sophisticated computers durin last few decades many computers will become obsolete theret putting the libraries to irreparable loss, it is but advisable that not on big computers are taken on hire basis but mini-computers and oth turnkey devices should be made use of for performing specific jo so that the risk-remains with the manufactures or it is mimimal a the library is assured of latest Computer to be taken into account the respect include the following.

1. Main-frame Computers VS. Mini-computers.
2. Capabilities of various Computers, especially in relation to library applications.
3. Reliability and Service of various makes of different manufacturing compames.
4. Hardware and Software.
5. Specifications and Accountability of various makes of computers.
6. Amenability to national and international standards.
7. Easy servicing and availability of spare parts.
8. Warranty & Safeguards.
9. Free training for hard ware & soft ware.

Kinds of Computers

Computers are of two kinds *i.e.*, *(i)* Analogue and *(ii)* Digital. The former is useful for scientific work as it helps in calculating the accepted information according to a pre-determined pattern which may be mechanical, electro-mechanical or electronic. In other Words, it helps. in processing the information in a physical from *i.e.* in terms of weight, volume or electric current. For example, it can translate temperature, flow, speed, attitude, voltage an other physical variables into related electrical quantities and for this purpose it uses electrical equivalent circuits.

The latter type of computer *i.e.* Digital Computer is a general purpose computer as it helps in calculating and processing the accepted data in digital form. In other words, it makes use of conventional letters, symbols and numbers for the purpose and is, therefore, suitable for processing of information in general and for various other commercial business and office applications. It is this type of computer which is used in libraries. The digital Computer can be further divided into two types *i.e.*, batch processor and Real-time Processor.

Batch Processor

It processes the data accumulated into batches or groups over a period of time. It consists of the following four component units:

(i) The hardware *i.e.* the machinery which is designed to carry out instructions necessary to perform the assigned jobs.

(ii) The Inputs Units help in converting the data passed on to them into a standard from acceptable to the Central Processor.

(iii) The Central processor of the heart of the computer consists of the storage unit, the control unit and the arithmetic unit.

(a) Storage Unit

The data in the store section of the computer is governed by the software the programme *i.e.* a series of instructions which are devised by the computer manufacturer or by the computer users or their agents. The capacity of the central processor is measured in thousands of units which may consist of one character of a byte or a computer word.

(b) Control Unit

The second part of the central processor of a digital computer is called the control unit because it not only helps in picking up one programme only at a time but also activates the necessary circuits so as to help other parts of the computer to perform the described jobs. However, a direct control over the operations can be exercised by the operator who comes to know as to what is going on inside the computer besides enabling him to key in massages necessary to run a programme.

(c) Arithmetic Unit

The third part of the central processor is known as the arithmetic unit because it carries out arithmetic calculations such as additions subtractions and comparisons.

(d) The Out Put Units

The results of the foregoing processes performed by various parts of the computer are called output units which may either be in print or in machine readable print or punched cards, paper tape or magnetic tape.

(e) Backing Store Units

The backing store provides the filing system for the computer and consists of magnetic tape reels. The input, output and backing store units are together called peripherals *i.e.* those which are outside.

Real Time Processor

The Real Time Processor is designed to process a large volume of data. In this system, the units called terminals have a direct connection or on-line connection with the computer in such a way that data can be fed to the processor directly. Generally, the terminal is an electric type-writer through which the operator keys in information or interrogatories. In this system, there is no need of presenting this information on machine-readable media *i.e.* magnetic tape punched cards or paper tape because in it the programme can directly control the processing of data received from a terminal *i.e.* an electric typewriter besides adding it to the files on backing store or sending back to the terminal the data already available on file and that is why is called real time processor because quick service even though the data is received from many terminals. As such, these two processors differ from each other on the basis of input and output units used by them.

The main advantage of a digital computer is its speed of processing the data. It carrier out the instructions of the programme in a fraction of a second. The speed of the peripherals expressed its one thousandth of a second or one millisecond while that of the central processor is indicated as one thousand millionth of a second or nanosecond. It is evident that the speed of the former is slower than that of the latter, the reason for it being than in the former electromechanical devices are used while in the latter electronic devices are made use of.

It is claimed that computers can serve as a panacea for all the existing ills libraries since these can be made use of for performing efficiently all sorts of jobs from the procurement of the reading materials to their organisation and use. In another words, these include the acquisition, classification and cataloguing and the circulation and use of the reading materials besides making provision for information and retrieval systems. The Computer-based book order System of the Michigan University library started with the use of 1401 Tape Computer and the present type of 360/40 computer. The system consists of the following processes:

1. The name and address of the book-sellers or suppliers are stored in a disk file and each one of them is assigned a number.

2. The book orders for the books to be procured are key-punched and each of the book-sellers is identified by the number alloted to him as stated in (i) above.

3. The orders are batched and sent to the data processing Centre on the campus twice a weak. On the following days, ten copies of the order forms are received by the library alongwith pre-punched cards in triplicate for each order and a list of orders according to each book budget a location besides an undated cumulative supplementary list representing all new orders placed in the library system and all transactions done against the orders placed earlier.

4. Out of the ten copies of the order forms, two copies are mailed to the book supplier and the third copy is field in the order by the order number, while the remaining seven copies are field in a separate file to be used for classification and cataloguing work.

5. The pre-punched cards serve various purposes, namely to indicate receipt of the book the need to pay the bill, to count the books added to the stock and to remove the order card from the order file in case the book is classified and catalogued.

6. The cumulative supplemental outstanding order file is passed against the budget allocation and statistics files every fortnight which helps in printing the up-to-date position of funds so as to help the Order Section Incharge to control new orders. In this way, two supplementary order tapes are printed every month for bringing up to date the master outstanding order file, indicating the position of each order at that time.
7. Letters for the unsupplied items are issued.
8. An Expenditure Statement is prepared monthly. It indicates the amount already spent up-to-date and the amount which is still unspent.

Advantages

1. Many repetitive jobs are performed at one and the same time, thereby reducing the number of staff members for the order section.
2. An accurate, up-to-date-and automatic information is made available about the latest position of each book order placed there by helping to avoid unnecessary duplicate ordering.
3. An accurate up-to-date and automatic information is made available about the latest position of each head of the book fund *i.e.*, how much amount has already been spent and how much is in balance thereby either to limit future orders or to accelerate the pace of orders so as to utilise the funds in time.

The Yale University Library System

This system provides for all the processes through which a book has to pass through the moment it is selected for purchase and is made available for use by the readers.

The Cornell University Library System

In the second system, an order-search from is used for placing a book order which remains there alongwith the L.C. cards upto the time of receipt of the book. In case, L.C. card is not available machine generated orders for L.C. cards are produced automatically.

On-line Systems

Besides in three other University libraries the On-Line Systems are in use. These include the "LOLA Library On-Line Acquisitions Sub-System Washington University Library "Rice University's On-Line Acquisition System and "The University of California at Irvine's On-Line Acquisition System".

Washington University Library System

The fires system has been designed to perform all technical services and processes consisting of various separate sub-stems of which one is the Acquisitions sub-system performs the following seven functions:

1. Preparing an entry indicating request for purchase.
2. Preparing a book selection entry and its checking.
3. Preparing a book order and its processing.
4. Receiving the book.
5. Processing Bills.
6. Preparing a standing order plan.
7. Preparing a report of the books received.

The Rice University Library System

The second system at the Rice University in based on MARC II tapes and holdings at eighteen libraries of the Gulf Coast which are cooperating in the project.

In this system, when a suggestion for the purchase of a book is received, the above record is first checked up to know whether the book in question is already in one of the libraries. If it is there, a report to this effect is generated but if the book is not available in any of the libraries but if the information is available in the file, the order for the book is added to database. Simultaneously, a multiple order from and receipt card in order to update the record are generated and the cost of the book is debited to book fund. In case the order relates to multiple volumes a card for each volume is produced.

If the information about the book is not available in the file *i.e.* data, the details of the order are included in the holdings and the non-order file. On receipt of the ordered book, a cataloguer work sheet is produced which is used to correct, and update the existing record before catalogue cards for the book are prepared.

In this system, a teletypewriter, called CONTROLMATIC Model 37, is used to supply to the cooperating libraries the current information received from the Library of Congress besides the preparation of classified extracts and the card listing to be used by Book Selection as a book selection tool.

The University of California System at Irvine

The third system at the university of California at Irvine makes use of IE 50 along with a central core memory of 512 K. It consists of two sub-systems *i.e.* book found accounting and purchase order writing. The first sub-system is to record, process and make available financial information regarding the book fund. The second sub-system besides writing purchase orders is to debit automatically the cost of book ordered besides conversion of the foreign currencies.

Computer-based Periodicals Acquisition, Processing and Control Systems

The acquisition, processing and control of periodicals have been eluding a permanent solution due to their idiocyncrasies. In many cases, the periodicals have been controlling the librarian instead of the librarian controlling the periodicals. The latest method to bring them under control takes the help of the computer, which is considered by many a panacea for various ills of library jobs including those of processing and controlling of periodicals and serials. Though efforts to develop a computerized system were started in the 1940's yet the first important system was designed and developed as late as 1962 only which was fully put into operation in 1964. The earlier systems were using computers for keeping parallel records on manually-run systems, whereas the latter system discontinued their use.

The periodical's work involves the following main jobs:

1. Ordering and Bill Passing.
2. Receiving supply.
3. Claiming the unsupplied periodicals.
4. Completing the volumes and sending them for binding.
5. Classification and cataloguing.
6. Preparing lists of Holdings and Union lists.
7. Administrative Control.

To perform these functions efficiently, various computer-based systems have been brought into use. In India also, computer is being used for the acquisition, processing and controlling of periodicals.

Most of these systems have the following components of records, inputs and outputs, with, however, minor variations besides converting the existing manual file onto a magnetic tape.

Inputs

(i) Location Mark.

(ii) Call number.

(iii) Title.

(iv) Periodicals holdings information with years and volumes.

(v) Month and year of the latest issue received in the library.

(vi) Source of supply *i.e.* either by purchase, gift or exchange.

(vii) Fund Allocation.

(viii) Supplier and his code number.

(ix) Period of subscription.

(x) Unique Identification number for each periodical title in the file.

(xi) Frequency of publication *i.e.* number of issues per volume and number of issues per year.

(xii) Expected dates of publication and receipt in the library.

(xiii) The existing position of a periodical *i.e.* whether it is active or not.

(xiv) Binding Code Numbers and other Binding Instructions.

(xv) Expected dates of the receipt of TCI, *i.e.* Title Contents and Index pages.

A Mnemonic Title, *i.e.* Abbreviated Title is used for the purpose of checking the receipt of a periodical issue.

Outputs

In most of the systems referred to above, the outputs consist of the following:

(i) *Master File List* which is an alphabetical list of periodicals, by Main Entry, received in the library indicating details of periodicals holdings of the library, is meant for staff use.

(ii) *Public Holdings Printout,* also an alphabetical list of periodicals by title or main entry which is meant for public use and consists of daily, weekly and monthly lists. These lists are very simple and contain only such information as is relevant to the users.

(iii) Supplement printouts which include daily receipts to be cumulated weekly.

(iv) Non-receipt And Claim List for all the overdue issues of periodicals.

(v) Titles List indicating the list of periodicals received in the library and their location but without the information regarding the total number of volumes held by a library.

(vi) Subject List for public use *i.e.* subject-wise list of periodicals.

(vii) Shelf List *i.e.* A classified list of periodicals with information about holdings.

(viii) Duplicate Lists *i.e.* lists of all periodicals of which more than one copy are received in the library.

(ix) Cross-References List.

(x) Subscription Agent List.

(xi) Active Titles List.

(xii) Inactive Titles List.

(xiii) On Order List.

Advantages

1. A Computer-based periodicals System enables a better access to the periodicals records to the staff.
2. It provides better service to the users.
3. It provides more accurate records.

Disadvantages

It involves huge expenditure for the conversion of the existing manually operated periodicals file onto the magnetic tape. Development costs of a computer system are exorbitant which are lost over a period of time. The cost of continuing operation of computer-based periodical system is not less than that of the manual system. Rather, in some cases, it may be even double of the latter, although final estimates are not available. In the computer-based system the time taken for checking a title is not less than in the manual system.

However the following few recent developments in the computer application to periodical systems which are under way may be helpful in improving situation:

L.C. MARC Serial Format

The library of Congress MARC Serials Format will serve as a communication format for periodicals between a reporting library and a receiving library in respect of the following:

(i) The national Union catalogue symbol for a reporting library.

(ii) Periodicals Holdings information.

(iii) The period of periodicals available.

(iv) Retention information.

Standard Serial Numbers

The second development is the use of an International Standard periodicals Number, officially called the American Standard identification Number, for serial publications which is specifically useful for periodicals checking work. This number is to consist of seven decimal digits besides an eighth check digit.

Periodicals Standard Format and Arrangement

This format provides guidelines as to where and how the bibliographical information which is essential to identify a periodical should appear. On the front cover of the format, the following information is provided.

1. Volume number.

2. Issue number in Arabic numerals.

3. Date of issue.

4. Code number of the issue for the identification of a periodical.
5. An abbreviated title.

Computer Based Cataloguing Systems

MARC Project

The use of computer in cataloguing *e.g.* MARC I Pilot project was started in November, 1965 by the Library of Congress. The main aim of this project was to distribute Library of Congress cataloguing in a machine-readable from to various libraries for the reading materials received by them go as to facilitate them to meet the. explosion of knowledge and the increasing demand for easy and quick provision of required information.

Working of the System

The MARC II was completed in 1967 with the development of a new format capable of transferring bibliographical data to the receiving libraries. The system consists of the following stages:

1. It presupposes the existence of a centralized or co-operative classification and cataloguing system on the pattern of that of the Library of Congress.
2. It also requires that the participating libraries of the programme should install computers and appoint programmers in their respective libraries.
3. The Computer-Based MARC Cataloguing System consists of the following main sections or programmes:
   (1) MARC Maintenance Programme for keeping the MARC file up-to-date- by means of the weekly tapes received from the Library of Congress.
   (2) MARC Selection Programme for selecting entries from the MARC tapes, converting character codes, preparing a record in a format suited to an individual

library and for printing two proof copies to be used by cataloguers of the library.

(3) MARC Correction Programme for editing the selected entries preparing the proof copy of the edited list, punching cards for using in converting to paper tapes and for typing book cards and spine labels in case a Flexowriter is used.

(4) MARC Card Print Programme for printing catalogue cards for the selected items may be presorted and alphabetized filing purposes.

(5) The Weekly Print Programme for printing the weekly supplements for the printed catalogues and the list of new books by call number.

(6) Update-Generate Programme for updating the Master file and generating the entries and changing for print files.

(7) The Monthly Pint Programme for bringing up-to-date the print files of the catalogues, and printing monthly supplements and a list of new books. These monthly supplements are cumulated to print the full catalogue.

Advantages of the System

1. A centrally prepared catalogue can be distributed to the receiving libraries in a machine-readable form.
2. In spite of increasing acquisitions the catalogue can be kept-up-to-date without employing additional staff.
3. The production cost of card catalogue on the computer is lesser than that of purchasing the Library of Congress catalogues cards.
4. The MARC tapes can be utilized for acquisition functions *i.e.* selecting and ordering and claiming unsupplied books without any additional cost.

5. The MARC tapes can be used for producing conventional card catalogue by the subscribing libraries as demonstrated by the University of Toronto.

6. The MARC data can also be used for producing book catalogues as demonstrated by the Washington State Library.

Limitations of the System

George Piternick points out the following few limitations of the Machine-Readable catalogue system:

1. The MARC record for any title is almost similar to the conventional bibliographic record, as such it inherits all its limitations.

2. The MARC format will be limited, at least for the next few years, to the English language books because the MARC character set is severally limited in respect of special characters and diacritical marks.

3. The time gap between the creation of MARC record and a catalogue record copy by the participating library which is inherent at present in the existing card production methods of the Library Congress, will not be removed until and unless both the cards and tapes are prepared from the same machine-readable record.

4. Expending on account of machine time by the participating libraries will go on increasing in view of the weekly shipment of about 1.200 records or about 62,000 records annually requiring 15,000 feet of magnetic tape.

Latest Developments in the System

The COMARC project has been taken up by the library of Congress with the financial help from the Council of Library Resources. Under this project, the Library of Congress receives records based on Library of Congress Cataloguing representing those of selected libraries which have converted their catalogues into MARC format. These records are to be checked with the Official Catalogue of the Library of Congress for updating and redistribution through the MARC distribution system.

Computer Output Microfilm

The Computer Output Microfilm (COM) was developed in the U.S.A. by Stromberg Carlson Company. It used the Charactron tube for projecting the computer output onto an unexposed film at high speed. The Charactron cathode ray tube was invented in the early 1950's which was responsible for displaying the results of computer processing on the phosphor-coated face of a television screen. Later on, a microfilm was attached to the screen of a television so that the information given by a computer was recorded. This device was responsible for the invention of Computer On Microfilm.

The latest types of computers which were capable of recording more than 100,000 characters per second were responsible for the replacement of electro-mechanical line-printers were, in their turn capable of printing 1,200 lines per minute each line, having a width of 132 characters. Further a COM is capable of recording photographically a full page at a time as compared to a line only printed by a line-printer. Moreover, a microfilm has another advantage over the paper in the sense that the microfilm has the capacity, of storing more information in a particular amount of space as compared to that of his paper equivalent as the microfilm of 105 mm × 148.75 mm size can store 225 pages of text with the reduction ratio of 42:1, into this computer, microfilms having 16mm or 105 mm width are fied.

The former are wound in spools or cartridges while the latter are cut into microfiche. The end product of a Computer Output microfilm is a magnetic tape which contains the requisite bibliographic; information besides ,the concerned printing and format control codes provided for the final images. This magnetic tape afterwards enters the said computer machine thus exposing a master micro-negative through which a microfilm master is developed and duplicate copies are prepared from the negative through which a microfilm master is developed and duplicate copies are prepared from the negative.

Pre-requisites for Maximum Output

In the following situations, the computer Output Microfilm can be helpful in ensuring optimum output:

(i) There is data file in a machine readable form.

(ii) The facility of a computer is available.

(iii) The data is of such nature which requires frequent sorting and reorganisation.

(iv) The data is to be printed out in cumulated from for mass distribution.

(v) The readers are ready to use the material in microfihn form.

Advantage of COM

If the library catalogue is to be produced in microfilm from instead of a book form, the following may be major advantages of using a COM:

(i) Easy to handle as compared to computer print-out the microfilm are less bulky and thus are easy to handle.

(ii) Compact storage Because of their lesser bulk, the microfiches & microfilms take lesser space as compared to card catalogue or printed book form catalogue.

(iii) Less Expensive Storage & duplication Because of their lesser bulk, the microfilm or microfiche catalogues are lesser expensive so far as their storages is concerned. Similarly, duplication of microfiche is much less expensive than their master copies once the negative are available *i.e.* their cost ranges between one tenth to one-hundredth of their master copies.

(iv) Cumulations are less costly As the catalogues are to be kept uptodate, so frequent cumulations are essential. In case of printed book form catalogue the cumulations take much time and are quite costly & still remain out-of-date, whereas the microfilm editions produced by computer are less costly.

(v) Requires no Binding The microfilm edition of catalogues being self-contained require no binding and hence lot of money is saved on that count.

(vi) Takes lesser time As compared to conventional printed book form of catalogues the production of up-to-date COM microfilm catalogues which are capable being used immediately takes much less time *i.e.* it takes between 24 hours to 48 hours only.

(vii) Less production and Distribution Costs Not only the microfilms are lesser costly than paper but their distribution is also much cheaper than a book because these can be sent by air mail at lesser cost as their weight is light than that of the book.

(viii) Easy availability of microfilm The microfilms are much more easily available as compared to paper.

Limitation of COM

The following are few limitations of COM when used for library catalogue applications:

1. **Needs Costly Apparatus.** Not only the COM equipment is costly and is out of the reach of each library but it also requires costly microfilm readers at various and places.
2. **Limited Supply of COM Apparatus.** Very few libraries in the world have COM service bureaus. Hence they have very little utility for majority of the libraries. Moreover, their rentals are so high that majority of the libraries can afford to avail of their services.

3. **Limited Number of Type Founts & Styles.** Similarly, very few stylised type-founts are available which restrict their use throughout the world. For example, except for few Japanese character sets, most of the COM machines use the Roman alphabet. As such, in the countries using other than Roman alphabet, the utility of COM machines is very much limited.

4. **Preparation of Paper Copies is Difficult.** In case paper copies of microfilmed matter are required it will cost much because the equipment for enlarging paper copies from film negative needs special equipment which is not only available at each point of service but is very expensive also.

However, these limitations of COM can be overcome.

The COM machines are being used by various libraries for other library purposes also which include the maintenance of circulation records in process ordering information for acquisition and feeding cumulation and publication of catalogues directories and yearbooks etc.

The OCLC started in August 1970 is a non-profit Corporation which was originally planned to be a net-work of academic libraries but now it has more than 700 user libraries with 1200 terminal including types of libraries including one national library *i.e.* the national Agricultural Library. Major portion of its budget is composed of fees received from non-Ohio Libraries *i.e.* in 1974-75, more than 62% or 1,213,330 out of a total budget of 1,956, 981 came from non-Ohio Libraries.

It is an line system. Its data base consists of the LC MARC records, catalogue entries contributed by its member user libraries. It is a shared cataloguing system in the real system. Its data base is more than 2.3 million out of which one-third is from LC MARC data.

Advantages

1. The system is very effective as the response time for title searches was 25-30 seconds.

2. Since it has adapted the battelle System the OCLC enables its users at remote places to search the central catalogue by author, title and subject approaches.
3. Its common products include computer line-printed catalogue cards besides spine & book labels accession lists & OCLC catalogue tapes for the purpose of producing COM catalogues.

The new systems which will provide genuine on-line cataloguing include the following:

(i) Washington Library network.

(ii) The university of Chicago Library System.

(iii) The New York public Library System.

Computer-based on-line Real-time library Circulation Systems

Many computer-Based On-Line real-Time Circulation Systems have been devised during 1960's beside many other data collection and batch systems. These include the following:

(a) The State University of New York at Buffalo's Real-Time Library Circulation system.

(b) The Illinois State Library On-Line Circulation control System.

(c) The on-Line Circulation Control System at Midwestern University.

(d) The Bell laboratories Library real-Time Circulation System.

In the first system an IBM 2741 typewriter terminal and the CDC 6400 computer are used. It needs borrower's Identification card but does not require any book card. To issue a book the borrower's identification card number and the call number of the book to be issued are passed into the computer by means of the typewriter and the typed matter is inserted in the book. Thus completing the charging of the book. This transaction needs 20 seconds. This systew handles more than 300,000 per annum at the State university Library of new York at Buffalo. It has the capacity of hooking into the system of the branch Libraries circulation work. In this system the computer can be asked through the terminal of find out the position of any item. Moreover, overdue notice and circulation statistics can be processed automatically. In this system the master circulation file consists of charged books only instead of the shelf list or other record of complete holdings of a library.

The Illinois State Library System

The second system which came into operation at the Illinois State Library operates on an IBM 1710 system using IBM 1031 terminals as inputs. It needs punched book cards and borrower's card. For issuing a book, the borrower's card and the book and card are inserted in the badge section of the terminal. To find out whether the borrower is a valid borrower, the programme calls for the master file of borrowers. In case the borrower is a valid user, his number and the information about the book are transmitted to the computer for final editing. After final editing, the information is put on the daily transaction pack in consecutive order to facilitate its further processing after few hours later on. Thus the issue work of a book is complete and the book is handed over to the borrower after due date slip is inserted in the book.

At the time of return of a book its call number and cutter number are checked from the book card and the reserve list and the returned cards are arranged in consecutive order with daily returns pack. If a book being returned is already reserved by a borrower the computer sends the information to the 1033 printer terminal which provides the call number, Cutter number, borrower's number and the date of reservation of the book. After, it, the returned book is handed over to the Reservation Assistant for further action.

In the evening the computer lists and punches one cards for each transaction of the day besides sorting them into Dewey Cutter and serial number orders. After this, a programme for updating the record is called in the computer for merging the sorted transaction with the master circulation record. This programme called CIRCUP takes up the transactions one by one for necessary action. In case of a discharge of a book it removes it from the master file but if it is a case of an issue of a book, it adds the information to the master file. The programme called DUE NOT prepares a new master file whenever it is updated besides printing the daily statistical information in the classified order by Dewey Decimal Classification.

This system is not only capable of printing the overdue notice for borrowers alongwith their mailing addresses, but also provides monthly statistics about the use of library. In this system, the book ID cards are generated from the shelf list kept on punched cards but it has not been made to serve as a basic record for circulation purposes. It is claimed that in this system the average cost per transaction comes to about 32 percent besides cutting down the number of staff members employed in the circulation section from twenty-two to nine only. Further this system works on a time sharing basis. In other words an interrupt feature controlled by 1026 controller, allows the central processing unit to work only when the information to be handled is fed into it.

The On-line Circulation Control System at Midwestern University

In this system, an IBM 1401, an IBM 1031 data collection system and 1033 printer are used, it needs book cards and borrower's cards badges. The IBM 1401 is shared by other departments of the University.

For issuing a book the book card and borrower's card/badge are inserted into IBM 1031 data collection system. Before the issue of the book, the processing of the computer is interrupted for finding out whether the borrower is a valid borrower which takes about second of CPU time. If valid the printer 1033 prints a book slip to be inserted in the issued book. Thus the book is issued. The total time taken in charging a book is about 10 seconds of returning a book, the information about its reservation if any is passed on to the circulation Assistant automatically because of the on-line updating of the circulation file.

Advantages of the System

This system automatically provides to the circulation desk information about the reserved book borrowers membership validity due date of return of the books fines due and other statistical data besides printing a daily circulation file.

Like the Illinois State Library's circulation system, this system also does not use the shelf list as the basic record for circulation purpose.

The real Time circulation control system invented by the Bell Laboratories called BELLREL is one of the latest in the series. It uses 360/40 computer to which are linked by Dataphone the terminals kept in three different libraries. Each of the three libraries keeps two terminal with keyboard, printer and card read facilities. In the system, a Union list of all three libraries is maintained which can help in finding out the position of every book stocked in the libraries of the system *i.e.* indicating whether a book is available in a library and can be got issued. Similarly, Direct Access Files maintained in the system provide information about the total book collection of a library *i.e.* shelf list and the position of the books issued and reserved.

The system can perform 22 transitions related to issuing, returning and reservation of books besides other queries about them. The system batch processes daily issue lists, pre-due and over due notices, lists of books in great demand and other related statistical information.

It is claimed that the system can handle more than 300,000 transaction annually. However, in charging it takes about 23 seconds which is more than that taken by the three other systems described above and many of the manual systems.

A Computer-based classification system is being experimented at the Documentation Research and Training centre, Bangalore. It is based on Colon Classification Schedules. The following procedure is followed for the purpose.

1. The schedules of Colon Classification are transferred on tape which include the schedules of Basic Classes Special Isolates and Common Isolates.

   For this purpose a punched card with 80 columns is used which provides the above-mentioned information a follows:

   (a) Basic Classes 1-8 columns

   (b) Basic Subject Terms 9-40 columns

   (c) Number of reels of tapes locating special isolates schedule 41-48 columns

   (d) Indication for card sequence 49-80 columns

2. The Kernal term of the document to be classified are fed into the computer.

3. In the synthesis procedure the compotents of a required class number are picked in the sequence in which they should be synthesized manually according to the set principle and postulates.

4. The computer assigns automatically the appropriate class number to the document in question.

Computer Based Inter Library Loan Systems

In order to facilitate the provision of material requested on inter-library loan basis, the use of computers and other latest telecommunication devices in being made increasingly in U.S.A, UK and Canada. These include the following devices:

1. Tele fascimile transmission.
2. Long Distance Xerox
3. Tele type.
4. Telex.
5. Computers.

The following are the important systems in operation which make use of one or more the above-mentioned electronic transmission devices for inter-library purposes:

Intrex

It is a device of facilitate speedy fascimile transmission of full texts of books, journals reports and other research materials requested on inter-library loan basis.

A. H. Robins Library Richmond Virginia Projects

The system started at the A. H. Robins Library, Richmond, Virginia makes use of the following equipment for processing inter library loan requests:

(i) IBM 360 computer

(ii) Four part Form using NCR Paper

(iii) Worksheet containing the names of its four major suppliers.

Other Systems

(i) LDX; University of California

The LDX is. a telefacimile system which provides 135 lines per inch and electrostatic printing on paper. Only single pages can be transmitted. It is a costly system. But it is speedy one.

(ii) University of Nevada Experiment.

(iii) Teletype

There are about 1000 libraries which use own teletype machines. Under this system, the massage is typed on teleprinter alongwith puncheq tape equipment. The message is produced in a visible form 100 words a minute.

Telex

The system of Telex is being increasingly used by libraries in the United Kingdom. More than 150 libraries have already provided this facility which include about 8000 libraries in their network. The rent is nominal *i.e.* about 5sh 6d. This is being used increasingly by the national Lending Library for Science and Technology, Boston, Spa.

A Computer-Based Information Storage and Retrieval System consists of the following two phases:

Storage, Feeding and Storage of Information In the Computer

It consists of classification and cataloguing 'of the books and other reading materials forming the input of the system and transferring the catalogue entries on to the magnetic tape and getting its print-out, if required. This catalogue on tape is to updated by adding new entries and correcting the existing entries, if necessary, and getting a print-out of the updated catalogue.

Retrieval-search, selection and answering the Query

The second phase consists of *(a)* preparing the Reader profile record *i.e.* the recording the Readers Queries and transferring them on to the tape and updating them, *(b)* arranging a dialogue between the reader and the computer through the language of the system, *(c)* selecting the bibliographical details of the relevant books from the catalogue on tape *(d)* transferring the selected entries on to the magnetic tape, and *(e)* getting a print-out of these entries, providing a copy to the reader and transferring them on punched cards if necessary.

In this process the following may be used:

1. **Computer.** There are different kinds of computers which might be used in the system *e.g.* IBM 360/50 and 360/67, ICL 1903 etc.
2. Magnetic Tape, punched cards or punched paper tape.
3. Magnetic tape deck, Card reader, line-printer, Electric typewriters.

However, these may vary from one system to another depending upon various kinds of input items, the kind of catalogue the kind of vocabulary of the kernel ideas used for identifying subjects of documents and readers queries the kind of computer used or available and the kind of output required.

Advantages

1. Facilitates retrospective and selection of documents as and when demanded by a user.
2. Provide periodically current awareness service in. Selective Dissemination of Information.
3. Facilitates the acceptance of reader's queries in the language of the system.
4. Provide the reader with a documentation list or a retrospective bibliography for his use.
5. Provide the service in an automatic and speedy way.

The following are some of the important Information and Retrieval System which are in operation in various parts of the globe:

1. Defence Documentation Centre (ASTIA) Arlington, Virginia.
2. Medlars.
3. Western Reserve university centre for Documentation and Research, Cleveland.
4. US Naval OTS, California's Uniterm Indexing.
5. University of Pennsylvania Institute of Cooperative Research.
6. National Bureau of Standards U.S.A.
7. Technical Information Centre, Electronic and Radar Development Establishment, Bangalore.
8. Autometed Data Processing System, INSDOC, New Delhi.

9. German Computer Centre of Machine Methods in Documentation, Frankfurt. 10. Ship Analysis and retrieval project.
11. VINITI
12. JICST
13. Technical Information Department Lockheed Aircraft Corporation Marietta, Georgia.
14. Documentation on Patents at Shell International Research, NV., The Hague.
15. Indian Institute of Petroleum Dehradun, U.P.
16. IBM Information Retrieval Satellites at the IBM Technical Information Retrieval\ Centre, Armonk, New York.
17. LC MARC System. It provides information and retrieval service also.
18. Project MAC at the Massachusetts Institute of Technology.

Information System and library Network

In this respect, the United States of America has made much progress besides the United kingdom and some of the European countries whereas India has yet to take concrete steps in this regard except that the government of India lias decided to establish NISSAT.

Critique of Computers

It is claimed that the application of computers to libraries would usher in a new era of progress and development as it will bestow the following advantages:

(i) It will make everything effortless.

(ii) It will perform the jobs with the speed of light.

(iii) It will help save money.

(iv) It will help transferring computer programmes from one place to author without extra expense.

(v) It will help in economising in future programming because programmes can be converted to later generation service by sharing computers with others.

(vi) It will help in saving money when many separate processes are integrated into a system.

(vii) It will provide better and more service to the readers.

Disadvantages

Among those persons who are sworn enemies of computers, the name of Ellsworth Mason is worth mentioning. Ellsworth mason, while discounting all the so-called advantages of computers, strikes a note of warning to those who want to use computers in libraries in the following words, Anyone who computerizes at this point time is hitching his wagon to a falling star... Computerizing library operations at present and projected costs and with foreseeable results, is intellectually and fiscally irresponsible and managerially incompetent.

Thought refuting most of the charges of Ellsworth Mason against computerization of libraries, Mrs. Henriette D. Avram, agrees with him in principle when she states that Mr. Mason certainly is correct in criticizing much of what has been done in library automation but is wrong to draw the conclusion that all efforts are misdirected doomed to failure. A poorly designed project does not prove that library functions cannot be automated; it proves that a disaster is a disaster. It is true that large amount of money have been expended and there have not always been positive or meaningful results.

Remedies

Lawrence Auld suggests the following ten practical and useful ways for preventing failure in library automation and for making it a success.

1. Motivation based on clearly defined goals;
2. Effective communication between librarians and computer people;
3. Logical and complete analysis of the system carefully executed programs, and abundant documentation;
4. Constant feedback of the system's day to day operations to the systems analyst and programmer;
5. Flexible and adaptable programmes.
6. A competent computer operator;
7. Computer machinery capable of performing the tasks required;
8. A high priority for computer services to the library;
9. Adequate budgetary support; and
10. Positive long term commitment by top management both now and in the further.

The first Indian computer was developed and built in 1956 art the Tata Institute of Fundamental Research, Bombay with some imported components while the second computer was built by the University of Jadavpur, Calcutta in 1963 in collaboration with the Indian Statistical Institute Similarly the Bhabha Atomic research Centre, Bombay has developed a small but high-speed digital computer for real time applications.

At present in India many public and private sector firms have started manufacturing computers. These include besides others the Hindustan Computers Ltd.., New Delhi and the Delhi Cloth Mills and Data products. Delhi. It is claimed that the Business Computer No HCL—8C manufactured by the former corporation costing Rs. 83,500 can repay its cost within two years besides providing various direct and indirect benefits.

The computer industry is likely to get a boost due, to the recent policy decision taken by the Government of India to reject the proposal by the American multinational computer firm IBM to continue to operate in India as a 100% foreign equity company under the foreign Exchange regulation Act besides establishing a computer Maintenance Corporation under the control of the department of Electronics to take over the servicing and repair activities of foreign computer the British company ICL has already agreed to dilute its equity. However, it has been reported that IBM has decided to wind up its business from India within the next six months.

The number of computers in India went up to about 250 in 1975-76 ranging from the small-sized Honeywell 400 to the largesized IBM 370/155. Twenty-nine universities in 17 States of the country have computer facilities which include IBM—1620 (5), IBM 360 (2), IBM 1130 (6), TDC—316 (8), TDC—12 (6), R—I020 (1), and B—5700 (1), besides, the Himachal Pradesh University Simla has procured for its Department of Physics a mini computer Model No. 1101 manufactured by the Delhi Cloth Mills and Data Products, Delhi which is being used mainly for mathematical and scientific calculation.

The important institutions which are at present making use of computers for information processing include the INSDOC, New Delhi BARC, TIFR. PRL, DRTC, IIT NIC; and IIT.

These institutions use the following of computers:

IBM 360/44; IBM 370/55;

IBM 1401; IBM—7044, IBM 1620;

ICL—1901, CDC—3600 and Honeywell—400.

Similarly they use the following programming Language PL1; SPS, COROL; Autocoder FORTRAV IV

However these different types of software programmes in various types of computes cannot be used without modifications.

In the Government of India the names of the following five Departments are worth mentioning which have been using one or the other type of computer for various types of application from the years mentioned in brackeds:

1. Planning Commission.
2. Register General of India.
3. Institute of Agricultural Research Statistics.
4. Department of Statistics.
5. Meteorological Department.

In short it is evident that since mid-fifties computers in India are not only being used increasingly in performing various jobs in libraries information centres and Governments Departments but are also being developed and built by public and private sectors. As future is bright in India especially due to the establishment of various such, their national and Regional Information Centres *viz* NISSAT DESIDOC besides about 600 Local Information Units located in the various government departments, industrial organisations and other Rand D establishments, Steps are lilso being taken for establishing sectoral Information Centres, especially FOSTIC, ICA, NICL, and MTIC besides various other industries.

Whereas the first computer was installed in mid-fifties of the century at the Indian Statjstical Institute, Calcutta mainly for the scientific and research purpose while for business purposes the first computer was installed in India by a U.S. oil firm, their number went up to 170 in June 1972. 15 are installed in Bangalore 46 in Bombay, 18 in Calcutta 20 in Delhi while remaining 68 are installed in other places in the country. Further out of a total of 170 computer installations 80 are used by business and industry while the Government, educational institutions research establishments and public, utility services and other organizations use 14, 20, 21, 23 and 2 respectively. This information has been revealed by a study undertaken by the NITIE which was sponsored by the United Nations Industrial Development Organization.

The complications of managing the sensitive and complex demands of the computer in libraries re infinite and incessant. Coupled with the fact that the computer in the hands of those derived from English stock tends to invest them with the emotional state of a Latin behind a driver's wheel this condition accounts for the fact that, even after twenty years, library computerisation not infrequently resembles the Place de l'Etoile during rush hour. While the basic problems of freedom from careful cost control, and decisions based on institutional egofulfillment rather than users' needs are still with us to a considerable degree, whatever its degree of success, the widespread application of the computer has brought changes in the way that libraries are run that were not anticipated. This chapter attempts to describe what tends to happen to the management and control of libraries when the computer is applied to library operations. Its generalisations emerge from observations of practice in the United States, mostly in academic libraries, with some reference to practice in Australia, Canada, and Great Britain.

The immediate impact on library management came with the creation of the computer unit in the library, which began in the early 1960s. Computers were introduced into libraries with all the subtlety of a spear thrust or the crash of a satellite in a back-yard swimming pool. Their rise in library economy coincided with the post-Sputnik decade, which spewed forth on education in the United States and elsewhere a flood of gold undreamed of in human history. Unlike the River Alpheus which cleansed the Augean stables; this flood left barnyards all over the land hip-deep in sharn. In retrospect, despite the material advantages which remain as residue, the 1960s was he most destructive decade of this century.

Computers came to libraries straight out of the technology of industry, and brought with them the mentality that characterized industry during an extremely confused and self-defeating period, marked in my experience most dramatically by the production of the Boeing 747 airplane. Repeated public statements by the presidents of all major airlines agreed without exception that this airplane could not justify itself economically (ten years before oil prices jumped), but conceded they would all have to buy them because they were the latest technological development, and they had to get with it. Why they had to get with it, and what they were doing in business in the first place were never discussed. This mentality of getting with it, totally disregarding cost justification, led to the observation in 1972 by one of our leading economists, Kenneth Boulding, that although productivity, in our economy had been increasing from two to four percent a year for a century, it had hardly increased at all in recent years, when at least 100,000. computers were being used in industry. His conclusion at that time "Automation seems to be a total fraud. There is not the slightest evidence of greatly increasing productivity in manufacturing processes." The year before, a survey of 100 American companies in eleven industry groups by a major New York consulting firm showed conclusively that investment in computers did not give a company any significant competitive advantage; in fact four of the eleven industry groups showed a negative correlation. The conclusion: companies that did well were not those with lots of computers but those with able management in depth.

Nevertheless, during the 1960s the computer industry was riding high, wide, and handsome, and in the process generating some of the most repulsive personalities of the century. At one time IBM home office managers would acknowledge privately that their salesmen were completely out of control, selling the moon with each computer, and the number of bankruptcies that attended the installation of computer processes in smaller businesses was alarming. These miracle-mongers swept into university computing centers on a wave of large academic budgets and pin-headed university president (who at that time in the United States tended to resemble industrialists in intimate ways), and they early brought pressure on the libraries to surrender to their lures. Their formula was simple, if brash-we can do anything you are doing in the library faster, better and much cheaper. Their persuaders were simple, if harsh-brass knuckles and billy-clubs. Librarianship was heralded as the whale-oil industry in petroleum times, and libraries were condemned as mismanaged, neanderthal units, dark blotches on the bright electronic screen.

Early specialists in library computerisation were for the most part recruited from the commercial world. They brought with them these simplistic views and attitudes and a very large burden of ignorance about library operations. They seemed to specialize in yanking fish out of water to teach them how to breathe air. Quite understandably, they were accorded the enthusiasm usually reserved for Martians at a high-church picnic or burnoosed Arabs in Grosvenor Square. From the beginning the computer unit in libraries was viewed as a foreign body, destructive to the larger organism.

In time, events proved this to be the case, and this first wave of computerisers was dashed on the rocks of its own ignorance-ignorance of library operations and the demands on them, ignorance of the complexity of computerizing bibliographic projects, ignorance of the complex variations that existed in seemingly repetitive operations. Discouraged and discredited by repeated notable failures, this first wave left or were replaced in library operations within a few years. During their tenure, there existed nearly total antagonism between them and the library staff, which they managed to keep in turmoil nearly constantly. There was no possibility of integrating them into the library in any managerial sense. The positive result of their failures was an understanding of the high degree of complexity involved in computerizing library operations.

The second wave of library computer specialists as kind of rebound tended to be librarians who had some experience with programming. In most cases, they did not have exposure in depth to an understanding of the computer, generally had not worked in other kinds of computer operations, and very few of them had high skills as programmers. They generally worked together with programmers from industrial, backgrounds. This was the situation when I surveyed computer operations in eleven major university libraries in 1969, when every university of significant size had its in-house computer staff, some of them larger than the whole the shortcoming of this generation of computerisers was inadequate programming skill, and, with the reduction of library budgets, in house-computer staffs largely disappeared in the early 1970s, although the last large staff of its kind persisted at the University of Maryland until 1978.

Although this second wave of specialists was far less antagonistic to librarians, they still were held at a considerable distance, partly because they were thrust into library operations by library directors and partly because of the long drawn out agonies inflicted to their colleagues by programming methods that they prevailed. The computer unit was still something 'out there', and if it no longer was engaged in guerilla warfare with the library staff, it nevertheless seemed to work largely at night in mysterious ways, and to slip things into operations that were not completely understood, often not needed, and even worse full of what were called 'bugs', for which there never seemed to be any truly effective exterminator. Though no longer considered the enemy, the computer unit existed for the most part despite the library staff, and could have done just as well, or badly, as a department of the university computer center.

There was much raging in the literature during this period of computer fumbling against the inherent rigidity of librarians who hated change and were obviously evil in many other ways, when you come right down to it. Re-reading these articles demonstrates how alienated computer people felt at the time, and rightly so. In thirty-five years of librarianship, which falls short of the introduction of the typewriter but encompasses the advent of microfilm, we have never seen any worthy librarian who did not embrace any new tool or machine that clearly helped do what he was doing. By its very nature, every library pullulates daily with change of every kind; nothing goes on the same from day to day in any operation, and the problems and demands shift constantly. There are few other agencies in the spectrum of human affairs so constantly involved in change. But at least until quite recently, librarians tended to be discerning, and if the tool or machine was not obviously useful it had to prove itself before being accepted.

The fact is that computer efforts in libraries from 1958 to 1970 contributed almost nothing to library computerization except disruption of libraty processes fantastic waste of money, and a heritage of bitterness through arrogance that has disappeared only in recent years. The Ohio State University Library circulation system we believe is the only significant in-house computerized system that has remained more or less intact until the present day, and it came on line late in 1970. By the end of 1970 OCLC was still in a batch card production system, BALLOTS (now ARLIN) still in its programming stage, the University of Chicago system, (offspring of the atomic bomb) was still under cloak-and-bagger cover behind vault doors, and MARC (the dinosaur with tiny brain that may yet devour us all) was still building up to solidity. The first interactive bibliographical system MEDLINE, which began in February 1972, was, in retrospect, the only highly successful library computer operation developed up until that time.

The achievements in library computerisation, then, are the product of the last seven years, and it is useful to speculate the changed conditions that made them deviate into sense and begin the Modern Age in library computerization, for which any sane operation would have waited before plunging. First and most important of all was the radical drop in library support that began to hit us in 1970 and has increased to the present day. It shook out the monkeys from the orange crop, and within three or four years stamped out library computerisation as cottage industry (every library it on IBM company). The fact, blatantly obvious in the failures of the sixties, that skilled computer programming is one of the rarest commodities in the world (and rarely, seen in a library setting), began to be recognized, and we looked for help to the few large computer operations outside where it seemed to have focussed.

The second factor, for which we had to look to England for guidance, was realization of the impossibility of local collection autonomy, and the promise of the computer as an information transmitter in a country as large and complex as the United States (conditions which influenced developments in Canada and Australia as well). This emphasized and in some ways exaggerated the importance of central production sources of basic library computer needs. Networking was in (and that rhymes with 'E' and that means Computers).

Third was the early success in producing the bricks with which we all were building-catalogue cards-by OCLC, in an area of service which we all were accustomed to buy from a central source. While MEDLARS had preceded OCLC in distributing a widespread computer service, it was remote because it serviced only doctors. But OCLC reached real people-librarians at a central point of their existence, and we quickly learned to love it, despite its additional costs, and to look to centralized production for a whole range of our computer needs. Enter BALLOTS, WLN and a whole series of new actors to provide that lovely element, competition, so long absent "from our economy, which is now getting intense.

Fourth was the development in the Library of Congress of a totally computerized cataloguing system, which came very slowly and at a cost that no one has ever dared to look at, for fear that it would overthrow our national government, but with national implications. Its totality now threatens to engulf us, as discussed below. With a new set of props under their foundations, libraries could now look sensibly, with much smaller resources, at what they could produce locally, with programming done outside the library, and the present status of the computer unit and its relationship to the management structure of the library emerged. It tends to exit in two conditions. In one condition the computer unit controls decisions on library computerisation, with the advice of concerned departments, and is itself the equivalent of a department. In the other condition, control over computerization is dispersed among the library departments, and the computer specialist provides centralized technology as a staff officer of the library director. Neither condition is totally satisfactory, and different kinds of tensions result from each.

The computer unit or computer specialist in either case represents a new type of power level within the library organization. It is central to the entire operation, a pivotal unit, with no counterpart in previous library history. It can impose' changes by design or inadvertently on departments with which it is not working directly, through the interaction of parts of systems and how they are affected by adjustments in the system. The computer unit, moreover, almost always reports directly to the upper library administration, generally to the director, and while, there are valid reasons for this relationship, it nevertheless places the unit in a privileged organisational relationship.

These two factors cause a change in peer relationships between the computer staff and the rest of the library staff, which are altered further by the mysterious nature of what computer specialists do, procedures which are amenable to simple examination or review by no one. The computer specialist is never as fully integrated into the library structure as other unit heads can be. For these reasons and others, the most successful computer units seem to be those headed by a librarian, with extensive knowledge of library procedures, who has accumulated the requisite systems and programming knowledge, although we know one spectacularly successful exception to this rule. Since he generally does not do the programming, academic knowledge that enables informal interaction with outside computer programmers will suffice. This kind of a specialist can minimize the impact that changes in computer applications make on library procedures and adapt them to desirable library needs most precisely. He also, since of the same stripe, will be more approachable to his colleagues and be engaged more intensively and more often in useful conversations with his colleagues about their work, totally aside from any practical need they have for his expertise.

Computerization has changed many relationships between departments in libraries. Its largest effect is the tilt in power balance between technical processes and public services divisions, which had been reasonably evenly distributed previously, in favour of technical processes. The most dramatic instance of this shift in my experience has been that registered in the Library of congress, where the proposal to close their card catalogue precipitated a major battle between the two elements that was finally resolved in favour of technical processes. Evidence of this shift is seen in the emergence in the past five years into high levels of library administration, including the directorship, of librarians whose career had been in technical processes, formerly a rare occurrence.

Within the divisions the independence of the separate units has been considerably loosened. Departments formerly based on rather clearly defined functions have now had those functions changed on the basis of new procedures generated outside of their unit, and to a larger extent than ever before the library organization is beginning to be described in terms of processes that are heavily overlapping in their reach. Boundaries have been blurred, and tensions have arisen over control of various aspects of computerization, such as the nature of processes and the demands they will impose on the department the kind of hardware and software to be used. The nature, location, control, and scheduling of computer terminals are often a matter of bitter dispute. Like elevators, they are far more economical if arranged in banks, but their cost strictly limits the number obtainable. All of these factors have greatly increased the amount and constancy of negotiation necessary to conduct relationships between departments.

A typical battle in American libraries occurs in locating the bank of DCLC terminals, which are likely, especially early in the use of the system, to be used by cataloguing, acquisitions, serials, inter-library loan, documents, reference, and even rare book librarians. While the early promise by computer-flappers in the early sixties was that every man could be his own terminal, with access to world information easily achieved by this point in time, there are a limited number that can be obtained by a library because of their cost. The matter of cost is the most frustrating aspect of the entire range of computers in libraries.

We know that it can do wonders for us in the hands of competent computer managers. The computer, in fact, presents the only longterm solution to the two most pressing problems in the entire range of librarianship-short-life paper of books, which is rapidly heading for shorter life with economic trends in paper manufacturing that are irreversible, and even shorter-life bindings (ironically called 'perfect bindings') for books, about ninety percent of which are held together by plastic smeared on the edges of loose pages at the present time.

These crack after seven or eight circulations, and twenty years from now any library committed to preserving books over time will be a mass of loosely-tied sheets. The computer, of course, could store all of our texts, and pump out on demand either microform or hard copy, but the costs of doing so are astronomically beyond our reach.

The promise of locating terminals everywhere, which of course is the highest desideratum in any information system, cannot begin to be realized, either now or in the long-term future in the declining state of library budgets. The future will see us with fewer terminals, rather than more, and struggles between departments for control will become even more acute.

All departments affected by computerisation (which includes most of them) become dependent on outside technology experts wIth the introduction of the computer, and this has markedly reduced their autonomy. While this often is not an entirely bad thing to happen, because departments can become rigid, it is futile to assume that basic decisions about what a department is doing and how it does it can be made better outside the department than in it, or better when having to accommodate the needs of other departments than when decided entirely on internal needs.

An automated circulation system, for instance can have an impact of considerable depth on the budget, priorities, and scheduling of acquisitions, cataloguing, and collection management, that is to say, it can rearrange their use of staff and funds, and churn up long standing policies that have emerged from years of negotiation and adjustment between departments within the library and the entire range of academic experts on a campus. The affected departments do not expect the circulation department to have an impact on them, and there is a tendency to resist or reject the new demands that should logically result from circulation information analysis. Nowhere in the costing of computer operations in a library is any account made of the cost of the time required for negotiations and the toll of these tensions on efficiency of departments placed in this new and far less secure matrix of organizational relationships.

Branches pose special problems to the main library in any dispersed system, and they are a special element in the interdepartmental relationship changes that follow computerization. Branches tend to go their own way to a large degree. They have their own support constituency in their academic specialists on a campus whom they can bring to bear on the library ad instruction. They are not constantly viewed, as internal library departments are likely to be, by staff passing through the library. Changes in their conditions to service can occur without being detected by the main library, and they impose large demands on the main library's central services for processing and information.

With computerisation, the branches become far more dependent on the main library. While they may gain access to the records of the entire library system collection, which is highly desirable, this may be in the form of microfiche catalogues which they may not like. They also will lose their card catalogues. However, centralization of the locus of collection records, if on line to branches with provision for defining whether materials are available, can remove a large burden of the curse of branch libraries to students, who are driven made by the dispersal of books among libraries for reasons that seem insane and on a rationale that defies acceptance. The branch libraries under a campus-wide computerized circulation system like that of Ohio State University, become access points for searching the entire system and reserving books for pick-up, greatly broadening the use of materials in all the other branches and in the main library.

The intolerable delay of a minute by telephone to determine current periodical holdings, which led nationwide to branch library check-in records duplicating the main serials record, yields to sense when the delay is only ten seconds by computer. So critical have fifty seconds become in this century! Computer application tends to standardize methodology in the branches, making transfer of staff easier and cheaper. In public library branches that must respond to rapid change in public demand for the most recent books, easy turnover of book stock is possible with a centralized computer catalogue and computerized checkout of books to the branch, instead of local card catalogues. It is also possible to generate management information about the branches for the library administration that will inform it more sensitively on a timely basis of what goes on in the branches, making them more amenable to central policy control. In general, computer applications tend to make the branches less autonomous, but in the near future we should see the processing of all their materials return to the branches, as it is facilitated by the system.

Although a the present time few libraries have more than a few operations computerized, throughout the land most library departments somewhere or other have tried their little trotters at some from of automation. The following discussion of departments most often involved in automation attempts to describe what tends to happen to procedures and demands on staff and management when their operations are computerized.

Early on, some of the wildest computer money was squandered by enthusiastic fools with keypunched brains in converting shelflists to machine readable form with no foresight about what was required for multiple use of these records, and no insight into the requirements for proper bibliographical standards. Enormous sums of money were spent in keypunching, and the resulting carloads of IBM cards lying around in closets throughout the land have scarcely been used and are mostly unusable. The University of Toronto library reports being confronted by "five separate files which had strong family resemblances but were not really compatible," resulting from keypunching that went back to 1965. Before the volume of MARC records at the Library of Congress grew large enough to dominate the scene, most computerized cataloguing records fell far short of standards for reasonable bibliographical access. The data base at OCLC still suffers from the fact that early entries into their computer from some libraries were not subject to quality control. At present computerized cataloguing information is produced almost exclusively by the few large central on-line data bases and bought by local libraries, who enter any local records not already in the data base as well as deriving records from it. When these data bases reached the critical mass that met most of the demands for current cataloguing in smaller libraries, their use increased greatly. This point was reached when two or three of the larger research libraries joined the system and began adding their records to those generated by the computer center. The rapid formation of regional networks with multiple members was accelerated by the need for smaller libraries to have contracting, access lines, and hardware procured by a central agency, and membership in such centers as OCLC has more than doubled in the past four years. The ease of joining these systems has tended to slow the development of local on-line mini and micro-computer systems, which pose many problems identical to those handled to badly during the first decade of library automation. Because of the mass of information in the card catalogue in the develppment of local on-line systems the card catalogue may be the first to be converted or the last.

The impact of automated cataloguing on the staff of cataloguing departments has been beneficial, since one of fits early results was the eradication of inefficient hand-cataloguing operations, of which there were many. The reason why libraries that joined OCLC early could show immediate cuts in staff was that many of them had cataloguing departments with very low productivity. Professional cataloguers who had been performing work easily accomplished by the support staff, practice that had stubbornly outlived the surge of acquisitions of the 1960s, were immediately obsolete and professionals now are restricted to original cataloguing. Except in those libraries expect in replicating inefficiencies, where professional cataloguers are used at computer terminals to summon catalogue cards. There has been retraining of the support staff, and some reduction of total staff in the cataloguing processes. Radical staff cuts in previously efficient cataloguing departments have not occurred.

On the managers of cataloguing departments there have been new demands requiring considerable ability to understand technological processes, radical new demands for training programmes, increased demands for supervision and work-flow adjustment, and infinite patience in coping with the peculiarities, changes, and failures of the on-line centers. These managers, once proudly suspicious of the flawed nature of humankind which generates the chaos in which they flourish, have now become total believers in the new magic that once the button on the terminal is pushed the catalogue cards will inevitably come and that all the cards required in the card-set will inevitably be present in the alphabetical cumulations they receive from remote computer centers.

These changes have resulted in cataloguing processes that are more expensive than efficient hand-cataloguing, but which produce much faster processing of the current flow of acquisitions to the shelves. The cataloguing department has become a much more central department than formerly, because it is the closest in need to the data base terminals. Its high priority demands on these terminals make it a host department to other departments using the terminals in most libraries. This department has experienced the largest change through computerization of any large library department.

Processing department, which is often absorbed into the cataloguing department, spent most of its time before computerized cataloguing maintaining files from which were drawn the bibliographical base for production of catalogue cards, an din producing the proper number of catalogue cards, in a variety of ways. This process has been entirely eliminated, and the largest cuts in staff produced by library automation have occurred in this unit. There still remains the task of filing cards in the various library catalogues, and the magnitude of this task is leading to the closing of library card catalogues in the large research libraries throughout the land. No satisfactory substitute for the card catalogue has yet been found short of local production of catalogues in microform or on-line access to local computerised catalogues, a process that is still excessively expensive.

This new condition has reduced the requirement of extremely high typing skills and high bibliographical skills in the staff of this department, making replacements easier to select, in a unit that characteristically has a high staff turnover.

Order department has been computerized in both its bookeeping and its order placement functions. One of the earliest applications of the computer to libraries, often generated by self-seekers outside of the library was to bookeeping records of the order department, which are fairly simple records sub-divided into allocations of the book budget by categories. While this is a simple, common place computer operation in business, we have seen more of them in libraries that did not seem to work effectively than one could imagining. By now, most of them have been straightened out, but in libraries that programmed their own systems, departure of the librarian programmer has generally left behind an undocumented system that had to be re-programmed. These systems involve payment of vendors through code numbers assigned to each vendor, and payments to the wrong vendor occur not infrequently. Fortunately, our bills do not run into millions.

These systems often make out the order forms, but the multiplecopy handtyped order form is still in common use. In the 1960s systems were designed to track the exact stage in the order process that each order has reached, but low use of this information has not justified its cost and effort. At present the on-line cataloguing data banks are used by order departments for verification, which has greatly speeded up the search process.

New processes have required staff retraining, but there has not been much change in the size of the staff. However, the nature of the searching, which formerly required educated, intelligent, and bibliographically skilled staff has changed, making it possible to recruit at a lower level of skill for these positions although they have not yet been downgraded in most libraries.

The new demands on the manager of this department require heavy interaction with the computer specialist, negotiation for the use of terminals controlled by others, and heavy dependence on outside sources for programme maintenance, re-programming, failures of the reporting schedule, and incorrectly paid bills. On balance, this manager has less control over this operation than before computerization.

Since computerized circulation records essentially involve manipulation of numerical data, they were among the very earliest to be automated. Like everything caught up in the forefront of the wild enthusiasm of early computerization, the butchery that resulted often made even computers. At one time information generated at this point was made the basis for all other computer applications in the library from cellar to attic, with disastrous. In 1969 I saw one large research library operation that updated its circulation print-out only once every four days because of the cost of paper. In the same year, we assured at one university that computerization had for the first time given them the ability to produce totally accurate circulation records. On my return a few years later we found their 13 IBM data collectors worn to the constant hiccups, occasionally collecting but frequently not (and IBM had discontinued their production).

Computerised circulation demonstrates nicely some of the basic weakening of control that can come in a library that automates. The library at the present time almost always depends on an outside computer for processing its data. It is not rare for these operations to wipe out completely the entire circulation record. While this can be regenerated to some degree of approximation by using previous computer tape records, there is no possibility of ever recovering completely from such a disaster.

One library was about "to shorten its circulation period from three weeks to two weeks, only to discover that the outside agency that handled its data was about to change to a new computer. This required total re-programming of every operation serviced by that computer, and two-and-a-half years later, when the computer operation had been converted and the library circulation system had worked its way into the re-programming schedule, it was possible to change that circulation. period. A prime example of that fact that although the computer initially can be a great accelerator of change, once imposed it becomes a powerful agent against change.

The difficulty of managerial control over programmers was demonstrated in one system that generated a daily Computer Output Microfilm circulation record. When you located a specific call number, it would tell you the date it was charged out and the date it was due, but both in Julian Dates, which completely defy normal human understanding. The record, you see, had been generated for the machine and not for the public although it was intended as a public record. This system also made it impossible to place a hold on a book currently charged out.

Although very small high school and public libraries that could in no way justify it either on functional or cost ground computerized their circulation records to get with it, there were nevertheless valid reasons for computerizing this operation in larger libraries. The volume of circulation had so swelled the bank of circulation cards. in larger libraries that adding and retrieving information from them was ponderous. In addition, the process of defining overdue books and issuing recalls would churn up the files for days. The computer eased both of these problems. It also imported new problems—the difficulty of the user finding the circulation record by himself (either in a wad of print-out paper or on microfilm), the lag in updating the filing of newly charged out books (in large libraries three or four thousand on busy days), which can reach two or three days if the timing of the system misfires, and errors in records caused by system lapses in collecting or discharging data. Not to mention the obscene condition that results when the machines break down completely, the counterpart of the log-jam I found at the airport in Rome last summer when no computer records of flight reservations or cumulated flight loads could be brought up on the terminals.

At present, most computerized circulation systems are remnants of local programming (some still the relicts of wild-and-woolly local library programming), and they yearn toward on-line systems, the simple and obvious condition for the solution of circulation record problems. Few can afford them. In the interim, lightpen collector systems are being used more and more, but instead of using packaged software programmes (with known effects and predictable costs) these often are subjected to local programming, with all its attendant evils.

Computerised circulations systems, once past the gargantuan task of keypunching cards for each book in the library, have eliminated the staff formerly used for filing and overdues, and have greatly eased the space-crush at the central circulation desk. They require very little staff training, and have imposed no great demands or the department manager. Except at times of re-programming, when dislocations in the records (until de-bugged) are so frequent and irrational that he must become a psychiatric social worker to avert hysteria on his staff, and an international diplomat to smooth the ruffled senses of library users. Once the shortcomings of computerized circulation systems have been absorbed by the manager, this operation becomes easier to manage than previously, since it involves far fewer workers, and so sizeable new problems.

This department has become the center for three kinds of computerized information services-on-line bibliographical data bases, specialized analytical programmes of statistical sources, and local service information in public libraries (occupational or carpool information, volunteer clearing houses, elected officials list and the like). These sources have in some libraries divided reference service into two sub-units for information sources and for in-depth traditional reference service.

There are now about 300 on-line data bases available for purchase. Larger libraries tend to subscribe to two or three of the most comprehensive in their fields of greatest demand with others added, as specialities and finances dictate. They are all extremely expensive, and the main-line bibliographical services are computerized versions of printed indexes with only slight extension of their coverage. Their virtue is the saving of time involved in manual searching of indexes, a factor of importance to advanced research workers. Costs of using them tend to be passed on to the user, which eliminates use by the ordinary library user or by the staff, useful as these services could be in routine reference work. They require extensive training, study, and experience in depth of veteran professional reference librarians, preferably educated in a discipline (science, social science) in the area on which the data base focuses. There is a certain amount of prestige connected with this retrieval that enhances the status of the librarian engaged in it.

The use of COM catalogues, spread around the university, or on-line catalogues with multiple terminals, reduces the use of reference departments for card catalogue assistance, which is provided at the other access points in the system. The extension of reference power that will be possible with the advent of on-line catalogue information accessible in all the ways now possible at the card catalogue, and with expansion of ways of approaching the data base, must wait for the day when libraries can afford such services.

The added computerised services have been assumed by reference departments without additions to staff and at a time when, indeed, public service staffs are being cut all over the country. They have required transfer of skills from the lower level users (typically at the student level) to the research level user at a time when services to students is deteriorating at an alarming rate. They have imposed no perceptible burden to managers of reference departments, and have equipped them with the new magic carpet—a computer terminal, to achieve which soine good librarians give up librarianship.

The man in the catbird seat, the runner between the redoubts of staff and higher administration has been affected by computerization more than the rest of the library put together. In the first place he is completely without choice as to whether or not to use it. In the view of one of its exponents, "[technology) does not permit the luxury of not using it." At the present time, it even forbids reasoned judgment in its application. In any sensible social or economic condition, decisions about whether to use technology or what kind to use depend entirely on what you are trying to achieve and what you should buy to attain the largest library service at the level of quality you require. In a condition where magic and w"itchcraft predominate in any of their manifold forms the arcane rituals must be applied, though they kill the body. With the radical decline of personal confidence of librarians who shudder at the thought of being labelled obsolete, not 'with it', defenders of 'the old manual system' and other cock-a-many nonsense, the magic words branded on our bosom are 'change' (for all changes are obviously good) and 'technology' (for machines are undisputed friends of man, ousting the dog from this once honoured status). Like the Boeing 747, the computer must be used in library processes, no matter how much more costly or what its degree of success, merely because it has been invented.

But once it is used, the Director is not off all of his hooks. There were more sound and mature directors squeezed out of their positions in the late 1960s in disputes over computerization than you could count. Ironically, they were fired for being on either side. If they did not apply the computer, because they saw the messes in library computerization throughout the land, they were pressured by the local computer boys and the administration; if they did apply the computer, with the level of results usually attained at that time, they were pressured by their agonized staff and users. The budget squeeze of the 1970s made university administrators look at the costs of what they referred to as 'free' computer time, and prudence in approaching the computers was allowed. In addition, as recounted above, programming had moved out of the library and conditions of choice had improved. The pressures on the director became less irrational. After all, any fool can join OCLC, and no one can possibly object to catalogue cards.

However, at the present time the directors of research libraries are heading into a major decision with very long term implications for the entire library, depending on which cataloguing data base they will choose to contract with. On this decision will depend a whole range of computerized processes for their library's operations (managed by an outside source), the scope of bibliographical retrieval possible within their library, and their standing in the research library cqinmunity. In some libraries this of will involve major commitments of budgets. This decision now emerges from what seemed to be simple decision four years ago of where they would buy on-line computer-produced catalogue cards.

Outside sources, as of this date, cannot to all of the work in the library, and dealing with local application of what is always an unruly technology presents the director with some of his most difficult problems. In many ways the director is the prisoner of his staff, dependent on them for information to cope with the bewildering range and numbers of complex problems that continually expand before him. However, a director with broad experience in library operations (and we are getting very many now who have very little) can review with some degree of sophistication the information supplied by most library specialists and question them when necessary.

In the case of the computer unit, however, this is virtually impossible, leaving this operation to a large extent on the honour system. The director is far more dependent on the technologist's expertise than on any other unit head. For reasons which range from frivolous to profound, the computer head's decisions are questioned by more peers in the library than are those of any other librarian. The director is left to unsnap these department rivalries. In many cases, the internecine disputes lead to hiring an outside consultant to help make decisions on a level above the emotional entanglements within the staff.

The ability to manage with any degree of sensitivity the development of a computer programme in terms of its time-table, its economy of machine time and storage, its documentation (so others can run it), the avoidance of programme-play (a speciality of professional programmers), and cleanness of the programme to minimize misfires is almost never within the scope of the director. Someone else controls it, in the library or elsewhere. Consequently, there is a looseness of control over the computer unit that would be inconceivable in the case of any other department.

And yet, this relationship is crucial in a library, especially in one dedicated to rapid change, since application of the computer can produce more change in less time than any other factor in existence short of total budget withdrawal. If the changes are not good, the resulting difficulties can take five years to repair. For all these reasons, some of the younger library directors who are beginning to emerge here and abroad are those with deep experience in computer applications.

Management information, which the computer can generate by the mile, is not used very much and generally not used effectively at any managerial level in libraries at the present time. The ability of the computer to identify exactly which books have circulated is not often used at a time when radical constriction of books budgets requires precise information about what kinds of materials to buy. At the director's level the computer is used for accounting purposes, but for cost accounting, work-flow scheduling, staff balance, collection management, resource allocation and budget preparation it is used sporadically and often very badly. A recent visit to a library discovered a monthly statement of management data about three inches high on the director's side table, including more statistics than anyone could digest and correlate in three days. Yet when the director produced for me his per-volume cost for cataloguing a book, an extremely useful statistic to have, we recognised it as being somewhat less than the cost for he catalogue cards produced by OCLC alone, the system he was using. We believe that slowness of movement into this important area of information is the result of poor results in programming that most of us have experienced in the past.

Many of the director's problems with the computer, including early detection of poor performance, could be relieved by one-line information systems, whose costs still place them a considerable way in the distance. Smaller operations, such as public library branches, with small demands for information storage can move to on-line micro-computers more easily than large and complex libraries with huge information demands, and to some extent this is happening, although movement into computerization by American public libraries has been very slow.

A sizeable portion of the library budget has been transferred to computerization and the staff to run it. Almost without exception, this constitutes additional costs, even after deducting cost savings resulting from the change. Only one major voice, Dr. Gordon Ray, President of the John Simon Guggenheim foundation in New York, has been perceptive enough to state in public that computer operations will have to be funded at the expense of conventional library services (at a time when these are being cut). This balanced view of what is giving way to supply computerized processes is seldom applied, and cost considerations seldom play a major role in decisions on library computerization. Costs experienced in system developments have a way of over running cost estimates by the experts by 60% not infrequently.

This looseness of careful cost control -in such decisions is best illustrated in the application of the computer to new academic libraries that began in the 1960s and even now are drastically short of collection strength, without regard for what could have been done with the money by forgoing computerization. This use of computerization as a public relations cosmetic to disguise basic inadequacy is illustrated in such cases as the Australian library 1,500 miles from the nearest substantial collection, supporting ten Ph.D. programmes on a collection of 60,000 volumes, which boasted of being computerized up to the ears. Or tiny public libraries in remote areas of the Rocky Mountains who have been forced against their better judgement into on-line systems using expensive terminals which have been foisted on them by the State Library. Or the proud report that 70% of English university and polytechnic libraries, most of them with inadequate collections, are using on-line bibliographic search services which are extremely expensive. These are computer diversions from library inadequacies. The sloppy management, or non-management of the costs of computers in libraries is not as bad today as it was ten years ago, but in the present state of library funding here and abroad, many of us should have been hung long ago for some of the things we have done. The lynchings still may take place. Computer costs are now visible enough in many library budgets to be targets for cuts by university administrations in the budget squeeze besetting the academic world.

Computerisation tends to divert more money into equipment than formerly occurred, and as we become more dependent on on-line access from multiple consoles this will become increasingly the case. As we move into microcomputers, where obsolescence is a daily rather than an annual fact, even more money will have to go into equipment replacement, and nothing short of short-term contracts at a fixed annual price on a lease purchase basis will be practical.

A final factor in the library budget is the competition generated against it on academic campuses by the computational computer center that serves faculty information needs. This is the only other large information source on campus, and it has a power base in the science and statistically-oriented social science, and language teaching faculties, and at the same time is critically important in generating research rant proposals. These departments have fairly consistently had better response to their budget requests than libraries in this country.

The critical change in the library-campus department relations brought by the computer is in our dependence on an outside computer, generally the one that handles administrative data for processing library systems. This dependence on an out house computer has reduced the library's control over its own operations to a noticeable extent. We are dependent on their choice computer on the skills of their programming staff on their schedule on changes in their programme systems, and on breakdowns resulting from volume of which the library is a small part. This outside computer tells us almost without exception that our work will be done on a batch system, interactivity as we need it being far beyond their capacity. It is a constant thorn in the side of all systems.

The demand by state legislatures for rapid response to requests for what they consider to be accountability data, which they always consider to be statistical and the mounting volume of such requests has been a large factor leading computerization in libraries. Yet the ability to respond has created additional demands for information, and has made public academic libraries even more subject to political control at a time in our history when this has become noxious. Legislatures have decreed by fiat a 20% blanket cut in all state computerization budgets. They have removed computer budgets from separate departments and centralized them in one local computer unit, with little knowledge of and no regards for the consequences. As computer budgets grow larger and state financing tightens as is likely to be the case in most states in the next few years they will be prime targets for a sweeping cut. All of these factors make for reduced control of the library over its own operations.

The very large computer systems with profound implications for libraries are MEDLARS, MARC, CONSER, BLAISE, OCLC, WLN, ARLIN, the University of Toronto system, the Canadian National Library system. Suddenly librarians are confronting big business, which these systems all are. Previously, it this occurred at all, it was on terms such as Blackwell North America's blanket order programmes, that gave a wide range of choice. Instead now a choice must be made among systems, all of which impose very large demands and have large rigidities which must be absorbed, if the benefits are to be obtained. This new situation, in which most libraries of any size are involved has considerably decreased our control over our own operations. Suddenly someone else is controlling how they will be done.

The networks which are the offspring of computer tie-ups and which are leading rapidly to a national library network again require the surrender of local autonomy with no clear realization of what balance of benefits and obligations they will produce. Already the grounds on which these stand are being shifted after a few brief years. Because of data base networks, the functions of the main bibliographical centers in this country are changing and their importance is decreasing. The centrality of DCLC is being eroded by the networks, and will erode further with the incursion of WLN and ARLIN aggressively into the field the latter two requiring total acceptance of their bibliographical structure and procedures.

Looming above all is the impact of the Library of Congress on the library economy of the entire country. For a long time its handling of library cards on while we have depended since 1902, has become less concerned with its clients and more concerned with its own internal operating problems. With the completion of computerization of its cataloguing processes and the expansion of its comprehensive coverage of books published, it has now become totally free from major influence by the entire library community and has gone is own way. For some time its subject headings have been changed to suit computer reading rather than user needs. Now that shortened budgets have made it totally impossible to break away from the bibliographical data that it generates, LC is imposing a radical discontinuity on practices of the past than within a year will churn up the entire academic enterprise to furies of frustration. While early in its development of computerization the library of Congress presented the glowing picture of their catalogue totally on-line. The financial realities dictate that the catalogue generated up to the present will not be computerized. The early promises of pushing a button to change the subject headings on all pertinent records when new subjsct headings, more in tune with changing times and terminology, were appropriate turn out to be something we cannot afford to do. Instead, we are confronted with a split catalogue that at the same time will consist of author and subject entries that break radically from practices in establishing these formerly. It is impossible for libraries of any size not to accept these changes, and equally impossible to prevent the Library of Congress from making them.

The loss of control over our operations involved in this development is immeasurable. Academic libraries ill spend the next five years trying to make their faculty believe that we in no way connived in the chaos that descended upon us on January 2, 1980 and trying to make them believe that there is some point in continuing to support our budgetary requests, and that money hitherto spent on libraries should not be diverted to some other more useful corner of the campus. It is the ultimate take-over of libraries by government, but not even that because LC will not have even token responsibility for any of us. After all, we are completely free not to use their cataloguing data directly thlough networks if we so choose, even though financially it is impossible not to do so. While the computer has helped us perform some of our tasks in libraries to a large degree its potential to help us has not been used, largely because of the extreme rarity of high quality programming skills and what was produced by lesser brethren in the past. Computerization has led to some reductions in standards in the error rate in circulation and bookkeeping records, in unchecked catalogue cards and has virtually eliminated prompt and accurate repair of errors when detected. The sum of what of the computer has done for us in the library has increased our total costs over efficient hand operations. Our achievements in the past seven years have consisted in getting up operating systems that work and in operating participatory networking data bases bit to only a slight degree are we doing things whose end results differ much from what we were doing before.

Balanced against these achievements have been major losses in control over own operations caused by dynamics of the computer in our libraries, In its connections to networks, and in national computerization policies largely uncontrolled by libraries. While libraries in the further may be managed from a remote center, local management has been greatly impaired. For a number of reasons among which the computer looms large, libraries will become in the near future less satisfactory for more people than before and their importance in their institutional setting will gradually decrease.

In this fast changing world information technology and information management are going to play an important role. Information has already been recognised as one of the basic resources for the socio-economic development of a country. Information has now rather acquired the status of the most sought after resource of the resources. The newly emerging 'high tech' disciplines such as computers, tele-communications, biotechnology, etc. are given importance because they store, generate, manipulate, communicate information.

We are experiencing the impact of the new technology on every facet of information handing. The advent of digital computer has opened up new possibilities in information management, and it is likely to change the information infrastructure by merging itself with other related technologies. The increasing use of computer systems for the control of management of information important implications for our thinking about information. And this information processing, storage, and dissemination with the aid of computer is probably called the Information Technology.

When the first computer, called ENIAC, was developed in 1946 it was a huge as it used electronic tubes with a slow speed and clumsy peripherals. It was the first generation computer. However with the development technology the tubes we re replaced by thee transistors and later the integrated circuits etc. and consequently the size of computer has been considerably reduced, while the processing speed has gone up marvellously. The computer systems we have in the late eighties or rather at the end of the eighties are based on Large scale Integration and very Large scale Integration. And with the availability of the microprocessors, we in India are on the way to developing computer networking.

In India computers have already invaded the library and information field and some of the liberties in the special and research organizations have introduced computer systems to automate some their functions. These functions include book ordering and acquisition, cataloguing serials control, circulation, generation and publication of bibliographies, indexes, and other documentation lists. The application of the computer system can also be extended to storage and retrieval of bibliographic indexes, and other documentation lists. The application of the computer system can also be extended to storage and retrieval of bibliographic information, and SDI services. The first computer in India imported from the UK, was installed at the Indian Statistical Institute, Calcutta in 1955. And in the first decade since as many as 16 computers were installed in different parts of India.

The first indigenous computer was designed in India in 1964 by the ISI, Calcutta in collaboration with the Jadavpur University,

Calcutta. This was the introductory phase for computer systems in India, and since then India did not look back in the field of computerisation. During the period 1965-72 the process of computerization speeded up with the installation of 170 more computer systems, although most of them were imported from the Western countries. Then the ECIL, Hyderabad took over the responsibility and installed as many as 94 indigenous computers during the period 1973-78.

Meanwhile, the Government of India gave the responsibility of the computers to the Department Electronics which looked into the question of computer acquisition and evaluation. In 1975 the Government of India set up the national Informatics Centre at New Delhi, and two years later NICNET which now is proposed to be extended to each state capital and district level. Besides, many more computer networks have been established in India during the last decade or so. These include, in addition to the NICNET, the INDONET it is the commercial net work for the country as a whole. We have the RAILNET it is the computer network for the railways; OILNET computer network for oil sector; EDUNET computer network for linking educational institutions; another related one is ERNET computer network for education and research purposes; IANET-computer network for Indian Airlines etc. Besides, there are others which are being. developed as the BANKNET for the banking services: STEELNET for linking steel works across the country to form a communications network etc.

The following operations of the library functions can be speedily processed by the computer These are outlined briefly.

A. Acquisition

(i) Duplication checking

(ii) Preparation of order lists.

(iii) Sending orders to book supplier/s

(iv) Monitoring orders and follow up action

(v) Verification with order file and invoices

(vi) Maintaining state of funds, budget control etc.

B. Cataloguing

(i) Duplicating cataloguing cards

(ii) Preparation of authority file/subject headings list

(iii) Sorting, checking, and filing of catalogue cards

(iv) Automatic generation of added entries

(v) Generating the monthly accession lists

(vi) Developing centralized and cooperative cataloguing system.

C. Circulation Control

(i) Registration of members

(ii) Charging and Discharging of documents

(iii) Updating the records file

(iv) Prepation of reminders

(v) Maintaining statistics

(vi) Information retrieval etc.

D. Serial Control

(i) Ordering of serials

(ii) Receipt and updating the record file

(iii) Receipt to vendors/publishers

(iv) List of holdings

(v) Preparing list of additions

(vi) Preparing list of binding

E. Documentation and Information Retrieval

(i) Indexing of micro and macro documents

(ii) Thesaurus construction

(iii) Abstracting work

(iv) Compilation of union catalogues/lists

(v) Bibliographic work

(vi) Searching and print-outs of queries of users

In addition to what has been outlined above, more library operations can be manipulated with the computer system to achieve efficiency, effectiveness, and to reduce per unit costs etc.

Advantages

Now let us have a cursory look at the advantages which can be accrued from the computerisation. The application of computer in libraries has enormous advantages. The various functions of a library can be extended further for the benefit of the users. Not that computerization will solve all the library problems with which it is infested today, but certainly it has great many potentialities as we have just seen above. If the librarian will be able to improve over the existing set of library services the image of the library and that of the librarian will definitely go up. Therefore some of the advantages of computerization are enumerated below:

(i) *Increase in Speed and Saving of Time.* Library computerisation saves time in storing the information, information handling and information processing information retrieval etc. because all these functions are done at enormous speed. As a result the time lag between the acquisition of documents and their availability to the user will be reduced considerably. And computer networking will further help in saving time of the library personal and the users.

(ii) *Computers system* will lend in updating the record files much more quickly and easily than in the manual system.

(iii) *Greater Library Cooperation.* With the installation of computer system in libraries in the country as a whole the opportunities of library cooperation will increase. These computer systems installed in different institutions can be hooked to each other via satellite and through a central agency and thereby can know each other's collection. Library cooperation can be achieved at various levels and for different functions including acquisitions cataloguing, inter-library lending etc.

(iv) *Better Library Management.* When properly planned, per unit operating costs will normally be reduced by computerisation. The money saved can be utilized for some other productive purposes, such as book purchase, or staring a new serve for users etc.

(v) *Staffing.* In order to meet with the increasing needs for services the use of equipment can further be extended as such scope always exists in the system. There is, therefore, no need for increasing the manpower.

(vi) *New Services.* Many new services can be introduced without any extra cost or manpower. And many library service can be generated only as a by product of the records already available on the system.

(vii) *Protection of Records.* Inputting the records in the system in machine readable from provides them greater protection against loss of these records by fire, earthquake, and other natural disasters. Recreation of the files from the machine readable from of re,cords is also, much easier.

(vii) *Report Production.* Various types of reports about library activities and other letters, follow up notices, sending of reminders etc. can automatically be generated.

Though much development has not been reported by the end of the 1980s, yet a beginning has already been made in various libraries, particularly the special libraries and information centres in this vast country of millions and millions.

INSDOC, New Delhi

This national level documentation centre has been compiling a national union Catalogue of Scientific serials in India with the help of a computer. Another application of the computer has been the compilation of the Author Index and the Key word based Subject index of the Indian science Abstracts. Thus computerization helps in the easy retrieval of information. INSDOC has also pioneered the computerized SDI service in 1975 when it started with software.

National Aeronautical Lab., Bangalore

In the library of this organization use of computer system has been made for circulation control, document ordering, acquisition of library material and information retrieval.

BARC Bombay

At this research centre of atomic energy computer has been put to use for cataloguing its technical reports. It is now servings as the inputting centre to INIS at the international level. It has developed a computerised system, AFSARI, for providing service from a general database on a magnetic tape containing bibliographic information.

DRTC, Bangalore

Computer is being used at the DRTC for document finding, and also for the training of its trainees. They also use computer for the purpose of giving short term courses to working librarians. They are also data about Colon Classification on computer for the production of schedules. It can also help in automatic classification.

SERC, Roorkee

For the retrieval of bibliographic information a computer system is made available at the library of the Structural Engineering Research Centre, Roorkee.

CFTRI, Mysore

A national centre or Food Science & Technology has been developed at the CFTRI. Its library provides computerised Current Awareness Services to the CFTRI and its work stations food industry and other R&D organisations. It also provides online search facilities on the database developed. At present it is serving as inputting centre to International food Information service for India.

Central Drug Research Institute Lucknow

The National Information centre here has developed a non-bibliographical database on medicinal plants. It has successfully developed and implemented softwares for library automation natural products and pattents search through online access. It has also brought out a computerized union catalogue of current periodicals on LUSLIC libraries.

Central Leather Research Institute, Madras

For its library it has planned computerised SDI service. It has developed a database for a variety of uses, particularly for information retrieval. It has been generating the annual cumulative subject indices for the service, Current leather Literature.

Central Machine Tools Institute, Bangalore

It has been using computer system for data storage retrieval, online processing of technical enquiries and library transactions.

ATIRA, Ahmedabad

A Selective dissemination of Information service is in operation using a computer system available at ATIRA, the national information centre for textiles.

IIT, New Delhi

It has developed and implemented a computerised circulation control system as apart of the computerisation.

SAIL, Ranchi

For its library and information centre, it has developed a computerised document acquisition system database.

DESIDOC, Delhi

For its library it has developed and implemented a computerized document acquisition system database among others.

BHEL, Bangalore

Here also a computerised book acquisition system has been developed and implemented. In addition to the above there are scores of more special libraries and information centres attached to the research organizations which have either developed computerised system or at the planning stage and would develop soon according to their requirements. Computer application has also gone beyond this percolating to the university libraries and in some of the university libraries in India computer systems have already been acquired and installed. Some illustration are given here.

Anna University Library Madras

The circulation service and the information retrieval functions have been computerized in this University Library successfully.

Panjab University Library, Chandigarh

It has also installed a microcomputer and has input the periodicals records in the system for efficiency and better control. It is planning to extend its applications in the library.

Gandhi Vidyapeeth, Ahmedabad

When this author visited its library in March 1988, it had already acquired a computer system and was at the planning stage.

JNU Library, New Delhi

This University Library has also acquired a computer system for automating its library functions. These are just some example.

There are other university libraries which are in the process of acquiring one or the other computer system for computerising the housekeeping jobs. In this region as per the knowledge of the author, some more university libraries are planing to go for computerization and for this purpose they are trying to give hands on training to their staff. Moreover, the UGC has already approved the development of information and library network for the Eighth Five year plan period, which will give incentive to other university libraries in the country to buy the computers. It is therefore hoped that during the Eighth Five year Plan all the 170 university libraries will acquire computer system as envisaged under the ambitions INFLIBNET network system were by all of them will be linked to each other in order to share resources and make the whole country a very vast library. This network will also be ex tended to include about 500 colleges and about 200 R&D centres to make it more worthwhile and network.

Bangalore in India is already on the way to be very rightly called the Electronic City of India. Besides, many big cities are now having such units to manufacture and assemble computers of various sizes to suit the needs of user groups in public and private sector. The other important places include Delhi, Hyderabad, Mohali, Madras, Trivandrum. Calcutta, etc. At the present speed it is hoped that by turn of the century, India might have taken many leaps towards computerization of library operations, there is now etc. need to train such manpower which would be capable of handling computers systems for information processing and management.

The computer is a tool with innumerable components, inter-connected in a very complex way. Besides the main machine, the central processor unit, there are many ancillaries called peripherals. Because of great computing power, speed, ability to execute complex processing functions, storage capacity and reliability, the computer is being used in almost all fields. Computer technology, both hardware and software, is deriving all benefits from the advances made in solid state physics and electronics. During the last few decades, the tremendous advances in these subject-fields effected such rapid changes in computer technology that it may be said to have ushered in a revolution.

The technological advances are discernible in the hardware materials used in the machine and its operational processes. The computer designed in different periods by using advanced technology has been specified by the term 'generation'; *e.g.*, the pre-1959 computer is called the first generation computer; the computer designed between 1959 and 1964, the second generation computer; the computer of the period between 1964 and the late seventies, the third generation computer; and so on. In different generations, the material used in the computer have been changed for each and every part of machine—the memory, the arithmetic and logic unit, input/output processes etc. In the first generation computer, dating prior to 1959, vacuum tubes were used and all functions were performed in the central processor unit. In the second generation, dating from 1959 to 1964, transistors were used. These had considerable effect on the computer which gradually became smaller in size and lesser expensive in cost. The third generation computer was built with integrated circuits by making use of micro-electronics for the components introduced in 1964. The magnetic media were used for the memory storage. The fourth generation computer came into being in the late seventies using advanced micro-electronic concepts to get further circuit densities. The new circuits were microscopic. The size became smaller still and the cost, less expensive. At the same time, the capability for storage and performance of the operational systems increased greatly.

Modern technological advances had an overall impact on the computer hardware in all aspects—the machine, operations and the cost. The primary'impact on the machine was the diminishing of size. The earlier computer was large enough. The weight of ENIAC was 30 tons. It consumed much electricity and produced much heat. The second and the third generation 'computers became smaller and smaller as a result of the use of electronics and micro-electronics. There are more than 50,000 integrated circuits in a modern computer, but the size is smaller than that of the earlier computer. The size of a modern computer has been reduced considerably by using a wafer-like material—the silicon chip. It is possible to pack over 2,00,000 components in one square inch of the silicon chip. It is expected that smaller chips will be able to accommodate even more components in future. The chip is an extraordinary material for the computer hardware, because of its low cost, compact electronics and capability to embody the logic and the memory units. A large umber of micro-electronic circuitry can be fabricated on a small chip which lead to 'very large-scale integration' used in a modern computer. A chip can store a very large amount of information, and so it is known as the memory chip A microprocessor is the 'computer on a chip' combining memory with logic functions. Using the chip the computer is becoming cheaper and more powerful, day by day.

A computer stores a large quantum of data in the memory and performs complex operations for various computations. So, it should be perfectly reliable. The vacuum tubes were not so reliable. The transistors had also certain flaws. They sometimes broke off from circuit boards. The chip has no soldered wires and each circuitry is more compact. So, the failure points are almost nil, and it has become most reliable. Furthermore, it is tiny and the electronic signals can move through it very quickly and thus save time. The probability of failure or committing mistakes is almost nil. Moreover, selfrepairing computers are also being produced.

The sophisticated magnetic media and the silicon chip brought about a major break-through in the storage of data and information. The magnetic media like the magnetic tape of offline service and the magnetic drum or disc for online service can hold more information than their counterparts in the earlier computers. Magnetic cores are proved to be efficient storage media requiring less space and working with greater speed. They are inexpensive and compact in size. Millions of magnetic cores can be accommodated in a small cabinet. Random access is provided much faster. The time for access to documents can be measured in nanoseconds. The early chips could perform work with greater speed than magnetic cores. The large scale integrated (LSI) circuit storage elements were used. In modern chips, very large scale integrated (VLSI) circuits are being used. It has increased the storage capacity in a comparatively smaller space.

Computers are becoming smaller in size, but of larger storage capacity owing to the advancement of hardware technology.

The speed in operation has become faster and the output, of greater reliability because of reduction in size. Now, least time is required by electronic pulses to travel because the distance is shorter in modern hardware. Thus, the speed of the processor has increased. The calculation time in the 1970's increased several hundred times more than what was in the 1950's. More than a million of calculations can be made in a second. The speed of the early computers was measured in milliseconds, *i.e.* thousandths of a second; the second generation speed was expressed in microseconds, *i.e.* millionths of a second and the next generations of computers in nanoseconds, *i.e.* billionths of a second. It does not come within human perception. The computer job of ten hours in the 1950's came down to a few seconds' hob in the 1970's and now the very same job can be performed in the tiny fraction of a second. This can be done also in a time-sharing and multi-programming operation.

The new innovations in hardware technology, particularly storage media, micro-electronics, VLSI, etc., have reduced the cost of the computer. Not only the cost of machines is reducing, but the cost of maintenance and operation is also being reduced because of the low consumption of electricity compared to that of the earlier computers. The cost of computer instructions has also been reduced because of greater speed. As the computer capability is increasing more and more, so the cost is becoming lesser and lesser.

A wide range of general-purpose and special-purpose computers is being used in libraries. Computers are also available in various sizes and with various systems adaptable to various specific-purpose applications. Mainframe computers, mini-computers, microcomputers, microprocessors etc., are the types which can be used in libraries. These can be used independently or in interconnected systems with master-slave relationship or network relationship. Computerisation may be implemented as an integrated system with a mainframe computer or part by part with mini or microcomputers to be interconnected in future. Such alternative make library automatic financially viable. Planning and management also become efficient, cost-effective and result-oriented. Mainframe computers are usually host systems for several libraries or information centres. These computers are timesharing and multi-programming, and an usually multiprocessors, being composed of many computers including microcomputer. All these operate in a connected was under the control of a central operating system. Modern mainframe computer are capable of address and several billion positions or more of memory with hundreds of registers. These are more than 32 bits in length. The channels between various parts of such a computer are capable of carrying upto 5 million bits of detain one millionth of a second. A mainframe computer has microcomputers to control specific hardware devices, such as printers, disc drives etc. These also help transfer of memory from one device to another through the bus. These microcomputer have central processing units with the large scale integrated memory system like the read-only memory or the programmable read-only memory or the programmable read-only memory.

RAM

It stands for Random Access Memory (RAM), and is a general-purpose memory to store data and programmes. It requires electric power to hold the content intact. So, it is known as volatile memory. In RAM, the location of the specific circuit is possible and can be accessed directly in the middle of the chip. One need not examine each circuit starting at the beginning and moving forward one by one.

ROM

While the chip is composed of specific circuits designed to execute a single programme, it is called Read Only Memory (ROM). Expect the designed programme, no other programme can be held by ROM. The entire chip must be replaced and redesigned for any change in the programming. But ROM is very much useful for any specific application, and when it is to be produced in large quantities.

PROM

The large scale integrated memory can be used for specific applications known as Programmable Read Only Memory (PROM). In PROM, chips are used singly for programming by breaking connections between circuits. PROM is very useful for specific programxnes and can be used for specific routine programmes.

EPROM

The disadvantage of PROM is that once a programme is recorded in the chip, it cannot be changed or revised. So a method has been devised known as Erasable Programmable Read Only Memory (EPROM) which is constructed not by breaking circuits, but by activating circuits between specific values within the chip and later de-activating the circuits with high intensity ultra-violet light. The chip for EPROM can be programmed over and over again without being replaced. The instructions programmed in ROM, PROM and EPROM can be held for years together, and are known as non-volatile memory.

The programming languages *viz.* BASIC, COBOL, FORTRAN, PASCAL, PL/I are available for microcomputers. All the programming languages have their specific fields of application for different purpose. In library applications, Beginners All-purpose Symbolic Instruction Code (BASIC) is most widely used. The advantages are that it is easy to learn; and the programming is rather simple. Moreover, the scope is wider and all the terms used in the library are programmable with basic. With the knowledge of a few commands and by manipulating them judiciously, one can construct fairly sophisticated programmes with basic.

It is possible to create numerous routines, subroutines and subcommands with BASIC. The usefulness of basic in library applications lies in its capability to handle strings. It is not always possible to determine the lengths and the characters for bibliographic data, and so, the undefined length area of a string allows flexibility in data input.

The original BASIC was limited in scope and command. But basic has been much developed since then. Now it is available in two modes-interpreted and compiled. The interpreted mode is better at the initial stage. It is slower, but helps the programmer to do his hob correctly. The compiled version is sophlsticated and meant for advanced users. For online interaction, the compiled version in more effective.

Library Network Hardware

Installing library network cards, cables, and connectors need not be any more difficult than installing the LAN software. The keys are to check your work each step of the way and use the right tools. This chapter provides information to help you install the network cards and cable connectors and ideas for running the network cards and cable connectors and ideas for running the library network cable.

If librarian follow a few safety rules, librârian won't damage anything. The worst that can happen is the installation won't work. The best that can happen is the hardware works and librarian are ready to install the software.

Preparing for the Installation

Time and energy spent preparing for the hob saves time and frustration while working on the job. There is nothing more discouraging than halting a project midway because librarian don't have the fight tools. Without the right tools, the result is sloppy, unreliable, and possibly dangerous. Preparing for the job includes knowing the basic rules of safety to protect yourself and the equipment, as well as making sure librarian have the proper tools. And don't imagine that librarian must complete the entire project in one day, regardless of how small or large your LAN.

Above all librarian must be aware of basic electrical safety rules when working with hardware. Electronic devices are sensitive to electricity, especially the nuisance of static electricity. For example, as librarians insert a card into the system, the static electricity in your body can travel through, and may damage, the card. Listed here are a few basic rules. Additional tips are included with each step of the hardware installation process.

(a) Always slow a system to become completely quiet after turning it off and before moving it. The hard disk is vulnerable to damage while it is still spinning.

(b) Always unplug any electrical device before removing any covers. Just turning of the power switch does not disconnect the system from the electrical current.

(c) Never consume liquids around and opened device. If, in the heat of the moment, librarians are sweating profusely, stop to wipe your brow. One drop of that salt water inside the computer could damage it.

(d) Always touch a grounded object before picking up a computer card or reaching inside the system.

(e) Leave the card in the protective antistatic plastic pouch until just before librarian need to use it. If librarian mist make changes to the switches or jumpers on the card, lay it on top of the plastic bag, which librarian have placed on a flat surface.

(f) Always use the right type and size tools. If librarian use a power screwdrive, be very careful not to overtighten screws.

(g) If librarian drop a screw inside the case, stop and immediately retrieve it. If librarian forget to get it and turn the system on later, you could seriously damage the computer.

(h) When working around electrical wire, be careful not to route network cable neat or over the wire.

(i) When cutting holes in wallboard, be very careful not to cut into electrical wire or plumbing.

Hardware installation can be very physically demanding. Librarians moving systems around and climbing ladders. Librarians will definitely be removing covers and bending over as librarians insert the cards. Remember to take it easy. The physical activity may increase your frustration level.

If librarian are doing the installation during nonworking hours, librarians may want to talk someone into assisting, even if that person doesn't know the business end or a screwdriver. Sometimes it helps to have someone to talk with as librarian work through the problems they encounter.

The Necessary Tools for Librarians

Before librarians take the first step of the installation, prepare as they would for performing surgery-place all the instruments within reach. Then, when librarians need a specific tool, they can just reach for it. Don't use a flathead screwdriver to remove a screw just because they can't easily reach the Phillips screwdriver. Computer toolkits are widely available at computer stores.

Keep in mind that librarians will need different types of tools for installing cards and for installing cable. Here's a list of tools librarian might need to install a library network card:

(a) Four screwdrivers-a small and medium size of both flathead and phillips. Better yet, secure a series of hex head drivers if your systems have hex head screws.

(b) Find something to extract screws dropped inside the computer. A medical clamp called a hemostat is handy. A doubled-up piece of sticky tape on the eraser of a pencil will also do.

(c) A small flashlight is useful as librarian peer down into the innards of the computer, especially if librarian are digging around for a dropped screw. A small, plastic flashlight is better than a large metal one in case librarian drop it into the computer.

(d) A power screwdriver saves time when removing and replacing screws in the back of the system. Remember to keep a loose grip to prevent overtightening the screws. If librarian use the power screwdriver to remove and install the screws that keep the cards in, be very gentle.

(e) A small mirror will help librarian see behind the system if librarian don't have the space to pull it out from the wall or can't bend over far enough to see the ports in back.

(f) A small hair dryer is handy for blowing out dust in the system.

(g) Small needle-nose pliers help move card jumpers.

The tool list for installing cable is a bit more lengthy. Not only must librarian cut the cable, librarian must also strip off parts of insulation and then properly clamp the cable connector, such as a BNC or RJ-45, on the end of the cable.

Be sure librarian have the proper crimp for the connector librarian are using. The crimp looks. like a strange set of pliers. Depending on the quality and the specific tool. If librarian are making BNC connectors, this tool is essential, if librarian are using twisted-wire, there is a way to avoid making cable connectors.

(a) Get and use large, sharp wire clippers.

(b) Find a sharp knife to cut away insulation. Better yet, there are wire strippers that will cut the insulation to the exact measurements librarian need before attaching the BNC connectors. The Rs 5000 is well worth the savings of time and greater accuracy if librarian are making more than four or six cable ends.

(c) If librarian will be going through walls, find a drill with along 1/4-inch bit.

(d) A small ball of string with a weight tied at one end is essential for pulling cable across suspended ceilings.

(e) Use wide masking tape or blank mailing labels to mark cable ends.

(f) Find a small keyhole saw if librarian need to make access holes in the wall.

(g) If the suspended ceiling has insulation, librarian and anyone working with librarian need gloves and a breathing filter.

(h) Borrow two tall ladders if librarian are running cable across the suspended ceiling tiles.

With the exception of the cable crimp and wire stripper, the tools just described are readily available. The cable crimp and wire stripper should be available from the same source as your network cable and connectors. Make sure you get the proper crimp size for the BNC connectors and cable.

Selecting Test Systems

If librarian purchased a LAN starter system already have the software, two cards, and the proper type of cable with connectors. This cable may be from 15 to 25 feet long. Even if that is not long enough for one of their connections in the library network, it is exactly what librarian need for the first phase of their installation.

One of the most useful and time-saving steps librarian can take is to move two systems next to each other, as shown in Figure, for the first part of the library network installation. In most cases, bring another system as close as possible to the server. Librarian will use these two systems at the same time to test both the server installation and the workstation's ability to access the server.

With the two systems side by side, install the first two cards, install the server, and then install the workstation. As librarian test and smooth out the process, you just shift from keyboard to keyboard to keyboard like a pianist playing a duet on two pianos. This beats running down the hall two dozen times to the nearest station to see if the server is working and if the workstation has made the connection.

As librarian would with any computer, make sure this temporary arrangement includes a sturdy table for the second system. Librarian may need another power strip if the receptacles are taken up by the server. Since librarian will have 15 to 25 feet of slack in the cable, avoid heavily traceled areas where coworkers could easily trip.

Installing Library Network Cards

Above all, before installing the library network cards, read the accompanying documentation. With luck, librarian won't have any surprises. Those surprises occure when librarian have two cards trying to use the same settings. In most cases, the default settings on the card will work. Try those settings. If they do not work, librarian will find out about if fairly quickly and can worry about those finer points later.

Make sure librarian have located and written down the technical support number. Find the page in the documentation that shows the specification, including the I/O base address and the IRQ. If all goes well, librarian won't need this information. If Librarian need to change some settings, it will be important.

Installation Steps for Librarian

Librarian should install any new computer part slowly and carefully. The smaller the changes, the less work librarian have to undo when problems arise. Here are the steps librarian should follow:

(a) Turn on the computer to make sure it works.

(b) Turn it off, unplug it, and remove the cover.

(c) Gently blow out any dust.

(d) Locate an empty slot in the motherboard.

(e) Remove the mounting bracket from the back of the system.

(f) Touch grounded metal to discharge static electricity.

(g) Remove the card from the antistatic plastic bag.

(h) Insert the card.

(i) Plug the system back in and turn it on.

(j) Test the card.

(k) Test the system.

(l) If librarian have problems, turn off the system and study the next section, "Network Card Problems".

(m) Install the LAN software.

(n) Turn off the system. Replace the slot screw.

(o) Replace the cover of the system.

Turn on the computer to make sure it works. Run through a few of the main programmes. Make sure the mouse works if librarian have one. If a printer is attached, make sure it prints. If there is a modem, check that as well. There is always the chance that something was not working correctly before your installed the library network card. It is maddening to try to fix a problem that librarian think was caused by the card but was actually present before the card was installed; checking the system beforehand eliminates that possibility Once librarian are satisfied that the system works as expected, turn it off, wait until it is completely quiet, and then unplug it. Librarian can disconnect it from the wall or from the back of the system. Remove the cover by unscrewing all the screws around the edge of the back. The cover may have to slide all the way forward before librarian can lift it off. Some covers just slider forward an inch or so and then lift off. Keep the cover screws together in a safe place.

If no maintenance has been performed on the system within the past six months to a year, Librarian will have an accumulation of dust. Use the hair dryer or other gentle; blower to push the dust out of the system. A vacuum is not recommended; nor is blowing with their moist breath.

In the motherboard, locate the slot for the library network card, using their flashlight if necessary. Make sure the slot has sections if librarians are installing a 16-bit network card. If it doesn't must install an 8-bit card or, alternatively, move an 8-bit card from a 16-bit slot into this currently open 8-bit slot, thereby opening up a 16-bit slot.

Remove the mounting bracket, shown here, by unscrewing the small screw at the top of the back opening in the case: As librarian loosen the screw, hold it carefully so you don't have to fish it out of the system later. Keep the screw handy, but save the mounting bracket somewhere else.

Touch grounded metal to discharge static electricity. Then stand very still while librarian reach for the library network card.

Remove the card from the antistatic plastic bag. Lay the card on top of the bag if librarian need to make any adjustments to the jumpers or dip switches.

The slots on the motherboard have small spring contact stirps that match the contact strips on the bottom of the card. As librarian insert the card, librarian may have to rock the card back and forth very gently to get it all the way into the slot. The mounting bracket on the card should be exactly at the top edge of the system back support. Do not use excessive force to insert the card. Librarian might damage the library network card or motherboard. If librarian knew for sure the card would work, librarian could just put the cover back on. But there is a chance that the card will conflict with other cards in the system and librarian may need to make changes on the card. With the cover still off, turn the system back on, be very careful here. Librarian have an open system with power in it. Anything, librarian touch or drop into this open system could damage you, the system, or both. If there is a major problem, librarian might get extra beeps or the system may not boot up. The odds of this happening are slim, but possible. If this occurs, Refer to the next section of this chapter. If the system starts normally, librarian are ready to test the card. Most card manufacturers provide a disk with utility software, including a programme to test the card. Refer to your card's documentation for the name of that programme and then run it.

If the card test programme runs, then try using the, major software programmes installed on the system. This step is essential because if don't and librarian load the LAN software. Librarian won't know if the problem is with the card or the LAN software. Make sure you test the mouse, the printer, and the modem by running programmes that use these devices.

If librarian had problems with their library network card or application software test, turn off the system and unplug the card again. Then refer to the next section of this chapter. If librarian did not find any problems, install the LAN software for the server or workstation. Librarian need not worry about setting up the entire directory tree.

If no problems were noted, turn off the system and unplug the cord. The temptation may be to jest replace the system cover, leaving out the network card retaining screw while the power is on. Don't! The screw must be replaced in the network card, especially because the cable pulls on the card. Attempting to do this work with the power on is very hazardous.

With the power still off, replace the cover of the system. If librarian use a power screwdriver, be sure librarian don't overtighten the screws in the back. Once librarian have installed one network card, don't assume that the installation will be the same for all the other systems. The only way this occurs is if all the systems are exactly the same brand, have the same cards, and use the same software. If librarian bought the computer systems one or two at a time, even from the same manufacturer, there may be different problems. The only difference on the second system, temporarily sitting next to the server, is that the software librarian install will be for a workstation, not a server. Even if librarian plan to make each system a server in a peer-to-peer scheme, start out with the simplest configuration settings later. Also keep in mind that when librarian attempt to start the workstation software for the first time, it will not complete the process until the two systems are attached with the library network cable.

Network Card Problems in the Library

Library network card manufacturers try to create card settings that work in the majority of computers. If librarian have a system with one serial port, one parallel port, and no unusual cards, there is a good chance the default settings will work. On the other hand, if librarian have a CD-ROM drive, a second serial port, a music or some other special card, the network card may have the same settings already used by one of those devices.

Most network installation manuals provide suggestions to resolve conflict between the library network card and other cards in the system. Those recommendations include changing dip switches and moving jumpers Dip switches are small sets of usually eight switch. By setting these switches on and software to use as a reference. The manual should show the numbers used for these settings. Make sure librarian know the on and off positions on the block. Use any small pointed device to move the switches. Here is an illustration of dip switches on a library network card:

Librarian may also have to move jumpers on the cards. These jumpers are small plastic blocks that fit over two metal pins. The inside of the jumper contains metal. When the jumper covers two pins, it closes the circuit, creating another setting on the network card. In many cases, there will be two rows of pins with four of five pairs. A jumper is to cover only one pair of pins. Here is a set of pins with one jumper.

Most network cards have just one set of dip switches a although there may be many sets of jumper pins. The network manual will have a drawing of the card with the different pin locations and names. On some cards, the setting are also printed next to the pins. Use the needlenose pliers to gently pull the jumper off the current pair of pins, and then push the jumper back on the new set of pins with your finger. However, before making changes to these settings, sketch the original location of the jumpers and dip switches. If librarian continue to make changes, make a new sketch for each setting. Also write down the value for that setting.

When librarian make changes to the card. Librarian will also make changes to the library network software. The whole purpose of making these changes is to avoid conflicts with other cards in the system. Since the library network software must be told those new settings on the card, librarian will need to reinstall the software or make changes on the command lines.

Making changes in the card settings to resolve conflicts can be a very tedious process. Librarian should make only one change at a time in the card. Two changes at the same time might cause additional problems. To make and test changes, follow these steps:

(a) Make sure the system is off and unplugged.

(b) Touch grounded metal to discharge static.

(c) Gently rock the card out of the slot.

(d) Place the card on the antistatic bag.

(e) Sketch the current dip switch or jumper setting.

(f) Make the change or the card.

(g) Insert the card back into the system.

(h) Plug in and power up.

(i) Reinstall the library network software or make the changes in the batch file to reflect the new card setting.

(j) Attempt to start the library network.

(k) If the library network appears to work, continue to test your applications. If not, return to step a.

Another effective but time-consuming approach to resolving conflicts is to remove all the nonessential cards in your system, leaving only the video, disk drive, and network cards. If the network card works, librarian then add cards one at a time until librarian locate the card causing the conflict. This information is very helpful for anyone providing technical support.

The number of possible settings and conflicts may seem overwhelming. Your ability to solve the problem depends on your perserverance and technical support. There are many sources for help. Don't be reluctant to begin working down your list, starting with the library network card tech support phone number.

As do all cards, the library network card uses a number of settings to work within computers. These settings include the I/O port address, the interrupt requests, the base memory address, and other settings, and they are a major reason why librarian might have problems with the network card installation. This is because no two cards in a computer can use the same IRQ, DMA, or I/O port address. While it is not essential that librarian know how these settings work, understanding the basics may help you try different values to get your network card to work.

The methods used to change these settings may differ. Older cards use physical methods, described in detail in the next sections. Newer cards, though, may these changes with software. Librarian run the special software programme to make the changes once the card is plugged in those new settings are then saved on the card. Librarian can run the software again to make further changes.

The I/O Port Address

Each card in the system has unique I/O port address. Many of these are reserved for specific types of cards, such as the video card. For example, librarian can't have two VGA display cards in the same system. Other card addresses are not unique to the card type. Network cards, as well as other cards, fall within this category. This is why these cards have dip switches to change the I/O address.

Any "extra" cards in the system, such as a CD-ROM, music speech input or output, digitizer, or scanner card, may already be using the default setting on the network card. If librarian have one or more of these cards, librarian will need the documentation for these cards to determine that setting. If that card works correctly, librarian are better off making changes to the network card instead.

The possible addresses for network cards range from 2EOh to 380h. The dip switches can be set either ON or OFF. With eight positions, that number expresses a binary number from 0000 0000 to 1111 1111, or 0 to 255 decimal. The catch is that the numbers used to represent the I/O address are in hexadecimal. Therefore, the number 300h is represented as 0011 1111 on the switches. Librarian need not know hex to make the changes, but librarians must make sure their switch settings match those in the network card manual.

Change the settings on the network card and software to aunique 110 address. If it still does not work, return the address to the original setting and consider changing the IRQ.

Interrupts

While the I/O address represents a unique ID to the computer, the interrupts are used to get the computer's attention. When the card. needs to send something to, or through, the system, it "Interrupts" the current processing. The system then checks the card to process that task.

The IRQs range from IRQO to IRQ15. As with the unique I/O, the interrupts also need to be allocated, one per card or action. The standard interrupts include IRQ4 for COM1 and IRQ3 for COM2. If you have an LPT2 port in your system, the IRQ5 is also being used. In most cases, though, the IRQ5 is a good choice if you have both COM1 and COM2 in your system. Librarian can try the IRQ2, but this interrupt may not work well in 286 or faster systems. On most cards, librarian change the interrupt by moving a jumper. One row of pins on the card represents all the IRQ settings the card can use. Some network cards have just three settings, while newer cards may have five or more pairs of pins. As with the I/O address, will have to check the IRQs used by other cards for potential conflicts.

Base Memory Address for Library Network

The network card contains its own memory to buffer the transactions on the network cable. This must "fit" within the memory addresses that DOS can use.

The network card memory fits in the reserved memory between 640 K and 1024K, called high DOS memory. The common settings for network cards include COOh, DOOOh and D800h.

Just like the I/O address and IRQs, this setting must be unique in the computer. For example, EGA and VGA display cards and some hard disk controller cards use the area starting at COOOh. Librarian will use another set of jumper pins to change the base address if librarian have conflicts here

Other Settings

Network cards have even more settings. These include the DMA, the channel, the cable type, the node address, the remote boot PROM, and the reconfiguration timeout, and they rarely need to be changed. Make changes to these settings only if advised by tech support or with specific directions from the network card manual.

Making Cable Connectors

Once librarian have installed two network cards, are ready to connect them with a cable. If Librarian purchased a network kit, typically you get one cable section already made. Librarian can use this cable to test their network with one server and one workstation. Once librarian are satisfied that the beginnings of a network. Librarian can run the cables and make the permanent connections.

Even before librarian begin tossing cables, he need to know what he must do to attach the cables. As mentioned, make sure you have the proper tools to make reliable connections.

Installing BNC Connectors for Library Network

Librarian use BNC connectors for network coax cable. Make sure librarian the specific BNC connector for the cable size. The connector is too large, the cable come apart. If the connector is too small, the coax cannot slide inside the connector.

When purchasing the cable and connectors, get specifications for the amount of insulation to trim. These measurements are very important for proper contact between the cable and connector.

The actual BNC connector Kit contains three pieces. The smallest piece, the tip, covers the inner wire or the cable. The second and largest part is the actual twist connector. The third piece is the sleeve. This slips over the cable insulation and clamps the cable to the end to the twist connector.

Making cable connector requires some practice. Cable connectors are not that expensive. Librarian may want to take a few feet of cable and few connectors and sit down to practice. This practice time helps later when librarian are in a rush to see if the whole LAN works. These are the steps for making a connector:

(a) Cut the cable, allowing several feet of a slack.

(b) Trim the insulation.

(c) Insert the sleeve on the cable.

(d) Attach the tip and crimp.

(e) Slide the connector on the cable.

(f) Bring the sleeve up and crimp.

(g) Tug on the connection to test its strength.

Make a clean cut of the cable with heavy duty wire cutters. If the end gets smasshed or hacked off with a knife, the connector is much harder to attach.

Using the guise, trim the insulation to the exact measurements. If librarian want to make the cleanest and most accurate trims, purchase a cable-stripping pliers. Work over a piece of paper; the braided portion of the cable sheds tiny wires as you trim it.

Insert the sleeve on the cable and move it up the cable a foot or so. If librarian forget this step now, librarian will work to get the main connector on the cable and then have to take it off again to put on the sleeve.

Attach the tip and use the crimp to bottom end slightly. The crimper tool has a special area for this purpose. This assures good contact between the wire and the tip. Move the sleeve up and over the end of the connector. The sleeve should touch the bottom of the connector and cover part of the insulation. Use the crimping tool to squeeze the sleeve, insulation, and braid against the end of the connector. Some crimpers create a six-sided crimp; other produce two edges on the sleeve.

Tug on the connection to test its strength. If it wiggles, seems loose, or comes off in your hand, cut whole thing off and try again. Do not try to repair your first attempt. Weak connections in library network cable will eventually drive you to despire.

Making solid BNC connectors is a real skill. As long as librarian accept the fact that librarian will need practice and librarian will make a mess of the first few, he can do it.

Using Twisted-Pair Connectors for Library Network

With the RJ-45 twisted-pair cable connectors, librarian have eight wires to handle. Librarian must strip the insulation from the cable without cutting the inside wires. Each wire must then be inserted in the proper slot in the plastic connector and then crimped with the special tool. If one wire is crossed or is not crimped properly, librarian may spend hours tracking the problem to that source.

The better approach when working with twisted-pair cable is to purchase the cables with connectors already made from the computer to a vendor. Librarian then run the cable connector from the computer to a receptacle librarian have installed in the wall. The receptacles are easy to wire because they use screwdown connections. Librarian strip the insulation, wrap the wire around the post, and screw it down.

Other Connection Methods for Library Network

The RJ-45 and BNC connectors are the most common for small library network. If librarian decide to have someone run the cable and make the connections, listen carefully to the method that person suggests. The cable and connector companies constantly improve their products and the ways to use them.

Do keep cable across an expanse of space is variously called tossing, pulling, stretching, stringing, or running cable. Each word describes the methods used to install cable. The most common ways to ceiling or pull it through the walls.

Even before librarian decide if librarian are going to toss or pull cable, librarian need to consider whether or not librarian need help with this part of their library network project.

When to Get help Running Cable for Library Network

Fire and building codes exist as safety measures for occupants or all buildings. When librarian begin using space outside the normal working rooms, librarian are affecting the construction of that building. One of the best and most serious reasons to get help with your cabling project is to work with someone who knows the what building codes. An electrician experienced with network cable knows what kind of cable the building requires. Not only can the electricians do the hard physical labor, they make sure the cable is properly routed to avoid interference and potential breaks.

Before librarian hire electricians to do the cabling, make sure they have experience and understand the limitations of the medium. For example coiled up in the ceiling—"After all, librarian never know when librarian will need it". This potential vendor does not understand the limitations imposed by network cable.

In some situations, placing the cable will just be beyond the capabilities of a novice cable installer. These situations require special tools and expertise, and might include the following:

(a) Workstations on two or more floors in the building.

(b) Cable layouts exceed the rated length and require repeaters.

(c) Building code requires special installation.

(d) Your library has strict work rules.

(e) The cable must be installed through duct work.

(f) Librarian want network outlets in the walls.

(g) The cable must be pulled through cable conduits.

When looking for a contractor, remember that librarian can supply the cable and finish the connectors themselves; some LAN specialists mark up the cost of cable 200 percent or more. Librarian will want the contractor to tag the ends or each cable and test for continuity before he or she is finished.

If librarian install the cable themselves, He'll need at least one other person to help. Someone needs to be on the receiving end as he pull the cable from one spot another. When working on ladders and around electrical equipment, it is also a good idea to have two people working together in the event of an accident.

Running Cable Over Ceilings for Library Network

Network cable is commonly laid across the top of suspended ceilings. If you've never poked your head up into a suspended ceiling, you'll find air conditioning ducts, phone cable, electrical wiring, and the top part of the recessed lights in the ceiling. The heavy items such as the duct work have suspension wires from the support beams, just like the frames for the ceiling tiles. Other cables may just be lying on top of ceiling tiles. Depending on your building code, this is also how you will install your network cable.

Your basic strategy is to lift the ceiling tiles every 15 to 20 feet between point A and point B. You then toss a weighted string from bole to hole. The better your aim and the fewer objects in your way, the further apart these access holes can be. Once the string has completed the route, your tie and tape the cable to one end and carefully pull the cable from point A to point B.

Ceiling tiles are made only to absorb sound, not to support much weight from above. Most tiles are made of pressed fiber and can be easily broken by hand. Don't lean on a tile from above and don't place anything heavier than a few coils of cable on the tiles.

You must be very careful when you push a tile up for access. Always push at one end. If that end resists, try the other. If that end will bot lift, something may have been routed over that tile that prevents it from moving. Move your ladder on tile over and try again.

Once the tile lifts up, you may be able to shift it over or tilt it up to provide access. There mayor may not be additional insulation on top of the tile. If there is, you should wear long sleeves, gloves, and a breathing mask. The material in the insulation very irritating to your skin and respiratory tract.

Based on line of sight, open another hole in the ceiling about 15 feet away. Assuming you have a helper, stand as far up as you can in the first hole and toss a small weight with string attached toward your helper in the other access hole. The likelihood of success with each toss depends on how much space you have between the suspended ceiling and the real ceiling, how many objects are in the way and how large they are, your throwing accuracy, and your partner's willingness to stretch in all directions.

The actual weight on the string is bot critical. It just needs to be heavy enough to carry the string for a 20-foot toss. The string should be attached to the weight so there is nothing to catch on other objects when you pull the weight back toward you. You'll miss your target once or twice and will have to try again. You may want to bring several weights in case you tangle the string so badly that you have to cut that section off and start again with another weight. A casting weight for fishing works well, as shown here:

Once you reach your first intermediate access hole, continue to open new access locations and toss to each successive hole. You may want to leave the tiles open to inspact the cable as you pull it through the ceiling. If the cable appears to have a very cleat path, you could replace the tile, saving yourself a trip back later with the ladder after the cable is pulled. Just tying the string to the cable is bot enough. Wrap a piece of wide tape over both the cable and sting, as shown here:

This helps prevent the end of the cable form becoming caught on another wire as you pull the cable through. Duct tape or wide masking tape works well. You may also find fire walls if you are running cable from one part of the building to another. These walls are typically concrete and extend to the roof. You'll have to route the cable through the access holes already provided for the other types to cables. Try to avoid routing through-pair cable, be careful to avoid fluorescent lights and electric motors that can cause interference.

Depending on the cable type, you may need to pull two sections of cable through the ceiling. For example, most of the workstation locations may be on a thin Ethernet cable path. But one office may be enough off the path that you have to run the cable to and from that office. You need not toss the string twice. Before you pull the cable through with the string from point A and point B, attach the end of the sting to the cable so you pull both the cable and another section of string. You can then use that second section of string to pull the second cable back from point B.

If you are routing the cable across the ceiling, you have to decide if you want the wires running down the wall, if building code prohibits it, you have no choice. If you want to hide the wires, you'll spend additional time cutting an access hole in the bottom of the wall. Again, depending on the latitude in the building code, you may be able to just leave to access hole, or you may have to install a cable receptacle. Use the keyhole saw to create the opening, watching carefully for electrical wire in the wall. Drop the weighted string inside the top of the wall until you can grab the string through the access hole. Pull the cable down the wall just as you did when pulling it across the ceiling.

If you choose to leave the cable outside the wall, you can minimize its distracting presence by using a corner of the room, especially if the corner is behind a door. You can also use cable tie-downs with self adhesive pads to hold the cable in place against the wall. Use a minimum number because when removed, the adhesive tends to remove paint and wallboard.

Running Cable Through Library Walls

If the library containing the workstations are next to each other you may be able to route the cable through the wall. Most library walls consist of two layers of fiber or plaster wallboard, separated by alluminum or wood studs. With a 1;4-inchwide, 6-inch-long drill bit, you cab easily drill a hole in a corner of the room. While there is little chance that the electrical cable runs to the corner, extreme caution is suggested. If, after the bit goes through the first layer, it hits something before reaching the second layer, quit drilling immediately. If it did not hit electrical wire, it might be water or drain pipes.

Installing cable through the walls may be a bit tricky and is a method more likely to require a professional installer. But if your route is through plaster walls and without the complication of concrete or metal, you'll require less cable and won't have the problem of cable hanging from the ceiling. Again, check your building codes and the local work rules before you drag out that 6-inch drill bit and begin poking holes in the library walls.

Other Routes for Cable

Running cable throughout buildings is an important consideration in the building's construction. Designers also recognize the need to add cable later and provide conduits and access areas for telephone, power, security, fire alarms, and other types of cable. Depending on the age of your building, routing cable from floor to floor may not be too difficult. But because this requires a knowledge of all the other cables in the path, this kind of cable installation is usually beyound the abilities of a small LAN installer.

If you do need to cross floors, you building owner may have contractor who regularly works in the building. If the building's contractor does not know how to run network cable, you may have to pay the extra expense of teaming up the contractor with a network specialist.

Testing Connection

If you like to measure success in small pieces, you may want to run a section of cable, install the connectors, attach it to the network card in the workstation, and see if it works. With some Ethernet networks, remember to move the terminator cap to each successive station as you build your network section by section. This methods helps you locate a problem system or cable run immediately.

Other installers place all the cable, put on all the connectors, attach all the systems and bring up the LAN, all at once. This approach is more dramatic and arguably more efficient for a professional installer. If you like this approach, you'll have to use a process of elimination to discover any problems you have.

In all cases, make sure there are no systems powered on and attached to the network when you work on cable or attach another station. If you use the "try each connection" approach, you must run turn of all the systems on the network before making further connections. You then need only turn on the server to test the latest connection. You then turn on the other workstations, one at a time, to make sure each one works. With larger networks, this connection-by-connection method would add a lot of time to the installation process, with your small network, the time is justified because you will know immediately where problem is.

Library Software Installation

Installing the library network hardware need not be any more difficult than installing the LAN software. This is not to imply that installing library network software is necessarily easy. Librarian'll need to take Librarians time and be prepared for any number of problems. The more complete Librarians plan, the better chance Librarian have of successfully installing a small library network.

This chapter covers the typical steps for software installation and testing that first connection. Once that test works. Librarian'll organise the server and set up the library network resources and accounts.

The information in this chapter is based on several library network programme. While specific steps and commands used in the installation process are covered, they are provided simply to supply background information. The actual procedures Librarian'll use to install his library network programme of choice will be detailed in that program's manual. In addition, the application programmes covered provide a perspective on just one of dozens of choices in each category.

Successful installation of any software requires a good understanding of the computer, careful reading of the manual, and time to test the results. Librarian must know the computer because, in many cases, Librarian must tell the software how to configure itself for example, Librarian may need to know the type of printer, the COM port with the mouse, and the type of monitor attached to the system. With library network software, Librarian need to know the card settings, the printer ports in use, all the user names, and other facts.

The manuals can range from one 160-page book with NOVELL, Netware Lite, to four manuals with Artisoft LANtastic, to over ten pounds of manuals with NOVELL Netware 2.2. The number of manuals reflects the complexity of the software. While Librarian need not read everything in the manuals, Librarian should read the basic installation instructions and have an idea of the contents of the other manuals. the larger NOVELL Netware package even contains a fourpage guide to help Librarian decide where to start in the stack of manuals.

Leave yourself plenty of time for the software installation. No matter how long Librarian think the installation will take, it will take longer. Installing software is not just copying files to the hard disk; it's also making sure the resulting software works. Thorough testing always takes days and it is too often left to the users to discover the problems. The longer Librarian spend testing, the fewer problems Library users will experience. Fewer problems results in a higher level of confidence and a willingness to use the library network effectively.

Some LAN software programmes start by erasing library hard disk. Librarian must have backup copies of files to restore the hard disk once the server software has been installed. Even with peer-to-peer library networks, making a complete backup of the server hard derive before starting the installation is essential.

Running a Test Installation

It's okay if this is Librarian first time inserting cards and running cable, but Librarian should be 'familiar with installing software before Librarian attempt to install LAN software. The inevitable trial-and-error method of solving problems requires a reasonable amount of experience with software installation.

The first step is to arrange two systems side by side for the installation of the server and one workstation. Librarian can use library network plan to begin setting up the server as Librarian make the installation choices. If Librarian re really prepared, Librarian have already arranged the directories on the server to conform to library network plan. Don't try to answer all the installation questions at first. Just set up the minimum to get the two systems to communicate. Librarian can then work back and forth between these two systems as Librarian build the library network according to plan.

The Server in Library

The first step for any software installation is to make copies of the disks supplied with the program. Make these the working copies-lable them and use them for the actual installation. Store the originals in a safe place.

To begin the installation, Librarian'll typically insert the first disk drive the type Install or whatever programme name is provided in the library network manual. From there, the installation programme will ask questions or provide a screen of settings. Once Librarian have answered the questions or changed the settings to suit the library, the programme continues by copying the proper files to the library hard disk. The specific responses Librarian provide affect the command-line settings and the initial defaults.

While the questions for library network may not be presented in the same order or using exactly the same terms, the concepts will be the same for all LAN installations. The information Librarian supply on this screen represents many of the decisions Librarian make while installing the library network software. Remember that this installation may take several attempts before it works the way Librarian want. Make changes now, while Librarian are in the test phase, and not later, when Librarian have users depending on the library network.

The more complicated programmes, such as NetWare 2.2, may use eight or more disks and start the server installation process by reformatting library hard drive. This step alone can easily take an hour or more. When working with these more complicated programmes, Librarian need to allow even more time to try different settings.

Every system attached to the library network must have a unique name (the machine name). Using library network plan, Librarian name the main server something like SERVER or HOST01. If Librarian will have more than one server on the library network, try to make each server name reflect the function of that server. For example, the accounting system might be ACCTSERV and the main server might be MAINSERV. Once other workstations begin using the library network, this name cannot be changed easily.

Machine Type

There will be only two choices for the machine type: the installation will either be for a server or a workstation. Make sure this settings is "server" for the first installation. Remember too that the server can also be a workstation in peer-topeer library networks. With a single-server library network, the additional choice might be whether or not the server is also to be used as a workstation—a non-dedicated server.

Installation Directory Librarian

Some installation software allows Librarian to specify the directory the library network files are copied into. In most cases,

Librarian should select the default directory name provided. The installation software will create the directory and place all the files within it. The selection of this directory affects other settings creared by the installation programme as well-usually the path and startup batch file commands.

Start-up Batch File for Library Network

Library network programmes create a batch file with all the commands and swithes necessary to start the library network. The default STARTNET.BAT is reasonably easy to remember, although it may be created in the library network directory and won't work unless Librarian move into that directory first. In most cases, Librarian'll incorporate that batch file into Librarianr AUTOEXEC.BAT file or call STARTNET.BAT from the AUTOEXEC.BAT file. Here is the STARTNET.BAT file created by LANtastic:

```
@ECHO OFF
PATH C: LANTASTI; %PATH%
AEX IRC=15 IOBASE=300 VERBOSE
AILANBIO
REDIR DAN LOGINS=3
NET LOGIN/WAIT \ \ HOST DAN
NET USE F \ \HOST\C-DRIVE
NET USE LPT1 \ \HOST\@LASER
NET USE LPT2 \ \HOST\@DOTMATR
NET LPT TIMEOUT 10
```

The startup batch file is also the best place to study the sequence of commands used to start the library network. If Librarian are having trouble, Librarian can print the file and then use that listing to type each command separately. This process can help Librarian identify which part of the library network startup process is causing trouble.

Library Network Card and Drivers in Library

The library network software must be configured for the specific library network card. If Librarian purchased the LAN as a Kit, those choices will be minimal. If Librarian purchased the software separate from the library network cards, Librarian may have a long list of cards to select from. If the card Librarian have installed in the computer does not appear on list, the drivers may have been supplied by the card manufacturer. Librarian may also need to call the card vendor to see if their card has an equivalent on the library network installation list.

Naming the printer connection is the first step in setting up the library network resources. This prepares the server to share that resource by establishing the printer port to use, such as LPT1 or LPT2. The name Librarian assign is just a convenient way to remember the printer attached to that port. If Librarian have two printers, a laser on LPT1 and a do matrix on LPT2, it makes the LAN easier to use if Librarian name these resources LASER and DOTMATR instead of PRINTER1 and PRINTER2.

The library network does not need to know what kind of printer is attached to it. It routes the printer data only through the server Librarian LAN or local application software must stiff be configured for the exact type of printer attached to the library network.

Defining Resources on the Server

Remember that each device to be shared across the library network is called a resource. Librarian library network plan determined what those resources were to be and what. names to use. When Librarian are setting up accounts, this information will be critical in providing the resources each specific user needs. In the first part of the server installation, Librarian named those resources. Now Librarian must allow those resources to be shared on the library network. When first installing the server, Librarian may want to just set drive C as a resource. This provides access to anything on that drive, a condition Librarian want only when first testing the server. Later Librarian will limit access to specific areas on the hard drive for the file security.

Librarian allow a drive or specific subdirectory to be used by expressing the full path and then applying a name to that subdirectory. Librarian do this in different ways with different LAN programmes, but once done, it allows users to access those resources by providing the full server name of the resource and then assigning a local drive or printer port. For example, the resource Librarian could have named ACCOUNT is actually C:/DATA/ACCOUNT on the server. To the user, it just becomes drive L.

If the server were to be linked to other servers on the library network, the drive connection area of the installation screen would contain one or more entries. If Librarian eventually set up a number of server on Librarian peer-to-peer library network, each servers is likely to have drive connections with other server. This entry becomes very important when installing a workstation.

The control directory stores the information for user accounts and resource information. Because this is a critical setting the default provided by the installation programme is recommended.

Once Librarian install the LAN software, Librarian'll have additional tasks, such as creating user accounts and managing the print spooler. In a peer-to-peer system, the installation software is the same for each workstation. Librarian'll create a unique name for each workstation, just as Librarian did for the server. The big difference will be that Librarian specify WORKSTATION instead of SERVER for the machine type. Once Librarian make the change, several others become more important.

With server-based to software such as NetWare 2.2, the user installation requires different software, but the questions and concepts remain essentially the same. Since the workstation may also be using a local printer, Librarian need to tell the installation programme which ports already have a printer attached and which ports will be redirected to the remote printer. For example, LPT1 might already have a printer one attached. Librarian might then set LPT2 as the printer on the server. To the user and the application software, the workstation has two printers, on LPT1 and the second on LPT2. The library network software then controls the redirection of the LPT2 printer data. Setting up the drive connection is critical for the workstation. If librarian are in a test phase, Librarian may just select a server drive resource such as C-DRIVE as library drive F. Once drive F is installed in the STARTNET.BAT file, the workstation seas it as the drive and directory named C-DRIVE. If C-DRIVE is the same as C:/ on the server, the workstation drive F has access to the entire hard disk drive C.

Once Librarian have the workstation software installed, Librarian are ready to test the library network. Because the library network installation software may have changed the CONFIG.SYS file, reboot the server and the workstation. Then run the library network batch file, possibly named STARTNET, assuming Librarian haven't already made ut oart if tge AUTOEXEC.BAT file. Run the server STARTNET first so the workstation can connect to the server.

If all goes well, Librarian'll have additional drive letters and additional printers from the workstation. Depending on the software, Librarian may have to log onto a library network drive before Librarian can do much with the server. For example, with NetWare 2.2, Librarian'll need to log on as SUPERVISOR. This gives Librarian total control of the library network. Or Librarian may need to run NET-MGR in LANtastic to set up the first user account. The requirements of this first step must be extracted from the library network manual.

If all does not go well, Librarian may have one or any number of problems to handle. In most cases, Librarian'll need to dig into the library network manuals to find ideas. Here are a few common problems with possible solutions:

No library network drive Drive F is the most commonly used drive letter for the first library network drive. If there is no drive F, try other drive letters. Librarian may have specified another starting drive when installing the software. Another possibility is that the library network did not start at all. In this case, Librarian'll probably see error messages from the library network batch file.

Can't Log On If Librarian do have the library network drive but can't seem to do much with it except look at the directory, Librarian may not be logged on. As mentioned, this differs among library networks. With NOVELL library networks, the logon name of SUPERVISOR provides system-wide access. With LANtastic, Librarian'll need to run NET-MGR from the server to create Librarian first user account. Then Librarian can log on under the account name from the workstation.

When the workstation first boots, it looks for server by name. If Librarian have changed the name of the server or entered a different server name when installing the workstation software, the workstation cannot locate the server by name. Check the server name on both the server and the workstation logon script. Also make sure the connectors on the cable are firmly attached to the cable and the library network cards.

System Locks Up If the system locks up, Librarian may have a conflict with the hardware or with other TSR software on Librarian system. These steps may help Librarian to isolate the problem:

1. Use the library network test software to make sure the card is functioning.
2. Create a book floppy disk that loads just the bare minimum in CONFIG.SYS. Determine this by examining the CONFIG.SYS file created by Librarian library network installation.
3. Boot from this "clean" floppy.
4. Try the library network batch file from the hard disk.
5. If the system does not lock up, Librarian know something loaded as a device in CONFIG.SYS or as a programme

running as a TSR in AUROEXEC.BAT is causing the trouble. Librarian'll have to add each line in the CONFIG.SYS and AUTOEXEC.BAT files one at a time to determine where the problem is.

The library network software run but the unable to locate the library network card address. Check to see that the card address matches the address in the startup batch file. Use another library network card in this machine to see if that solves the problem. If Librarian have only two cards, swap them and see if the problem follows the card or stays with the computer.

Finishing the LAN Installation

Now that Librarian have made the first test connection, Librarian are ready to configure the server to suit Librarian library network plan. This include creating user and group accounts, creating user work areas (if necessary), assigning additional resources, and testing the applications to be used on the server if it is also to function as a workstation.

User Accounts

Librarian control the user's access to the library network's resources via the user account. The library network supervisor (Librarian) creates accounts that can include the user's name, a description of the user, a password, hours and days access is allowed, special access privileges, and more. This data is important for keeping track of the many users on the library network and to prevent users from accessing files in. other user's areas.

As supervisor, Librarian must set up an account before that user can access a server. On a peer-to-peer system, a specific individual's name must be in the user account file in order to access the resources of that server. This is how the local supervisor at a server/workstation controls access to the resources on his or her system. To remove access, the supervisor of that server deletes the user's name.

Group Accounts

With LANtastic, group accounts have all the features associated with a user account. Librarian can set up a group account to be used by a number of people at one time. For example, if three people in marketing need exactly the same access to programmes and files, Librarian could create a group account named MARKET and allow those users to log on as MARKET. Librarian could then restrict library network access to areas only the marketing department needed to use.

NetWare 2.2 uses group sin another way. For example, when the library network is first installed, all users are automatically made members of a group named EVERYONE. The group contains access to the library network sub-directories necessary to run the library network. Librarian can create and name additional groups. with different access areas and resources. Once the group is created, including that group name in an individual user account gives that user all the same settings as the group.

Finishing Resource Installation in Library

If Librarian plan to reorganize library server hard drive, this is the time to do it. Using Librarian library network plan, Librarian should create directories, move files, and do whatever it takes to create .the planned directory structure. If Librarian have enough hard disk space, Librarian can simply copy files from one directory to another and then delete the files in the first directory.

If Librarian have a lot of directory and file re-arranging to do, Librarian may want to consider a utility programme such as Central Point's PC Tools 7.1. One of the man functions in this programme is directory pruning and grafting. With this feature, Librarian can select and move entire directories, with all files intact at one time.

Completir g the installation also includes setting up Librarian additional resources, such as the fax board, the CD-ROM drives, or other devices Test those as carefully as Librarian can before Librarian turn the users loose on the library network. These are even more delicate to install and manage than the library network software.

Testing the Applications

If Librarian plan to also use the server as a workstation, test the applications Librarian plan to run on it. These applications, probably left over from the preserver hard drive configuration, must be able to run at the same time that the server software is running. The server software requires more memory and "steals" processor time. Once the server and workstation software are loaded, Librarian may not have enough memory to run the applications Librarian intend to run. If this is the case, Librarian'll need to look into a memory manager programme and possibly purchase more memory.

If the applications run too slowly on the server/workstation, Librarian may need to change the library network plan and allow that computer to function just as a server. The alternative is to accept the loss of speed. Librarian'll also need to test the performance later when users begin accessing the serve, which slows down the speed even further.

When setting up the remaining workstations, Librarian may discover differences that affect the library network cards and the library network installation software. be prepared to solve a whole new set of problems with each workstation connection. The only exception to this rule is if all the computers are exactly the same there are several approaches to actually getting the library network software on the additional workstations. Librarian can use the original library network software and answer all the installation question again. Or to save time, Librarian can copy the library network files from the first workstation to subsequent ones. With a few exceptions, those files from the first workstation will be exactly the same on the remaining workstations.

The first exception occurs if Librarian changed any of the settings on the library network card. If Librarian have, Librarian'll have to make changes to the startup switches in the STARTNET batch file on the new workstation, if Librarian installed the card with the default settings, Librarian do not need to make any changes.

The second exception applies to all the workstations. Since each user must log on with a unique name, the command-line parameters must be modified for the user's name. For example, LANtastic uses NET LOGIN \\SERVER\USERNAME. Each workstation batch file must have a unique USER-NAME. If the library network startup batch file does not include the logon, then this does not need to be modified, although Librarian may want to include the logon command as part of the startup batch file for the workstation users.

A final exception occures if the library network software is purchased one user at a time, such as NetWare Lite. Each of these disks has a unique number and must be installed on only one machine.

Testing the LAN for Librarian

At this point in the LAN installation, Librarian may have spent a long day or more installing cable, inserting cards, copying software, and testing the LAN connections. Librarian may be ready to declare the library network operational and go celebrate-but don't. If Librarian want to earn even a modicum of trust, he must spend more time testing the applications on the LAN. While Librarian cannot begin to simulate all the possible conditions that can occur on a library network, Librarian can attempt a few. As Librarian went from station to station and tested the LAN, each may have worked well. But the purpose of a library network is the handle multiple actions. With one or more assistants, Librarian need to put the library network under some kind of load. This includes loading files at the same time Librarian use the library network printer. User try as many combinations as Librarian can think of.

Don't have the extra time? Too many library network installations leave out this last step or reduce it to a 15-minute test drive. This puts the users in the position of testing the library network. These are the people Librarian want to sue and benefit from the library network. Do as much as Librarian can. If Librarian also want to let Library users know what Librarian tried, make a short list of these tests and provide a copy. Even if some of these combinations subsequently fail, the users will know that Librarian considered the situation and that it appeared to work at the time.

As Librarian'll quickly discover, the users will create many different combinations, some of which will result in problems. If Librarian have provided an adequate orientating for the users and can offer a reasonable response to their problems, the users should be able to see the library network as another way to extend their computer processing power.

If the server is to contain programme files for multiple user, Librarian need to purchase the LAN version of Library application software of test the single-user version very carefully. Keep in mind that newer programmes may not be designated as LAN versions but may still be "library network aware" and can share files across the library network. For example, Borland's SideKick 2.0 is a personal calendar and utility programme. While he programme package does not state "LAN version," the third paragraph on the first page explains that the programme allows files to be shared across a library network. In this case, a group calendar can easily be kept on the library network for everyone to access.

Installing LAN application software may not be any more complicated than installing any software. On the other hand there may be a few additional considerations or problems that develop during and after the installation. The following sections provide a thumbnail sketch of several applications to illustrate the installation steps. These examples provide a quick idea of what installing this type of software may involve on a LAN.

As with any software installation, Librarian need to remember the basics:

— Install from backup copies or at least write-protect the originals.

— Make sure Librarian have enough disk space be fore beginning the installation.

— Know Librarian equipment well enough to answer any installation question.

— Make backup copies of the AUTOEXEC.BAT and CONFIG.SYS files prior to installation.

— Send in the registration card.

— Library network software requires some additional precautions and steps:

— Install the programme files in an accessible area on the server.

— Make that area read-only to prevent accidental deletions.

— Provide an area for each user's configuration files.

Each LAN or library network-aware programme has its own requirements. While Librarian may not always read the manual when installing single-user software, the potential for multiple problems with multiple users suggests the need to read the LAN manual.

Also note that some of the applications discussed here may already be included in the LAN software Librarian select. For example, LANtastic has a small mail programme and can access a CD-ROM drive on the library network. As always, Librarian need to evaluate the features offered in each package to determine if that programme, or another, would best serve the needs of users on the library network.

CD-ROM Drives

Using a CD-ROM as a resource across the library network may require special software, depending on the type of LAN. One programme Librarian can use with NOVELL NetWare 2.2 is CD Connection from CBIS. The programme provides up to 21 CD-ROM drives on a library network, contained in a dedicated CD-ROM drives on a library network, contained in a dedicated CD-ROM server. A major advantage of this dedicated CD-ROM server is that CD-ROM device (SYS) drivers need not be loaded on the local workstations.

Installing this software requires an understanding of CD-ROM drives. The CDROM drive should have been tested first on the local system. An extensive knowledge of device drivers and the ability to modify the CONFIG/SYS file are also required. Access to the CD-ROM is not limited to the number of users; it is limited only the availability of the library network resource.

Communications

A popular communications programme, Procomm plus, produced by Datastorm, also has a LAN version. This allows multiple users to access a modem in another system. The five-user package includes five complete manuals, a feature not typical for most LAN programmes.

This product requires and additional programme in the NetWare environment before it can be used. The NOVELL ACS (asynchronous communications server) software must be installed before Procomm Plus LAN can be used. NOVELL ACS requires a dedicated server containing one or more modrms attached to a NOVELL NetWare 3.1 library network. This example demonstrates the need to know the software's requirements before purchasing for the library network.

Electronic Mail

cc: Mail from Lotus is a very popular electronic mail programme for library network for all sizes. The software comes in a basic platform package for DOS, Windows, Macintosh, and other operating systems. The platform programme creates the post office and provides the user interface. Librarian can add additional users in increments of 8 to 25. Additional cc:Mail programmes, such as Gateway, allow transmittal of messages from server to server and through a modem.

The software installation is relatively easy for someone familiar with the concepts of E-mail. As the system administrator Librarian must establish a post office ans set up individual users. All the mail messages are kept in one location on the server, with password-protected access for each user. Users can be notified when new mail arrives in their mailboxes and access the messages from within other applications.

Windows

Microsoft Windows 3.1 provides popular interface for newer, more powerful systems. It uses graphic images (icons) to represent programmes and files making access easier and more intuitive. The user may not even know whether the files are located on the local directory or a library network directory.

Windows is very efficient on a library network. When it is installed on the server, all the files are copied to the Windows sub-directory. When it is installed on a workstation from the server, only the files required to start Windows locally are copied to the local drive. When additional programmes are needed from the server, Windows accesses those shared files. The user's data and files can be kept on the local drive.

Windows requires fast 386 systems with at least 4MB of memory. This latest version, is very stable and very library network aware. Installation to the server takes some time and a considerable amount of disk space.

Basic Databases

Database programme, such as PC-FILE 6.5 for LAN, .are "basic" only because they do not include a programming language. They still have all the features Librarian need to manage large files of Data. The LAN version provides record locking, an essential feature required when more than one person uses a database at a time. This expands the individual management of a database to the group level on the library network.

The documentation includes a separate booklet explaining how the LAN version is different from the single-user version. It explains the minimal differences and changes necessary to adjust for various library networks. The library network. booklet also provides a clear explanation of record and file locking.

Programmable Databases

Programmable databases, such as dBASE IV version 1.5 from Borland, provide all the features in basic database programme, as well as a programming language. With this language, a programmer can completely control the use of the data on the library network, including the required file and record locking. But these programmes can also be written to guide the user through the process of adding and editing data and printing specific reports.

dBASE IV provides individual LAN Packs to be used on the library network. Each package contains a dBASE manual and a disk to increase the number of users able to access the programme on the library network. With this method, a copy of the single-user version is installed on the server. Then, for each additional user access, the LAN Pack software is run to increase the count on the server copy. For every disk from each additional LAN pack, the user access count is increased by one. For example, the purchase of dBASE IV and three LAN Packs allows four users the share one database at a time.

User Training

Library network planning document should include user training as one of the several steps to a successful library network installation. The administrator of a small library network has the advantage of keeping directly in touch with all the potential users. If the users have been part of the planning process, they already know something about the library network. Additional training will help them learn the details and help Librarian when Librarian have to solve problems.

Training Basics

Arrange the user training as soon as possible after the library network has been installed. Better yet, provide basic instructions even before the library network is active, and then follow up with a problem-solving session. Here are some additional ideas about the training:

- — Announce the specific times for training as far in advance as possible. This allows everyone to work around that established date.
- — If possible, provide the session away from the library if this is not possible, don't allow interruptions during the training session.
- — Encourage attendance by providing a meal or other incentive.
- — Sessions should involve management, even if they are not using the library network directly.
- — Provide handouts geared to the users on the library network. Always include a summary of commands on one sheet.

Training Outline

The training details very with the user's level of experience and how much they really need to know. The training Librarian provide will be based on library network design. For example, the results of a server crash affect the users differently if everyone depends on the server for files than if they just use it for printing.

Problem Solving

A LAN training session provides an opportunity to review with user the basic steps for problem solving. While being covered as part of the library network training, there steps apply to any problem associated with computers. These are the three Rs of problem solving: Recover, Report, and Re-create.

Too many computer users have learned only one way to solve a problem—they turn off the computer. On a library network, this "Solution" is disastrous if the user is using a server as a workstation. Since the server also has open files for other users, everyone may be affected by this rash solution. It is important to recover from the mistake, not ignore it. Develop and publish a list of steps when problems are encountered on the network.

Those steps might include the following:

1. Read the screen for indications of the next step or keypress.
2. Press the F1 Key for help.
3. Read the manual for the software. (With LAN software, this may require the arduous task of locating the manual first.)
4. Ask others who may have had the problem before.
5. Call or locate the support person (probably the system administrator).

If a reboot or power down is required on a server, warn the other users and allow them to exit from their programmes on the server first.

Report the Problem

Regardless of the recovery or restart, the problem should be noted somewhere. An E-mail or paper not to the administrator is very helpful. Because LAN problems can be intermittent, these reports may provide a pattern the administration can notice when the information comes from several sources. The report can be very minimal. It should include the user's name, the date, and the time of the incident. The user should explain what happened prior to the problem, what the problem looked like, and how the problem was resolved. While one or more of these elements may be missing, anything provided by the user can be helpful. A sample report might look like this:

Re-create the Problem

The best approach to solving problems once and for all is to re-create them. In the example, Sehgal R. thought the problem might be related to the library network, so he waited for a few hours and tried again, with the same results. In case, the problem is more likely to be the printer setting within word, possibly still set for Sehgal R. local laser printer. By re-creating a problem, Librarian can learn to avoid those circumstances in the future or at least be prepared for the problem when it occurs.

Before sitting down to begin the installation, make sure Librarian have:

— Read enough of the manuals to understand the installation steps and additional information provided.

— Left enough time to install, troubleshoot, and test he installation.

— Gathered enough floppy disks to make backup copies of all the programmes.

— Completed library network plan, including a list of users.

Once Librarian have finished the installation, Librarian need to make sure Librarian have:

— Documented the resources on the server, including all LAN programmes.

— Scheduled training for the users.

— Filled out and mailed all the warranty cards.

— Provided the users with a contact for technical support.

When Librarian. are setting up first library network, the software installation should be a bit less intimidating than the hardware installation. If Librarian have a good idea of the basics and have planned as much as possible, yes. As long as Librarian get over any aversion to manuals, take time, and rely on library list of technical support names. Librarian can do it.

Keeping the library network running smoothly requires constant effort. The more stations and software running on the library network, the ore area you will need to watch for problems. This chapter provides an outline of library network maintenance tasks, such as backing up data, disaster preparation, and hard disk maintenance user training and technical support are also emphasized in the chapter. This chapters checklist helps librarian in maintenance schedules. Librarian will discover that library networked printers need additional attention' from both the users and the administrator. As library network supervisor, librarian'll manage the user list, directory resources, and the massive number of files that accumulate on the server. Librarian may also want to improve performance on the library network. And librarian'll definitely want users to continue to learn and benefit from the library network.

Even before librarian begin thinking about library network maintenance. Librarian may want to consider the attitude of the users attached to the LAN. These users may perceive themselves as part of a group and share the responsibilities of managing a library network or they may see themselves only as users, served by "someone else." Librarian approach to library network maintenance should be as carefully planned as the installation. He need to determine which of these two approaches you want the library network users to take. Do you want them to become dependent upon you or to accomplish as much as they can on their own?

Librarian'll need to decide who will be responsible for the daily and extended maintenance on the network. Someone needs to keep printers supplied with paper. Someone needs to create and delete users and user .file access. Someone needs to manage the server files. And someone needs to provide general support for the inevitable library network and application problems.

❒

6

Communication Network in Library

A computer network is intended to connect together a wide range of information technology equipment, which varies in the design and operation of the equipment itself, in the information types it handles, and in the internal processing which it undertakes. In order to be able to communicate successfully, these various systems must have a common 'language' for the exchange of information, while retaining their local independence.

As well as an agreed form for communication the network units must also agree on the process of communicating the rules which govern the procedures for the exchange of information and the co-ordination of action between participants. In daily communication we use a language to express our ideas and intentions, and the voice as a means of transmitting this information to other people.

To ensure that the communication is successful, we must converse in an agreed language which the hearer is able to understand, and we must be able to respond to messages asking for clarification, repetition, and so on. In any conversation, there are well-understood rules which govern the process of communication-taking turns, allowing others a chance to speak, indicating that one has finished speaking, waiting until another has finished before speaking oneself, and so on. These signals are often given implicitly, through signs such as gestures or tone of voice.

The data communication process has to be much more structured and organized in style, spelled out in every detail, since these tacit factors are missing from a machine-based process. The rules for communication must be well defined and standardized; there is little room for 'working out' what a participant in the exchange really meant to say. This process underlies the development of sophisticated and 'user-friendly' applications which depend on network communication, even though this may not be immediately apparent.

A goal of information networking is to allow users to work in this medium as naturally as possible, finding the least obtrusive fit with the natural work environment. A dialogue which is mediated by computer communication places certain structural constraints on the process due to these underlying factors; the task of design is to find ways of incorporating the equivalent of the contextual factors which inform human communication while working within these constraints.

A basic model of the communication process identifies the entities involved, and their respective roles. There are three main elements:

(a) a sender, which originates the message, and is responsible for representing the content of the message in an agreed format;

(b) a channel, which carries the message from sender to recipient through some physical medium;

(c) a recipient, which receives the message, and is responsible for interpreting the format in order to extract the information content.

The communication is not simply one way, and the roles will at times be reversed: the recipient may wish to send a reply to the original message.

In network communications explicit signals and format rules are vital to the success of the communications process. For a computing machine to manage this role effectively, rules governing these issues must be highly detailed and agreed in advance, and encapsulated in software programmes. Data and communications software must be able to deal with management of the exchange process, not only by sending and receiving messages for transmission but also by encoding and decoding between the internal format used by the computer and the format used for external communication. It is also necessary to monitor the quality of the exchange and to co-ordinate activity between participants at each end of the process for longer data exchanges. This is problematic because the channel which links the participants will have characteristics of its own which may affect the communication process.

The sender and recipient exchange the encoded message as a physical signal transmitted in some way through a common channel. The environment of this channel can potentially interfere with and distort the signals in the process, resulting in the loss of some information content and delivery of a corrupted message. This kind of interference is known as noise—the general effect of corruption and garbling of the signal which occurs after it has been transmitted, and before it is received. For example, noise may result in the appearance of unreadable characters on a computer screen in the midst of a normal text message, as the re.ceiving system attempts to interpret corrupted signalling codes.

Although the use of more reliable technology for the transmission medium has reduced the problem of noise in recent years, the rules which govern the process of communication must still be capable of detecting and recovering from the effects of noise by returning a message to its original form. This requires the communications software to have some means of matching the two versions of the message that sent and that received and entails the addition of control information to the actual data content by one means or another. Thus the exchange will consist of more than the simple data content of the message.

Techniques for dealing with the effects of noise are concerned to preserve the quality of the message by ensuring that the integrity of the signs used to represent the information content have not been compromised. The communication process must also therefore be concerned with co-ordinating the system of codes which is used to express the semantic qualities of the data exchange what might be loosely called the 'meaning' of the message; with the physical representation of the chosen coding system as transmittable signals; and with any control information which binds different elements of the message together.

There are various different coding systems for the task of mapping information generated by user applications into the binary codes used by the computer. For text, the ASCII (American Standard Character Set for Information Interchange) is widely used both within a computer and for data interchange purposes; however, completely different character sets are used in some circumstances, for instance the EBCDIC character set which dominates the IBM mainframe world.

There are several different representation formats for graphics, which may be either bit patterns or geometric coordinates, and for other forms such as video signals and multimedia information. For meaningful information to be exchanged there must be agreement between the end systems on the method by which the message is represented for transmission, even though this may not affect the actual exchange of data symbols through the channel. Since there is little standardization in the internal processes of computer equipment itself, the actual physical signals which the end systems generate must also be standardized for inter-operability, and may need translation between different physical forms in order to make use of different communication channels.

Synchronous Communication

The additional control information which is appended to the user data content carries information used in processing the message, and must also conform to some agreed system. A simple text message, for example, may contain an, overhead of information which is used to indicate boundaries between characters or chunks of text; this will appear as binary digits apparently identical to the data content unless there is some common method of 'reading' the stream of symbols.

A multimedia message which contains both sound and video elements requires control information to synchronize timing of the audio output with the screen display, which must be interpreted correctly.

There is a need to synchronize the flow of information between the two end systems, so that signals which will conflict with each other are not generated simultaneously, and so that the receiver is ready and capable of processing the incoming signals at the rate which they are sent-controlling the 'turn taking'.

Communication can take place in one of two alternative patterns, and in each of these synchronization is achieved in different ways. Asynchronous communication might be characterized as 'on demand' use of the communications channel. All network users have equal access to the channel, and use it to send messages at random intervals, characterized by short bursts of activity with quiet periods of varying length in between. The receiver waits passively once the connection is made, and is activated by the receipt of some message. A typical example of this type of activity would result from a user seated at a terminal screen, alternating interaction with a remote computer with periods of planning and thinking.

Synchronous communication depends on a fixed cycle, in which each user, and both sender and receiver, have access to the channel at defined time intervals for a fixed period. A typical use for this approach would be for large data file transfers in situations where the transfer is being managed completely by the computer systems as a background process, with no human intervention, or for the synchronization of composite sound and video signals in video-conferencing systems. This synchronicity characteristic delineates the time/response dimension of the process, defining the appropriate activities in the end systems to control the process; there is also a characteristic of the communication channel which will affect the process.

Channel and Network Communication

Communication through a transmission channel can occur in one of three different modes determining the allowed direction of, and activity in the transmission. Each of these requires a different level of sophistication in control of the communication process:

— in simplex mode, the communication is in one direction only;

— in half-duplex mode, the communication can be bi-directional, but at alternate times only;

— in full-duplex mode, the communication is bi-directional, and both end systems may transmit simultaneously.

The term channel is normally used to denote the more abstract concept of a logical channel rather than the actual physical media. One physical link may potentially offer several logical communication channels, which can be thought of as separate entities.

Since a network is a medium which is shared by many users, management of the communication process is a more complex affair than is suggested by the simplified one-to-one model. As well as agreeing on the terms by which the exchange will be conducted, the communication programme must be able to supervise and regulate the dynamic elements of the process, making necessary adjustments as the exchange develops and operating conditions fluctuate. The communications programme must be able to:

— establish and maintain a connection across the communications channel between the sender and recipient, agree the terms on which the exchange is to be conducted, and terminate the connection-once the transaction is completed;

— regulate the flow of information, between the two participants to prevent overloading of data by the recipient, if it is unable to process it quickly enough, causing a possible loss of information;

— control the quality of information received by checking for the presence of errors and taking corrective action as necessary, perhaps by requesting a re-transmission of corrupted information.

The term bandwidth is an indication of the information capacity of an individual element in the process: the higher the bandwidth of the channel, for example, the higher is its information carrying capacity. The overall communication process (including the end systems) can only utilize the information-carrying capacity of the element with the least available bandwidth in any particular situation; either the transmitter, the receiver, or the channel will have a more limited bandwidth and will define the overall information exchange rate. In many situations, the bandwidth of the communication channel will be the limiting factor.

The capacity of a channel is normally expressed as the number of distinct symbols per second which can be passed along it. This maximum data transfer rate is usually given as a figure measured in bits per second, since the number of bits which make up a useful 'unit' of information will differ according to the information type-between characters of text and scanned images in bit-map form, for instance. In this way, a channel which is described as having a particular data transfer rate can be matched to different information transfer processes through a common comparable measure.

In some circumstances, particularly in modern communications, the term baud rate is popularly used as an equivalent to this measure of bits per second; although this is not a strictly accurate use of the term, it can normally be taken to mean the same thing. Transmission channels can also be characterized by the method of signalling which is used. In baseband signalling the capacity of the channel is monopolised by a single message for the duration of the transmission, typically by varying the voltage along an electrical cable in a pre-determined pattern.

Broadband signalling enables a physical medium to be shared by more than one transmission by varying the frequency of the signals to ensure separation of one from the other-as a radio can distinguish different frequency transmissions. Broadband offers a higher bandwidth, and is therefore more associated with information networking applications which require higher capacities, such as multimedia. A goal of advanced network technology is to support a flexible, use of bandwidth among multiple users according to fluctuating demand, changing the allocation dynamically according to the transmission needs of the moment.

A communication channel is a logical concept that can be implemented on a variety of physical media, each of which has its own particular characteristics, such as bandwidth. The choice of which to adopt depends on the purposes of the network and the kind of applications it must support, the predicted traffic and data rates together with required response times, and a cost/benefit calculation on the relative importance between these factors. The most widely used physical transmission media are mentioned here:

1. The twisted pair is the simplest form of transmission cable, two simple electrical cables carrying small voltage signals. This is a very cheap method of connecting individual computer devices to a network, and is easy to install, but is not suitable for carrying traffic from many devices due to the limited bandwidth which it possesses, nor for applications which require more than a 1 Megabit per second (Mbps) data rate.

2. Co-axial cable uses a more substantial copper cable to offer a higher bandwidth suitable for multiple access from a limited number of nodes on a local network; and for the transmission of information forms which require a higher throughput of data, such as video signals, at data rates of up to 10 Mbps. This higher capacity is bought, at the expense of a higher material cost and a more complex installation process.

3. Optical fibre cable provides a means of transcending the physical limits of electrical cable, by conveying signals on

a fluctuating light beam enclosed within a very fine glass fibre. Since light waves have a much higher potential bandwidth than electrical waves, data rates up to and beyond 100 Mbps are possible, as well as providing a lower susceptibility to noisy or sensitive environments.

A single glass fibre, smaller in dimension than a human hair, is provided for each signal, and an installed optical cable may consist of several hundred fibres bundled together, providing a high throughput for existing services and spare capacity for future growth. While optical fibre provides a means of building very high bandwidth networks which can support sophisticated multimedia services, it is expensive and more difficult to install, requiring special interface equipment between cable and computer.

4. Microwave transmission offers a non-terrestrial alternative to a physical point-to-point link. Data is conveyed on radio waves through free space, and is normally used in conjunction with geostationary satellites. The data is transmitted from a ground station, called an uplink, to an orbiting satellite which is in direct line-of-sight, and the signal is bounced back to a receiving station (the downlink) at some different geographical ground location. These re-transmissions can be broadcast over a wide area for receiving by many destinations simultaneously, or be highly focused onto a single site.

   Satellite relay is commonly used to leap across long distances, such as in establishing connections between the United Kingdom and North America or the Far East, or where the laying of a physital cable would be costly or impossible across difficult geographic terrain. Microwave transmission may also be used on a ground-toground basis, between stations situated on high ground within line of sight of each other.

5. Network communications have also been achieved by the use of infra-red and broadcast radio signals; there is a growing interest in the use of such 'wireless' communications. Some use is also made of radio data broadcasting at a national level.

Protocol

Essentially, a protocol is one attempt to address the basic problems of data communications which are relevant to networking within a particular arena. Since there is no universally applicable solution to these problems which will be effective in all situations, a range of protocols have arisen which have proved effective in specialized areas within the current feasible limits of technology. Since the development of communication protocols has been carried out within the context of perceived practical problems, there is a tendency for the available offerings to be predicated on the use of particular types and make of equipment.

Computer manufacturers have devised their own proprietary protocol suites intended to interconnect only their own Computer makes; and more generally applicable protocols have emerged for broader categories of computer, such as for local networks of microcomputers. Although a protocol is a logical specification rather than a particular implementation in software, the protocol is likely to make assumptions about available levels of functionality and processing capabilities.

As both computing technology and information applications have led to more complicated and sophisticated systems, so the communications process between systems has also developed a parallel level of complexity. The complexity of modern networking has led to the use of a layered approach to protocol specification. A layered protocol aims to analyse the overall communications process into well-defined and semi-autonomous functional modules, each of which provides a specialized service in the overall scheme and works in conjunction with the other modules.

Network communications can then be split into constituent activities, and these may be implemented on different parts of the system in different ways, not necessarily all together on the same piece of equipment. Any particular layer may potentially contain alternative specifications for reaching the same goals, each of which is more appropriate for a particular environment or system arrangement.

As long as the module provides the appropriate service to its co-operating modules in the process, the way in which it achieves this, need not concern the other elements involved. This kind of arrangement provides a greater flexibility in inter-connecting different types of system which conform to the same layered framework. There is not, unfortunately, any universal or even dominant agreement on one scheme for dividing logical functions up into different layers.

The growing need for the capability of inter-connecting computer systems and networks whatever their local characteristics has led to several initiatives aiming to develop a degree of standardization between the major alternatives, and to encourage the conformity of new products to these standards. These initiatives aim to develop a framework within which the most widely accepted and established 'industry standard' protocols can fit as alternative options. At the present time networking protocols fall into two main groups:

— those emanating from or supported by national and international standards making bodies, which are more 'open' in nature with published specifications;

— those emerging as proprietary standards from major computer manufacturers, which are 'closed' by virtue of their confidential specification and non-participative development.

A set of protocols will deal with aspects which are more closely related to the physical aspects of data and network communications and those which are more related to the information transfer aspects of user activity. At the lower layers, the data communications aspects can be seen as falling into three main areas: the physical connection, basic data management, and routing through the network.

The physical level is concerned with producing, receiving and monitoring the physical signals which are actually transmitted between systems, and with the standardization of methods for representing data in this form. A well-known example of this is the RS-232C standard, which defines the electrical interface on equipment as a multi-pin connection and assigns a particular function to each pin. The data link level is concerned with error control and recovery, and with flow control. In order to achieve this, most protocols encapsulate the user data in frames by dividing the stream of data into units of a pre-defined size and adding control information for use by the receiving system.

Since the network connection will be conveying data frames from other network users, the frames also contain header information ensuring delivery to the correct destination. Special frames may also be used to send only control information, for example to establish and terminate links with a remote computer. The frames produced by this layer are passed down to the physical layer for transmission. Error control is important at this level, since noise on the channel may result in the loss or corruption of frames; one purpose of splitting the whole message up into data frames is to retain control of the transmission as it develops, and take any remedial action necessary. Error control takes a number of simpler or more sophisticated forms, some of which require feedback from the receiver, for example:

— echo checking reflects characters received back to the sender for display on the user's screen, so that any corruption can be noticed and re-transmitted;

— acknowledgement schemes require the receiver to send an acknowledgement token back to the sender for each frame, before the next is transmitted;

— check digits can be added to the data frame by the sender, based on a computation carried out on the user data itself, and which the receiver can also use to check comparability.

Flow control is concerned to ensure that the data is not sent faster than it can be received; this function can make use of some of these devices, for instance acknowledgement schemes, or add features of its own to the exchange process. The network level is concerned with the management and control of routing through the network. The extent to which this is relevant will depend on the type of network in use and the mode in which it is operating. There are two broad modes within which a network can operate, providing two types of service:

— connectionless mode, in which the data is dispatched by the sender with the appropriate destination address, but no direct connection is made between them;

— connection-oriented mode, in which the two end systems behave as though directly connected by a physical medium and work in cooperation with each other.

A network may offer both these types of service as alternatives, but cannot normally support mixing between the two types. The network layer will typically organize the user data into packets, splitting up a long message into several units in this way and adding source and destination information to each packet to control its path through the network. The user data is then made transparent to the network itself, which is only concerned with the 'external' address information. Different packets which constitute parts of the same message are then treated as independent units, and may travel through the network at different speeds and by different routes.

The receiving system takes delivery of the packets and reconstitutes the message in its original format using the control information added by the sender. An X.25 network is an example of this arrangement. The network layer passes the packets down to the data link layer for the addition of error and flow control information, once it has completed its own responsibilities. In this way, user data is passed between layers between both sender and receiver, with only one actual physical network connection among them. In wider area networks, these three layers are also contained within the intermediate stages internal to the network, as well as in the end systems.

The specific protocols which implement these broad functions within an individual context will depend on the particular elements of the system which is in use, and the equipment available to it. A range of protocols are implemented either as software in communications packages, or as hardware built into data communications equipment. Some have achieved a greater popularity and therefore a de facto standardization over time.

In order for the communication process to be successful, both systems which intend to exchange data must be capable of running the same protocol, and therefore require communications packages or hardware which are compatible with each other; larger systems may offer a range of communication alternatives which can sense the method used by a caller and select the appropriate option. The types of device which have a role to play in the entire networking process can be placed into two categories:

1. Data Terminating Equipment (DTE) describes the devices which originate, or provide the final destination for, a transmitted message; either that operated by an end-user, or a computer system working autonomously. Typical examples of DTE devices would be a desktop microcomputer, a mainframe computer system, a visual display unit terminal, a printer, or a facsimile machine.
2. Data Communicating Equipment (DCE) describes the devices which are used to support onwards communication of a message received from some DTE device type-acting as 'steps in the chain' rather than as end-controllers of the process. This may be a device attached to the end-user's system, or some intermediate step within the network itself.

The data communicating equipment acts as a common interface for unlike data terminating equipment, they even out the differences through the common use of a standard protocol. In this way, dissimilar types of information technology equipment can be used for information networking without requiring an end user to be aware of the physical characteristics of the receiving system; the more widely used and open the standard protocol which is used, the wider range of equipment which can interface in this way. The kind of equipment which falls into this category fulfils specialized roles in the communications process: some of these are integral to the internal functioning of the network element itself while others are associated with user end systems. Some of the more commonly found types are described here, as indicative of the range.

The multiplexor is a device for concentrating a number of terminal devices onto a higher bandwidth line, to make the most effective use of this capacity and to remove the need for installing many duplicate lines (one for each device) in parallel with each other. This arrangement would typically be used to connect several terminals situated near each other to a central computer which is located at some distance.

The multiplexor is responsible for apportioning the line on an equitable basis between all the terminals connected. There are two main methods of multiplexing:

— time-division multiplexing, in which each terminal is allotted the full capacity of the channel for a fixed period of time, in a rotating sequence;

— frequency division multiplexing, in which the full channel capacity is divided between users by allowing simultaneous transmissions on different frequencies.

The most appropriate form to use depends on the applications which are using the system; commonly asynchronous enquiry-type applications, where activity is in unpredictable short bursts, use a time-division form of multiplexing. A multiplexor must be installed at the receiving end, to separate out the different terminal signals for processing.

A modem is another communicating device which allows one kind of DTE equipment, typically a personal computer, to establish a temporary connection with another remote computer system by using the normal telephone line. Since the telephone system was originally designed solely for voice traffic, which is analogue in nature, some conversion process must be used to translate digital computer data into a form suitable for analogue transmission. Digital signals are in a binary form, having two states-on and off-which can be represented as changes in voltage signals on a cable.

Since the normal telephone line is designed for transmission of sound waves, these binary signals must be transformed into an audible tone by the modem. This process is known as modulation; a modem (modulator—demodulator) must be placed at both ends of the telephone link, acting as the interface between the end systems and the line, encoding and decoding the digital data signals. A series of standard recommendations have been produced by the CCITI (Comite Consultatif Internationale de Telegraphie et Telephonic), a Geneva-based international organization concerned with issues in telecommunications development, for the use of modems.

The cost of modem technology falls steadily, faster transmission speeds are achieved at a higher expense due not only to the price of equipment but also to the additional communications processing which is necessary at higher speeds. Higher transmission speeds are achieved by a panoply of special techniques which require more sophisticated error checking capabilities to counter the increased influence of noise. While the ccrn recommendations are standard within Europe, the existence of a separate set of standards in North America, developed by the Bell Communications Corporation complicates the international situation. The most common of these are the Bell 203 (1200 bps) and Bell 212 (2400 bps) standards; although working at the same speeds they do not have an exact correspondence to V-series standards and are not compatible. A final example of data communicating equipment is the use of an independent computer processor to handle the communications loading of a large computer system. This would typically be used where a mainframe computer is accessed by a large number of remote callers; for example, a system which makes an online bibliographic database available to users on a global basis through the use of modems over a telecommunications network.

A smaller computer—such as a minicomputer—is dedicated to the task of dealing with the network communications, so that the mainframe does not become overloaded by this task, and is free to concentrate on database activity. The front end processor handles the external contact, passing queries back to the database machine and forwarding results to the remote caller. The remote caller is, of course, not aware of the separation of functions.

❑

7

Fundamentals of Telecommunication

In the past, telecommunications has largely been regarded as a natural monopoly in the same way as gas and electricity. The long-term nature of the investment needed to create a national infrastructure, and the massive amounts of capital involved, have discouraged private initiative and relied upon governmental support and backing.

During the 1980s, in many countries around the world, this arrangement began to be perceived as too parochial and inflexible; liberalization of telecommunications regulation was seen as a means of stimulating innovation, by encouraging the development of market forces through the introduction of new service suppliers.

The Impact of Liberalisation on Telecommunication

The liberalization of telecommunication has taken two main forms, they are the following:

(a) **Privatization.** In which the monopoly authority is established as a private corporation, which competes on the same terms as any other business;

(b) **Deregulation.** In which the new service operators are allowed to offer competitive services, by the removal of restrictive practices which legislate against this.

Many countries have opted for a mixture of these two forms, often with a transition period setting special conditions which alternative services must adhere to. The extent of deregulation has also differed considerably; since the telecommunications infrastructure is seen as so essential to economic development, the total abolition of all regulatory mechanisms is not considered desirable. For this reason, many people speak of re-regulation, stressing a change in the conditions of government control rather than their complete removal.

The United States has historically been different from most countries, as their telecommunications have always been controlled by a private corporation, licensed under government monopoly. The AT&T corporation which provided the telephone systems prior to liberalization was forbidden in a 1956 ruling from entering the computer or information business, in which it would be considered to have an unfair advantage. In this period, two major corporations, AT&T and IBM, dominated the telecommunications and computing industries respectively, but did not directly compete with each other. A Federal Court ruling of 1982 ended this arrangement by requiring the divestiture of AT&T under the corporate anti-trust laws. This resulted in the creation of seven independent regional Bell operating companies out of the former AT&T conglomerate, each of which provided the public telecommunications service in a separate geographical area of the United States.

AT&T itself remained to compete for the traffic between these regions with other long haul private network operators, such as MCI and US Sprint. AT&T was also permitted to enter the computer and information business in its own right which, as the original developer and licensor of the Unix operating system through Bell Laboratories, was an attractive new direction for its corporate development. This 1982 judgment did not, however, end all regulation over the sector. The divested AT&T was prevented from entering 'electronic publishing'—the provision of information services on their networks—for a period of seven years while competitor network suppliers developed their strengths. This restriction was removed in 1989. Tne regional Bell Operating Companies (RBOCs) are now permitted to offer:

(a) electronic messaging;

(b) audiotex;

(c) electronic gateways to other information services;

(d) integrated billing for online information through these gateways;

The AT&T corporation, however, acting as the carrier of inter-exchange traffic, is increasingly interested in developing information services through co-operation with the regional operating companies; for example by using national customer databases of names and addresses for credit card and target marketing schemes.

The exact relationship between monopoly and non-monopoly services has been the subject of debate and conflict between the Federal Court and the Federal Communications Commission throughout this period, with the former championing a more restrictive approach. Realizing that the computer industry which telecommunications serves has global interests, both AT&T and the RBOCs have also diversified into foreign markets, both as telecommunications carriers and as providers of online services, following the creation of new opportunities through liberalization abroad. Although the trend has had an uneven development, there has been a steady blurring of the distinction between information provider, information vendor, and telecommunications carrier which will continue in the present decade.

The Impact on Europe

The same global trends have affected the structure and development of the telecommunications and information industries in Europe, but here the influence of the large multinational corporations has been diluted by a more robust government policy concerned to afford some protection to national and regional interests.

Within the European Community (EC) public data networks evolved independently in separate countries, resulting in a smaller overall market for each and a relatively higher cost of equipment than in the United States. This concentration on a national scope has led to the development of somewhat different technology, in particular the installation of different digital switching systems, which reduces the potential for European connectivity as a whole. The European Commission has taken an active interest in the development of the telecommunications facilities within the member countries, where the role of the PITs has been crucial in the growth from fledgling services to sophisticated international networking.

The EC commissioned the national PITs to create a packet switching network capable of supporting access from all the member countries, and itself mounted a variety of information services on the network under its own auspices as well as encouraging the development of others. This initiative gave a boost to the developing of information industries in Europe, helping to create a market sector in which information vendors could establish themselves, while the PITs were engaged in building up their own national packet switching networks to an adequate standard for a reliable international service. Once these had begun operation, Euronet was discontinued in 1984. This period saw the development of Packet SwitchStream in the United Kingdom, and similar ventures in France, the Netherlands, and Germany. These developments were driven through at the national level, with little detailed co-ordination between network suppliers who increasingly came to view each other as business competitors. This has resulted in the duplication of services and multiple international links to the United States and the Far East, with the network suppliers effectively competing to capture the market for data traffic entering and leaving Europe. The European Commission has been concerned to develop international research and development programmes, and has used the liberalization programme to stimulate innovation and corporate investment, in order to build a compatible European communication infrastructure capable of supporting the open internal market from 1993.

The creation of a European Telecommunications Standards Institute and the progressive reform of the PIT authorities have pursued explicit actions taken to support the declared EC objectives of:

(a) opening all network services, except the basic phone and data transmission services, to full competition;

(b) opening the terminal market to competition, within accepted operating standards;

(c) establishing uniform telecommunications charging across the EC;

(d) creating European standards for equipment to increase compatibility and remove trade barriers.

To support research and development, the Commission has embarked on programmes intended to develop the economic power of the region through advanced telecommunications technology. The RACE programme is a ten year effort, begun in 1985, to develop the standards and technology for integrated broadband communication through EC funded project teams drawn from industry and the academic world. The less favoured regions of the EC are supported by the STAR programme, which funds in part the development costs of upgrading communications infrastructures in the more rural areas of Greece, Ireland, Portugal, Spain, France and the United Kingdom.

The development of narrowband ISDN, however, has not progressed as fast as considered desirable by the EC, which set itself a target of 5 per cent market penetration by 1993 a decade earlier; in early 1992 there were only five commercial ISDN networks in operation in the EC and it was forecast that only 1 per cent would be achieved, failing to impact small and medium sized enterprises and the residential sector. This slow progress is due to a lack of standardization in ISDN technology, a consequent lack of cheap equipment available for the mass market, and an unwillingness on the part of network operators to take committed action in the face of this uncertainty. Within the EC, individual countries have taken a path of deregulation; rather than of complete privatization. Many former publicly owned PTTs have been transformed into private companies, but often with a majority shareholding still held by the State; and although these compete with private corporations in some areas, most still retain a degree of monopolistic privilege and control which in some cases can be quite substantial.

In the United Kingdom, changes in telecommunications occurred within a more general perspective of a Conservative government free-market philosophy committed to reversal of state monopoly industries in general. The successive Telecommunications Acts of 1981 and 1984 separated telecommunications from the postal authority, establishing British Telecom (now BT) as a private corporation.

At the same time, licences to offer similar services were granted to other companies, with the intention of creating a competitive market which would encourage innovation and efficiency. The principal competitor was Mercury Communications, founded for this purpose by Cable and Wireless; two other licences have also been granted for the establishment of cellular radiophone services. A curiosity of the British situation was the third licensed operator, the city of Kingston upon Hull, which for historical reasons already ran its own local phone system; so successfully, that it was able to provide free local phone calls. This was privatized in 1987 as Kingston Communications, eventually becoming part of a larger corporation. The 1984 Act also created OfTel, the Office of Telecommunications, charged with administering the regulatory structure and overseeing the implementation of the licensing conditions imposed on operators, to protect the public interest and ensure fair trading. These included, for instance, a requirement for Mercury to develop a commitment to geographical coverage of the United Kingdom as well as more specialist business services.

Mercury Communications was originally targeted at large corporations, but since obtaining the right to interconnect with the BT network, and thenceforth the ability to provide complete end-to-end services has extended beyond its limited geographic base to provide data services to medium and smaller businesses. As well as digital phone services, Mercury now provides a packet switched data network under the name of Mercury 5000, and an ISDN service called Premier 2100. In this way, it is now competing with BT in all major areas, and is actively co-operating with foreign companies such as AT&T to provide advanced satellite network services. While Mercury has built an all-digital network from the start but has limited geographic coverage, BT has a completely national service but is only just becoming fully digital in operation. At the same time as upgrading its national network, however, BT has developed international networking capabilities, for instance by the acquisition of the US-based value added network Tymnet, and has developed a range of value added services for delivery on these networks. There are two levels of integrated digital services, ISDN-2 and ISDN-30, with connections to ISDN networks in many other countries. In conjunction with this, BT provides video-conferencing and 'narrowcast' television services for intra-corporate communications. There is no restriction in the UK on the development of information services by the carrier operators, and BT in particular has developed many such services. The Prestel system was an early venture in videotex or viewdata, but has had little long lasting success despite being one of the first examples in this field.

Although successful in niche areas such as travel and insurance, after ten years of operation Prestel had only 95,000 terminals in use, and had failed to fulfil its original objectives of serving a mainly residential domestic market. Business oriented information services have proved more successful in areas such as financial, currency, market, and company information. Despite deriving some benefit from a loose regulatory structure which in practice has shielded BT from some of the effects of direct competition, the lack of a unifying structure under which services are offered, and a general philosophy of 'let the market decide' has retarded the development of a strong direction for telecommunications in the UK.

The relatively low cost of leased lines, for example, favours the building of private networks and encourages third-party suppliers of value added services, while discouraging the take-up of national services such as ISDN. BT must therefore compete on the same terms as these third party suppliers, and increasingly on an international basis. A further round of liberalization has opened up the possibility of other interested organisations applying for a licence to offer telecommunications services. These potentially may include:

(a) cable TV franchises, which have extensive links to customer premises, but no national infrastructure,

(b) cellular phone services, which are now allowed to build trunk networks, and could offer a packet switched radio-based network;

(c) recently de-regulated satellite services, able to both receive and transmit from small and cheap terminal devices;

(d) other national industries, such as British Rail, which have extensive rights of way for laying cable.

Telecommunications Network

The cost of entering the telecommunications market in a competitive age is likely to mean that any of these options would be likely to seek an alliance with a foreign network provider, with particular interest expressed from United States Bell companies.

The relationship between the telecommunications authority and the State has been markedly different in France. The national PIT was established as France Telecom in 1986, a private corporation owned by the State. The organisation largely retained control over equipment approvals policy and operating conditions, able, for instance, to levy a 30 per cent surcharge on leased lines used for value added services by competitors and to prevent certain kinds of services altogether. The Transpac X.25 public packet switching network is claimed to be the largest in the world, and has extended its value added services across Europe, including the recent acquisition of the London Regional Transport network in the United Kingdom. Transpac is already used by some United Kingdom companies for facilities such as electronic data interchange, in preference to leased lines from BT or Mercury, and is expected to be a major competitor in the European open market for telecommunications services.

The best known success of the French PIT has been the Minitel service. This videotex service, in contrast to the British Prestel, is now the dominant videotex system in Europe and has been sold to many other network operators, including NIT in Japan, the Italian PIT, and the Bell company US West.

From its first operation in 1983, Minitel grew to 4 million connected terminals in its first five years, and nearly 6 million in 1992, of which at least half are business users. Videotex is generally seen as providing access to large databases of information, presented through an easy to use interface which is accessible without special knowledge or instruction.

The system was originally developed by telecommunications interests as a suitable information service for linking the telephone with a domestic television set, but is now often supplemented by an intelligent terminal or personal computer.

A major reason for the initial success of Minitel lay in the policy of freely loaning the specially designed Minitel terminals to telephone subscribers, at the same time as replacing the printed telephone directory with an electronic version accessible only by videotex.

The Electronic Directory, provides access to a national database of phone subscribers through a simple enquiry language, as well as Yellow Pages information. The great success of this service very quickly created a substantial user base for Minitel, which encouraged other information suppliers to participate by offering other information services. These other services now cover a wide range, aimed at both the business. and domestic markets, and including:

1. Electronic messaging; professional services; business and financial information; domestic shopping and banking services; and chat lines.
2. The Pancatalogue comprising the online catalogue of the Bibliotheque Nationale and of the SIBIL user group of 22 universities is accessible *via* Minitel; the new French national library, due to open in 1995, plans a Minitel link which will enable the user to reserve materials from home, and book a reading place for a particular arrival time.

3. Newspaper publishers offer a package of services including news bulletins; information on sport, entertainment and leisure; classified advertisements and games.

4. Professional level services include access to a range of online databases with sophisticated search interfaces. Services are organized in a kiosque system, in which the user has the available services displayed, but pays only for actual use with no fixed subscription fee. There are seven different levels of charging for information used, priced per hour of usage regardless of distance, ranging from almost nominal fees to typical online database searching rates. The vendor is responsible for mounting the information, and chooses the applicable charging rate. Teletel, the service umbrella under which Minitel is managed, provides access through the Transpac network, and includes the user charge in the normal telephone bill on behalf of the vendor. An international service is being introduced which interlinks with other national videotex services, and with Teletel hosts abroad.

France Telecom opened its Numeris ISDN network in Brittany in 1987, and established a national network by 1990. The development of suitable applications was encouraged by a partnership scheme in which France Telecom sponsored pilot projects with commercial and client organisations, paying half of the research and development costs.

Many of these applications involved the transmission of high definition images, such as the transfer of X-ray and ultra-sound images between medical sites in emergency cases, the transmission of satellite weather images, and the distribution of high definition house pictures around a network of estate agents.

In Germany the PIT authority was turned into a private corporation, owned by the State, in 1989. Prior to this, the Deutsches Bundespost had resisted the encroachment of competitor services by keeping prices high for leased lines, charging by volume rather than by fixed rental, and by refusing equipment approval.

The 1989 reform following re-unification created a Bundespost subsidiary Telekom, and allowed private companies to compete in establishing value added services, although it has been reluctant to change this policy. The Deutsches Bundespost established a basic rate ISDN in eight major German cities in 1989, and expanded this to a broader national network, using the promotion of applications as a development device in a more limited way than the French experience. Telekom currently offers the following services:

(a) a videotex system, called BTX, similar to Prestel;

(b) an electronic mail system, called Telebox;

(c) a facility for remote monitoring of industrial plant and processes.

The development of the telecommunications infrastructure has stimulated the growth of the information industry, creating a larger potential market for information suppliers by bringing many more people into the communications web, building a more reliable and higher quality service.

The European informatics organisation, Eusidic, organizes an annual monitoring exercise on the reliability of international packet switching services by asking its members to record a typical week of use. This has recorded a steady increase in reliability, showing a 25 per cent failure rate in calls in 1988 compared with a 14 per cent failure rate in 1991; a large proportion of these faults are believed to occur when a dial-up connection through the PSTN telephone line is used as a local link to the packet switching exchange. An increase in, the total number of packet, switching exchanges in many European countries has reduced the importance of this link, and simplified the installation of new network connections. More dependable communications together with a network infrastructure which is capable of offering a connection to all potential customers has led to a substantial growth in the number of databases produced in both

Europe and the United States, and in the number of host systems which offer access to them.

By 1990, there were estimated to be 1048 databases produced in EC countries and 2214 produced in the United States, excluding those only available in videotex model; this represented an 11 per cent growth rate per annum in EC countries and a 7 per cent growth rate in the United States. Within the EC the same report counted 227 hosts offering access to a total of 1256 databases, and 299 online hosts giving access to 3348 databases in the United States, although this is counting some databases more than once when they are accessible from several different hosts.

Compared with earlier surveys, this figure indicates that the number of hosts in Europe is growing while those in the United States are remaining stable. A similar growth has taken place in the professional and business database usage sector of the videotex market in Europe, although the trends here are not so marked.

The French Minitel system dominates the area, with just over 85 per cent of the total number of installed terminals across Europe (6.6 million) in that country; some 50 per cent of the estimated 5 million or so Minitel customers are professional users compared to about 80 per cent of the 100,000 Prestel users in the United Kingdom.

Overall the European Commission estimated that there were 15,000 information providers on European videotex in 1991, although once again most of these are mounted on the Minitel system which provides the predominant means of access to professional information services in France.

The distribution of the online market is uneven with the United Kingdom, France, and Germany accounting for about 70 per cent of the market share, the majority of which is held by the United Kingdom. The large number of potential databases, of which many can often be consulted through competing hosts at varying charging rates and using different command languages as the search interface, is a source of confusion and uncertainty for the end-user.

The diversity of choice has led to a growth in the use of gateways, links through from one system to another. Gateways in telecommunications networks can take one of three main forms:

1. Conversion facilities which link dissimilar systems and information types by translating back and forth between the two, typically used for the forwarding of electronic mail between systems.

2. Hosts which have a link through to other relevant hosts in their own area of interest, so that the second can be contacted directly through the first: the user can drop out to the second host, consult the services available, and then return to the first host on completion.

3. Value added services, which provide a 'front end' to a range of databases on different hosts, to ease and enhance user access by masking detailed differences between hosts in a common presentation and interface.

The use of value added networks has been an established part of the online scene for many years, especially attractive in situations where the reliability of the public telecommunications network cannot be guaranteed. The Dialnet value added network used by Dialog Information Services is an example. This offers regular users a local network connection point with billing for telecommunications costs integrated with that for database usage, as an alternative to dealing separately with international telecommunications vendors.

A third-party gateway service takes this a step further by offering integrated access to many different hosts through one connection.

A well-known example is the Easynet service, which allows users to access more than 900 databases on various hosts; the user may select a database directly or enter the relevant criteria for the service to select automatically the most appropriate one itself. The service offers one command language (the Common Command Language) to all the host systems made available, so that the user is not required to learn new search languages and unfamiliar systems are made more accessible. The Common Command Language reduces the degree of sophistication possible in search statements by imposing commonality, so there are facilities for the experienced user to express the search in the native host language. The Easynet gateway also provides management facilities for monitoring the most effective database usage, and for controlling the costs of use throughout the process. This growth in the online information market in both provision and usage is predicted to continue at increasing rates, with market research forecasts continually revised upwards.

The expanding availability of information services and the almost ubiquitous presence of telecommunications networks is beginning to have a substantial impact not only on the way in which traditional information consumers such as libraries and information units are conducting their activities, but also on the development of new information-related occupations which can take advantage of these new communications features.

The practice of teleworking—the conduct of work related business and interactions over a distance and through the telecommunications networks: with the employer, with colleagues, with customers and contractors is one of these areas.

The development of information networking, in both the informal and personal sense as well as a formal substitution of electronically-mediated work relations, is fundamental to the growth of distance working. A major plank, in the telecommunications development programme of the European Community has been the encouragement of teleworking through funding of the necessary infrastructure, as a means of economic development in rural and less-favoured regions of Europe. An example of this is the development initiative conducted in conjunction with BT to provide digital exchanges and line plant for the installation of integrated digital services in the Highlands and Islands region of Scotland in the Hi-ISDN project.

A complementary project, called Hi-VANS, provides an easy to use interface to national and international services and to the public data network, as well as local information services for the development of tourism and community enterprises. An example of one such enterprise is the use of the network to transmit scanned images of articles which require abstracting from the Elsevier journal publisher in the Netherlands to distance workers in the Highlands. The articles are scanned in the Netherlands from the print version and sent to abstracters in Scotland; the completed abstracts are then returned for publication to the Netherlands with no production delays arising from postal delivery times.

Similar pioneering efforts have seen the foundation of 'telecottages' in many rural areas of the United Kingdom. A 'telecottage' is a generic term for a rural information technology centre, which provides easy access to IT, usually in a public building and on an informal basis. The telecottage can provide formal and informal training, and can act as a catalyst for small enterprises by providing cost-effective access to equipment, as well as supporting the work of community groups.

Apart from public funding, this concept has found sponsorship in the United Kingdom from BT in the form of four Teleservice Centres, established as well-equipped telematic service centres; the first of these to begin activity was in the Shetland Islands in 1991. The willingness of a major telecommunications corporation to become so involved in stimulating the development of a networking infrastructure for information enterprises testifies to the potential possibilities for the future.

In Europe, the concept of teleworking was developed first in Scandinavia, spreading quickly to the United Kingdom, and is now strongly favoured by government and EC initiatives in France, Spain and Portugal. The Telecottage Association, formed to support the growth in teleworking through personal networks of groups and individuals by means of seminars and newsletters, estimates that there are about 590,000 self-employed teleworkers in the United Kingdom. Many of these people are professional workers to whom the production, use and exchange of information is vital to their work.

The recent acceptance of distance working indicates a trend towards more skilled information workers, and the replacement of traditional office work by advisory, and consultancy-based work which does not require fulltime attendance at a particular geographical location to be carried out. This is demonstrated by the Telemedicine project in northern Norway, for example, which provides specialist medical services from a central hospital in Tromsoe to isolated local hospitals and health centres through the telecommunications network. This links together services such as pathology, radiology, and cardiology with access to medical databases and patient information systems for remote diagnosis, without requiring the patient to make a difficult journey to the central hospital facilities.

Generally, teleworking can take a number of different organisational forms:

(a) home-working, in which the workers are based at their own home, making few visits to an employer premises;

(b) telecentres, which offer new information technology facilities for workers from various different organisations;

(c) satellite work centres, which are owned by a large company but are geographically dispersed;

(d) flexible working, in which the work is carried out partly at the organisational premises and partly at home.

These new organisational forms imply changes in the overall structures for, organisational communications, and an increased emphasis on the development of networks which are capable of stretching beyond the physical confines of organisational premises alone.

Private Network

The backbone of the private network is often provided by leased lines rented on the basis of sole use from the local telecommunications authority. The costs and conditions which are imposed on the lease differ quite widely between countries. Where lines are cheaper, as in the United Kingdom for example, a large corporation may now be able to justify a leased line on the basis of voice transmission only, using one Megastream line to replace several analogue phone lines, and be able to transmit data 'for free' on top of this usage since a fixed annual rent is paid. High bandwidth circuits such as these supply point to point connections, and are appropriate between sites which have a high data traffic flow. Dial-up lines may be used where small amounts of data are sent at infrequent intervals, possibly using parts of a public packet switched network.

Since 1989 organisations operating private networks are allowed to resell spare capacity on their bandwidth, so that linking in with an existing private network already in use elsewhere may be one option; for example, banks may make network capacity available to some of their corporate customers. While terrestrial lines are normally controlled by a telecommunications authority, since the liberalization of services, non-terrestrial transmission offers a wider range of choices. Microwave links can be installed in line of sight between tall buildings, and satellite services can be employed to carry audio, video, and data services within a wide geographical area.

In the United States an 'open skies' policy, under which any qualified organisation can apply for a licence to operate a domestic satellite service, has been in operation since 1972; in the United Kingdom, however, the granting of full licences has been more reticent. Satellite capacity is available from a number of specialist data communications companies, and in Europe through the Eutelsat consortium of PIT authorities.

The pricing for Eutelsat usage is differentiated by member country with wide discrepancies in national rates; recently, clients have been able to book capacity through any member offering the best service. The development of very small aperture satellite transmission (VSAT) has lowered the relative costs of this medium, since a receive only dish uses the same technology as satellite television, and can be installed with the same case without the need for formal planning permission. This can provide a low cost 'point-to-multipoint' data broadcasting, for fast updating of many sites simultaneously; and is also used as a stop-gap measure for establishing a network link quickly, or to link sites which are separated by difficult geographic terrain.

Cellular network radiophones can also be used for non-terrestrial data links, but are not yet ideal for this purpose. This method appears attractive for linking a portable personal computer fitted with integral modem into a corporate network from uncertain locations; however, the cellular channel is noisy, and the transition between cells introduces delays in which contact may easily be lost, preventing truly mobile data communications. Although the transmission of packet data over the VHF radio waveband is feasible, its widespread use has not yet developed in the United Kingdom; licences have only been granted to radio data companies for quite limited and specialized markets. The wide area networking elements also take on an international dimensiol1 if the organisation needs to link into sites in other countries.

Larger organisations have diverse information needs, and sometimes specialist but vital performance requirements, demanding the development of a networking strategy which is flexible and controllable. For information networking to support corporate communications, the organisation has three main choices.

(a) To build a private network, using network elements from different sources.

(b) To send data over one or other of the public data networks.

(c) To hand over all network management aspects to a third party specializing in this field.

These choices have varying significance for different sizes and types of organisation operating in different fields; these disparate demands will lead to differing perceptions of the technology which is at the leading edge for a particular situation.

Smaller organisations, or those in which the information and technological infrastructure is less developed, may be well satisfied with options which are already considered obsolete by those in which information has a high strategic or mission importance. The use of public telecommunications in one organisation may have as far-reaching effects within that context, as are sought by another which is planning frame relay and broadband networking as replacements for X.25 and ISDN.

Some significant advantages of the use of public data services are given below:

(a) The development of private networks demand the use of scarce personnel with technical expertise in networking skills, and a high capital investment; while using public networks leaves the organisation free to concentrate on its main activities without draining off resources.

(b) Once a private network is developed it is hard to change, and expensive to upgrade with technological advances. Information activities may demand a high capacity at critical times, but may not justify this permanently (for example, with seasonal peaks in retail transactions); variable use of the public data network will smooth out peaks and troughs of this nature.

(c) The broader scope of public services can develop targeted services for particular needs in a cost effective way, and save on the duplication of effort.

(d) In a similar way, organisations can take advantage of the emergence of international standards through participation in a more general service, without the cost of individual development; for example, electronic data interchange standards for basic business documents.

The use of completely private networks, can have important attractions especially to a larger organisation which is able to amortise costs over a longer period.

(a) The strategic importance of information to the organisation may demand control over the data at all stages, without fear of compromising security and confidentiality.

(b) Control of the network enables technological decisions on speed and efficiency, the use of proprietary protocols, and flexible changes in response to need.

(c) Control also extends to economic factors, where the unpredictable nature of changes in public services are avoided while spare capacity can be resold to other clients.

The third choice available to organisations is the use of third-party services to take over the management of all network facilities on its behalf. This removes the need for specialist expertise and keeps the technology up to date, while retaining some control and security, by making this the responsibility of an expert networking company. This is an attractive option to a medium sized organisation where communications is important for its business but not of vital strategic importance particularly if this involves the use of international connections and the consequent complexity of dealing with different national authorities. Network management companies may offer project management in the development of a network for a specific problem within a defined budget, or full facilities management of all networking arrangements.

Liberalization of telecommunications has encouraged the growth of management services from both private companies and the telecommunications carriers, while the increasing complexity of networking has made their services attractive to the client. The operators have often evolved from organisations which have established their own extensive private networks.

❐

8

Use of Videocassettes in Library

In today's electronic, on-line catalogue environment, cataloguing materials is analogous to putting a jigsaw puzzle together blindfolded. All bibliographic records must be accessible through multifaceted searches in order for patrons to have success. Quality control, standards, and real-time testing arc some ways that librarians can use to assure that success.

Historically, the number, correctness, and inclusiveness of cataloguing records for videorecordings has been less than satisfactory. When these unsatisfactory records are imported into a local database without correction or modification, they can cause substantial difficulty and chaos. Charles Osburn speaks specifically to these difficulties in his five barriers toward acquiring any library item, three of which are appropriate to this discussion:

(a) difficulty of cataloguing [or obtaining cataloguing information];

(b) difficulty in acquiring certain materials (and verifying their existence and vendor availability]; and

(c) difficulty in processing that item once acquired [*i.e.*, multiple cassettes, multimedia kits, oversized cases, supplemental materials].

In 1989, the Rockefeller Foundation Video Distribution Task Force surveyed a number of libraries across the United States for their views and practices regarding existing videocassette collections.

Librarians in charge of the videocassette collections were in widespread agreement that videos should be catalogued, and many of those libraries were already using OCLC as the major bibliographic source utility for cataloguing information. Those same librarians felt that videocassettes acquired from mainstream vendors, rather than those purchased from independents, vanity presses, and other, alternate sources of acquisitions, would require very little original, primary cataloguing because of the likelihood of bibliographic record appearance in various national bibliographic databases such as OCLC, NYSCAT, and WLN.

Furthermore, the survey indicated that 73 percent of all libraries serving populations of more than 25,000 catalogued their videocassette collections; 46 percent used full MARC cataloguing, but 3 to 23 percent of those libraries video titles required primary cataloguing because of their non-existence in a bibliographic Utility. Such non-existence of videographic records and the resultant time-consuming process of primary cataloguing is, at the very least, costly for the library and tends to increase the time from actual purchase to shelf-readiness. When a match is found on a bibliographic utility such as OCLC, the record is often done incorrectly and/or is incomplete, thus necessitating local verification of the information and substantial modification of that record.

Also, a title such as The Wizard of Oz may be listed in a database several times because of incorrect cataloguing or varying copyright dates/manufacturer information. The cataloguer must search a number of records before a "hit" can be found. This process costs the library valuable search time and excessive database charges (*e.g.*, OCLC charges a set fee for each record accessed on the screen, not just the one chosen for local database downloading and eventual modification). Fully 27 percent of those libraries surveyed in the aforementioned Rockefeller Project felt that it was not necessary to catalogue videocassettes. Twenty percent of surveyed libraries chose to produce alphabetical title lists of videocassettes instead of cataloguing those titles in a card catalogue or public access catalogue (PAC).

Even today, there is a great need to educate librarians about the philosopy and methods of cataloguing all library materials. The ultimate goal of library acquisitions is to purchase as much of any needed product to satisfy intellectual demand and/or need within budgetary limits. If budgets are mismanaged and community responsive collection development strategies are not followed, the worst that can happen is that certain titles may not be acquired and the collection will suffer. Much more of a travesty, however, is the inaccurate/incomplete cataloguing or omission of cataloguing for titles already owned by the library. The ultimate goal of any library is to make materials available to patrons. When patrons and library staff alike are not able to locate and access these materials when they need them, the entire fabric of a library's reason for existence is undermined. Ralph Hunzinger, Audio Visual Director for the King County (Seattle, W A) Public Library System, feels that "if an item is not fully catalogued and patrons cannot find it, then the library does not own it."

Historically, the fact that has set libraries apart from other information businesses/agencies is that of organized bibliographic access. If this characteristic is compromised for videocassettes, then libraries are on the verge of a great demise. The cataloguing of videocassettes in libraries has advanced much since the early 1980s. The revision of AACR II, new rule interpretations from the Library of Congress Cataloguing Services Bulletin, Yand MARC/OCLC format integration have all contributed to the greater availability of cataloguing for videocassettes. However, problems still remain in terms of adequately policing databases for record input consistency and standardization and unnecessary duplication, as well as modification of the record on the local end.

Because there are many fine textbooks detailing the policies, procedures, and specific rules for cataloguing videocassettes, this text will not duplicate those efforts. Instead, this chapter will discuss some of the specific problems related to adapting the videographic record to the local database to produce more refined access points.

It will also detail problems in the following areas: *(1)* the connection between Circulation/patron reserves and the videographic entry/holding's record and *(2)* the consistent use of various fields, as well as standardizing terms and subject headings within those fields. The end result of such cataloguing will yield a highly "patron friendly" catalogue. This is not an easy task, however, and will require much effort, time, and deliberation on the cataloguer's part. While it is recognized that there are many libraries possessing a physical card catalogue rather than the electronic equivalent or "on-line database," this discussion will focus primarily upon the unique needs and characteristics of bibliographic records in an electronic environment.

Specific examples from OCLC MARC records will illustrate various concepts, but the text will not detail, in step-by-step fashion, the correct methods of cataloguing. Furthermore, this chapter will seek answers to the following questions:

1. How much detail in the videographic record, both in book catalogues and other types of on-line catalogues, should be available?
2. To what degree does the cataloguer have to go to catalogue videocassettes?
3. Are Library of Congress subject headings and other types of subject headings useful, and how can they be modified to be more suitable for the video format?
4. To what degree can the cataloguer depend upon the information supplied by the video jobber, distributor, producer, or bibliographic vendor (online, CD-ROM or other)?
5. How do book catalogues differ ftom their card catalogue and on-line patron access catalogue (OP AC/P AC) counterparts in terms of bibliographic needs and patron access (usefulness)?

A Brief Historical Perspective

Many of the video formats bibliographic problems stem from the general neglect historically given to audiovisual materials by cataloguing departments. In college and university situations, film and videocassette collections/ services were frequently developed outside of the library infrastructure.

Audio-visual services in these agencies were separate entities from the library with their own budget, buildings, staff, and clientele. It was not uncommon for these audiovisual centers to be managed by non-librarians. Their "catalogues" were printed title listings with brief annotations and sparse subject indexes prepared by clerical staff from vendor catalogue information. During the video explosion of the mid-1980s, patrons thronged to the public libraries demanding videocassettes NOW-they wanted them in great variety and in large quantities. In order to supply the patrons' insatiable demands, these videocassettes were ordered, received, and hurriedly shelved without proper cataloguing.

When audiovisual materials were organized in some fashion, librarians often used homegrown classification and cataloguing procedures rather than relying on LC or AACR II standards, or utilizing LC or DOC schemes. The arrival of the half-inch VHS and Beta formats was to have an unforeseen and profound impact on all libraries and how they dealt with the problem of bibliographic access. The number of videocassettes available for purchase became much larger, patron demand increased dramatically, prices started to drop, and collection sizes soared. A public library that once purchased 30 to 50 16mm films in a year could now purchase hundreds of feature and non-fiction videocassettes. In order to give better service and increase access to these collections the cataloguing and processing of these materials had to be upgraded.

Today, there are two philosophies in providing access to non-print resources: the departmental approach and the "omnimedia," integrated approach. Full cataloguing is seldom necessary in the departmental approach, where simple title, series, and/or subject lists have traditionally sufficed. The omnimedia approach, on the other hand, stresses uniform treatment for all types of library materials and continues to influence revision of cataloguing rules with respect to nonprint media. It is this omnimedia approach with which this chapter is solely concerned.

Regardless of the philosophy or machinery used to catalogue videocassettes, the access points are only as good as the information originally input into the title record the "garbage-in, garbage-out" syndrome. Bibliographic utility records, such as those existing in OCLC, WLN, and their CD-ROM counterparts, should always be viewed and modified after uploading in the local PAC to meet local needs for term inclusion, consistency, and standardization.

What is Cataloguing and Why Bother?

Even though many readers of this text may not per form original, primary cataloguing of videocassettes, at some time in their career they many be involved in the setup and organization of audiovisual cataloguing procedures or be asked to evaluate a library's or a vendor's cataloguing performance. From an administrative standpoint, videocassettes are more time-consuming to catalogue, which ultimately results in cataloguing backlogs, resistance from print-biased cataloguers, and a significant time delay in getting the material on the shelf ready for circulation. Usually the cataloguing of videocassettes involves much interpretation of cataloguing rules rather than just their written application. Standard bibliographic databases such as OCLC and WLN often contain inaccurate and incomplete information, or do not contain the item being catalogued at all.

Knowing something about the process and problems of cataloguing videocassettes is helpful in making cataloguing policy, procedural, and staff-task decisions. Cataloguing serves two functions within a library. The first, an in-house function, is to provide a comprehensive inventory and bibliographic control. The second, a public service function is to provide multiple access points within a logical, consistent, and standardized framework enabling patrons to locate library-owned materials. It is in the melding of these two discrete functions that the librarian must find unity and compromise-to provide all the information useful to the librarian while also providing a clear, concise access path for the patron. This juxtaposition of different needs results in a basic conflict patron needs and demands versus local and international standards such as MARC, LC, OCLC, and AACR II (Anglo-American Cataloguing Rules 11), revised edition.

The term "cataloguing" actually comprises three distinct activities:

1. Descriptive cataloguing wherein the actual extant of the item is described in accurate detail. This task also entails describing the contents through a descriptive annotation and choosing analytical entries and added entry points. Descriptive cataloguing for videocassettes can present problems because, in some instances, the cataloguer is describing attributes of the physical cassette, while other instances demand detail of the intellectual property contained within.
2. Assigning subject headings-Library of Congress, Sears, or other standards.
3. Assigning a classification or accession number. One number/letter sequence which effectively distinguishes a single item from another, possibly placing it within a subject framework like the DDC (Dewey Decimal Classification Scheme, 20th ed.), the Library of Congress Classification scheme, ANSCR (Alpha-Numeric System for Classification of Recordings) and others.

The catalogue entry or "record" may be a full MARC record comprised of numbered "fields," or it may be a very brief "short entry" with only bare bones information such as title, imprint, collation, and subject headings in it. This short entry could be in the form of an incomplete MARC or OCLC record, or a local database, non-MARC record.

The AACR II recognizes three distinct levels of information inclusion, while the Library of Congress (LC) has adopted a minimum level for cataloguing audiovisual materials. The previously mentioned assumption of mainstream titles most likely being catalogued by LC is not valid because LC has not undertaken a comprehensive plan to catalogue videocassettes. They have a serious backlog of titles and their cataloguing is often incorrect and inaccurate, occasionally to the point where original cataloguing at the local level would have been more efficient and cost-effective than searching, choosing, and downloading an inaccurate record. The level of cataloguing which the technical services staff selects for a library's videocassette collection can be dependent on several factors:

1. How does the video collection fit into the mission of the library?

2. How do the patrons access the collection currently, and what are their needs?

3. How large is the collection now, and what is its projected growth over the long term (five to ten years)?

4. How is the collection currently displayed/shelved?

5. How is the collection currently circulated, and what kind of automated system is available for use with this collection?

6. What is the staffing situation? (*i.e.*, the availability of professional cataloguing staff)

7. What type of catalogue does the library possess?

8. What level of cataloguing is standard for print materials at the library?

9. What classification system is currently used for features and for non-fiction videocassettes? Is the same one used

for print materials and/or can either be adapted for the videocassette collection?

10. Are there circulation policies that may impact upon the cataloguing process or procedures?

11. What is the current administrative support for the video collection and service (inclusive of budget, staff, housing, etc.)?

12. What kinds of materials are in the collection (features, documentaries, local production, etc.)?

Factor 12 may be the most important in establishing an accessible, professionally catalogued collection. Without the active support of the library's administration and a committment to develop and nourish the collection as an integral part of the library's collection development plan, the videocassette collection will remain "ephemeral." It can be easily cut out of the budget and easily disposed of—after all, who knew the collection even existed without those titles accessible through a "real" catalogue?

Finding and Verifying the Videographic Data

Pre-recorded videocassettes are mediated formats, meaning that they require some form of equipment in order to be viewed-unlike a book, which can be opened and read without the aid of audiovisual equipment. Another problem unique to videocassettes is separating the physical medium from the intellectual material contained within.

The videocassette itself is only a format. Very often, the "programme" magnetically reproduced on that videocassette is a different format altogether (*e.g.*, any theatrically released feature film is originally produced on 16 or 35mm film) possessing a different copyright date as well as other information. Therefore, many times there is a need to view the video, at least in part, to ascertain some vital pieces of information, even if the only purpose is to compare that information to an already existing videographic record. The

AACR II rules acknowledge that fact, requiring information from both the extant (physical videocassette) and intellectual property (programme contained within the format).

TABLE 1

LOCATION OF IMPORTANT VIDEOGRAPHIC ELEMENT

E,I	Title, variant titles, analytical titles
E,I	Series title(s)
I	Original copyright date
E	Manufacturer's copyright date, manufacturer's order number
E,I	Manufacturer
E,I	Producer/production company
E,I	Director
I	Other important credits - writer, musical producer, narrator, etc.
I	Major performers
E	Audience indicators, MPAA ratings
E	Running time
E	Closed captioning
E	Other attributes colour, B/W, letterboxed, dubbed, subtitled, etc.
E	Descriptive annotation
E	Titles/pagination of supplementary/accompanying material

The extant item includes the physical videocassette labels (spine and face) as well as the art box (front and back). The intellectual property information can be found in the opening and closing credits (the title, copyright date, producers, director, and major performers).

Table 1 is a listing of important information and where it most often can be found (E = extant video; I = the actual programme).

Table 2 illustrates the findings of a library science graduate, student at Northern Illinois University (DeKalb, IL) regarding the percentage of videocassettes, divided into four disparate "types," possessing certain vital videographic information as well as the time necessary to locate that information. It should be noted that, many times, there are inconsistencies in the title credits on the intellectual property, the videocassette extant label, and the extant art box. This presents a problem in the discernment and prioritization of the elements concerning which one source to use.

As a general rule, AACR II recommends using the information on the credits first, the extant label second and the art box last.

The AACR II also has a prescribed manual of style determining the order and appearance of the videographic information. Table 3 is a brief outline of AACR II rules dealing with videocassettes. Although rule interpretations arc not necessarily the same within AACR II and LC, the Cataloguing Service Bulletin from the Library of Congress and its index should be consulted for further rule clarifications. Originally developed for physical catalogue cards, the electronic equivalent of a main entry card is often reproduced within a PAC system. These elements are outlined as follows:

TABLE 2

PERCENTAGE/TIME TABLE FOR SPECIFIC VIDEOGRAPHIC ELEMENTS

Documentary	
66%	date only at end; 26% no date
66%	producer name at end
66%	publisher name within 1 min.; 20% at end
66%	title in 1 min. / 33% 2 min.

Contd.

Children's Videos	
53%	title in 2 min.
47%	publisher in 2 min./ 40% in 1 min.
73%	date at end / 20% in 2 min.
46%	producer name at end / 33% in 2 min.
Instructional "How-to" Videos	
66%	producer name at end
46%	date at end / 20% in 2 min. .
53%	publishers name at end / 46% in 1 min.
80%	title in 1 min.

All catalogue card and OCLC record figures have been created by the author for this text; A the DYNIX record figures are taken from the Elkart (IN) Public Library database, Bear in mind that, as a general rule, most videocassettes will have a title main entry rather than an author (*i.e.*, a performer: producer, or director) entry. There are three areas of title location on a videocassette. The title frame within the intellectual property is the primary cataloguing source, which is mandated by AACR 11 in determining the title main entry. Secondary variant sources include the commercial packaging and the videocassette label.

TABLE 3

AACR II RULE INDEX FOR CATALOGUING VIDEOCASSETTES

AACR II

Chapter No.	*Rule Description*
1.0	General rules - where to find sources of information, punctuation, cataloguing levels

Contd.

Chapter No.	*Rule Description*
1.1	Title and statement of responsibility, punctuation, General Material Designator [GMD)
1.4	Impring information (place, producer, date)
1.5	Collation (physical description area)
1.6	Series area
1.9-1.10	Items made up of several type of materials and supplementary items
2.1	Items without a collective title
2.7	Notes area
7.0	Motion pictures and videorecording general information
26.4	Uniform titles

Analytical entries play a vital role in linking the four short titles/ authors to the main title. The analytics are also mentioned in the descriptive annotation. It is important to note that in many electronic databases, repetition of titles/terms may yield duplicative search results. Thus, putting a title analytic in the MARC 505 field [NOTES) and the 740 fierd [TITLE TRACED DIFFERENTLY) for Jane, Wishing, for example, will yield two entries under that title, both leading back to the same videographic entry, A Tale of Four Wishes. This is confusing to the patron, and may be avoided by modifying the local database display/search profile. An issue which cataloguers labour over is deciding upon tile main entry and the use of, uniform titles. To a large degree, tile emergence of the electronic Catalogue has lessened the importance of the main entry and uniform style cards.

The main entry is also the deciding factor for Cuttering. Also, if the main entry chosen differs from the title on the videocassette label(s) or art box (inclusive of back, front and spine), they must be relabeled to be consistent with the title frame and main entry. Two examples will clearly illustrate the need for this practice. A cataloguer views a video with the title frame reading Walt Disney's Cinderella. LC and AACR II treat an entry of this type in a similar manner, stating: 7.1131. [New). When credits for performer, author, director, producer, 11 presenter, and so on precede or follow the title in the chief source, in general do not consider them as part of the title proper, even though the language used integrates the credits with the title.

Twentieth Century Fox presents Star Wars

Steve McQueen in Bullitt

Thief with James Caan

This does not apply to the following cases:

1. the credit is within the title, rather than preceding or following it; CBS

   Special Report

   IBM Puppet Shows

2. the credit is actually a fanciful statement aping a credit; Little Roquefort in Good Mousekeeping

3. the credit is represented by a possessive immediately preceding the remainder of the title.

However, even in light of rule 7.1B1, the cataloguer has sufficient latitude to determine the main entry along with added entries. A main entry under Walt Disney's Cinderella should also have, as an added entry, a uniform title expressed as [Cinderella]. In this manner, all Cinderella adaptations could be accessed together. Although cataloguers widely agree, both in practice and theory, that videocassettes should not be given a main author entry, because the responsibility of "authorship" in a video rests in more than one person, they do not often agree on who should be listed in the notes field (found in the film credits). LC provides the following rule clarification:

> 7.7136. [Rev]. For audiovisual items, generally list persons (other than producers, director, and writers) or corporate bodies who have contributed to the artistic and technical production of a work in a credits note.
>
> Give the following persons or bodies in the order in which they are listed below. Preface each name or group of names with the appropriate term(s) of function:
>
> photographer(s); camera; cameraman/men; cinematographer
>
> animator(s)
>
> artist(s); illustrator(s); graphics
>
> film editor(s); photo editor(s); editor(s)
>
> narrator(s); voice(s)
>
> music [composer(s)]
>
> consultant(s); adviser(s)
>
> Do not include the following persons or bodies performing these functions:
>
> assistants or associates
>
> production supervisors or coordinators
>
> project or executive editors
>
> technical advisers or consultants
>
> audio or sound engineers
>
> writers of discussion, programme, or teacher's guides
>
> other persons or bodies making only a minor or purely technical contribution

The cataloguers entering these records could not even agree on the exact title [245], much less the imprint statement [2601, notes [520], topical subject headings [6501, or added name entries [508, 7001. The general media designator (GMD) in the brief entry was not even correct, being entered as two words rather than the accepted one—"videorecording." Furthermore, the brief entry even left out the fact that the video was closed captioned for the hearing impaired. What is even more amazing is the fact that the more complete video graphic record was entered into the database before the brief record; therefore, it can be assumed that the cataloguer did not perform a very comprehensive search of the database initially.

Cataloguing Videos in Series

Videocassette titles in series seem to create havoc for cataloguers. Before a discussion of cataloguing suggestions can be undertaken, it is important to define a series and describe the various series types. Basically, videocassette series fall into four distinct types: a publisher's series; a producer's series; a television serial; and a programme issued as a multivolume set (two volumes or more). Examples of a publisher's videocassettes are videocassettes produced by different producers, possibly following a similar "formula" format but packaged to look the same, marketed together and sold as a package. Examples of publishers' series are The Traveloger Collection, National Geographic Society Specials, PBS Video's The American Experience series, and National Audubon Society Specials.

A producer's series such as Films Incorporated's The Story of English or PBS Video's The Civil War are examples of a producer's series-dependent and sequential programmes dealing with the same subject, all produced by the same company. This type of series may have episode or volume titles. The third type of series is the television serial, possessing an overall serial title with one or more episodes on a videocassette. Each episode may possess its own title. Examples of these titles would be The Outer Limits, The Twilight Zone, I Love Lucy, The Fugitive, and The Prisoner. Miniseries such as The Thorn Birds, Brideshead Revisited, I, Claudius, and Shogun may also fall into the third category if each volume Possesses a discrete title, rather than just a multiple set with one title.

Many cataloguers have difficulty in determining what constitutes a series title. One example is the proliferous recurrence of the PBS Home Video label in the [440] and [490] fields as a series. A true series is neither a label or a trademark, like PBS Video (under Pacific Arts). The cataloguer must decide whether *(1)* to include the main entry of the series title in the [245] field with each volume listed as a separate title within the [5051 and [740] fields or *(2)* to enter each volume as a distinct videographic record, linked only by the common series field [730]. Depending upon the local database search characteristics and space, the advantages and disadvantages of either choice are as follows:

Advantages. True series are known distinctly by the series title rather than individual volume titles. Usually, the volumes are closely related in subject content; therefore, individual annotations are not needed. Also, producers and copyright dates are the same throughout the series. Programmes can be listed in any pertinent order, such as alphabetical, volume number, or viewing order within the contents field [505], which may prove helpful to patrons.

Individual annotations for each volume cannot be entered/ displayed easily. The listing of the individual volumes in two fields simultaneously may result in duplicated listings for a resultant search, ultimately confusing patrons—Each volume is essentially treated like a copy. Many computerized circulation systems such as DYNIX allow holds/reserves to be placed *via* two methods: *(1)* first available copy and *(2)* specific copy. The patron must choose the specific copy if a specific volume is wanted instead of the first available volume. The problem becomes exacerbated when there are multiple copies of each volume. The only alternative to the patron is to put all copies of that specific volume on hold in the hopes of getting one.

Individual MARC records for each series volume, part/title solve the hold/reserve problem mentioned above.

This form of entry uses much more database space and requires more cataloguing time for creation of the records, as well as creating a greater error rate regarding consistent cataloguing for multiple entries (however, some systems allow the use of one record as a template to recreate another record). Many times national databases and CD-ROM cataloguing products will not have separate records for series titles; therefore, primary cataloguing is the only solution. Also, using this method, the series entry cannot not be given a generic annotation.

With the above definitions and discussion of the MARC record and local database search parameters in mind, the following series test is given so that cataloguers may find it easier to determine main entry (*i.e.*, 245 field entry).

1. Series with a series title and each title possesses a unique episode title, programme number, or volume number (*i.e.*, Tell Me Why, Video Aircraft Report, National Geographic Society Specials,' National Audubon Society Specials). A decision must be made as to whether all series titles should be shelved together or individually based on their subject content/genre similarity.

   A. as a group, catalogue as in 2A.

   B. individually, catalogue under episode title [2451 with added under series [440/490]. Include, as part of the tit.1e any volume, part, programme number, etc. Cutter under episode title.

2. Series with one episode title (subtitle) per video, dealing with the same subject/genre (*i.e.*, needing to be shelved/ cuttered together-The Outer Limits, Doctor Who, plus series with volumes needing to be viewed in sequence). Individual programme annotations [520 Notes] desired.

   A. Catalogue under the series title followed by the[GMDJ subtitle (episode, programme, volume, etc.). Added entries in [7401 (episode title) and [440J or [490) (series). Include, as part of the title, any volume, part, programme number, etc. Cutter.

3. Series with one episode title (subtitle) per video, dealing with the same subject/genre

   A. Catalogue under the series title. Added entries in 740 (episode title with any program, part, volume, number), 440/490, and 520. Cutter under series title.

4. Series with more than one episode title per video, dealing with the same subject/genre (*i.e.*, The Twilight Zone, The Story of English, Cosmos, The Civil War).

   A. Catalogue under the series title followed by the [GMD]: subtitle the first subtitle (episode, programme, volume, etc.); the next subtitle; and so on. Include, as part of the title, any volume, part, programme number, etc. Added entries in (7401 (episode title) and [4401 (series). Cutter under series title.

5. It is also recognized that patrons desire the following things:

   A. They want access under title exact/title keyword for certain serial/series titles like I Love Lucy, because they will not remember individual episode titles.

   B. On some series (TV fiction programmes and same subject series (such as Doctor Who and The Story of English) titles, the patron must be able to distinguish one unique title from another at the OP AC title list. Also, there should be no double entries for the same title under the same search list.

   C. Titles listed under B should be cuttered similarly and shelved together as a group, permitting easy browsing access.

   D. Do patrons desire unique, descriptive annotations (notes) for each title?

In many computerized booking systems, such as Tek Data Systems' DMAX software designed specifically for media, the system allows the input of individual titles with annotations as well as a separate database of series with its software designed specifically for media, the system allows own annotations and title listings. These databases are then merged for searching and book catalogue production, giving the patron the best of both worlds. A record from the DYNIX database of the Elkhart (IN) Public Library, which graphically illustrates the concept of a series main entry for a television miniseries, multivolume videocassette with individual episode titles. Each volume has become a copy in the DYNIX system and is barcoded and circulated separately.

The cataloguing effects the circulation and shelving/arrangement of the title as well as the access points, but the title is catalogued under the series title with one series annotation. Contents notes list individual volume titles, A local library database record actually has two parts—a bibliographic/videographic record and a holdings record. The videographic record relates descriptive detail to the item for search access, but is not copy specific; the holdings record is copy or barcoded item specific, detailing call number, item barcode, copy number, status (on shelf, out, etc.), and other coded information useful for gathering library circulation statistics.

A copy number refers to multiple copies of the same title. However, some unique circumstances commonly occur in videocassettes to upset this rather straightforward concept. Many times, titles have multiple parts, such as The Godfather, issued in two or more separate parts. Even though these parts form the whole and circulate together, libraries may choose to barcode each part for greater inventory control. Series titles such as The Civil War, The Story of English, and Brideshead Revisited possesses multiple volumes, but do not necessarily have to circulate together.

Within a local database, circulation is bar code specific. Therefore, it is inherently tied to the holdings record which is accessed (*i.e.*, searchable) through the video graphic record. In many cases the patwn can actually view the holdings (copies, volumes, parts) and place a hold/reserve on anyone copy or all of them. Circulation modules such as DYNIX provide the patron with a "selected copy only" or "first-available copy" selection. The cataloguer must make a choice of how the title is to be catalogued relative to how it will be circulated, thus choosing to catalogue the entire set under the series title if the series title is better known-than its individually titled parts. Each volume would receive analytics and/or a [740] field entry if titled.

The collation would reflect the number of volumes within the entire series as well as the series running time. The holdings screen would show the individually barcoded volumes. Advantages to this method are a savings in cataloguing time (cataloguing a series and adding holdings is faster than cataloguing each item in its own video graphic record and adding a holdings record) and conservation of database space. If a patron wishes to place a hold on a specific volume, he/she must remember to be copy specific. Furthermore, if multiple copies of one or more volumes are added to the holdings, the patron must be sure to place multiple, copy-specific holds.

As a further example of local database modifications for series, the Doctor Who PBS television programme is presented: Most OCLC MARC records list the individual episode titles in the (245] field with a series entry in [440/490]. Most vatrons do not know individual episode titles and want the entire series shelved/cuttered together. They search under title keyword and title exact for "Doctor Who." It is also important to have a computer default set to recognize "Dr." and "Doctor" as being the same term. Most databases have a string limit on screen/print output when showing resultant search titles. Therefore, it is important that each episode be distinctly identified.

In keeping with the series definitions and cataloguing recommendations, The Elkhart Public Library has chosen to catalogue each episode separately, modifying each OCLC record [245] field (Dr. Who) to contain a title and subfield b title (episode title). A [7301 series entry and variant title entries [7401 are also entered as well as subject headings [650) for multiple point access. In this manner, all the Doctor Who episodes are standardized, containing consistent information and allowing a comprehensive list of all titles in the series be listed at once.

As previously mentioned in the series discussion, it is important to discern a volume title from a series title in both the videographic and holdings records. The practical side of this concept reveals itself when holdings records are attached to single barcodes for circulation. A film such as The Sound of Music may be produced on two videocassettes which need to be circulated together. The videographic collation might read: -2 videocassettes, part 1/11 (280 min.)." Part I might contain the bar code, with part II rubber-banded to its partner (or boxed together in another manner).

A distinction must be made by both the cataloguer and the public service librarian in determining a part from a volume, as wen as whether to circulate the set as a whole or as separate parts, which will effect both the videographic collation and holdings record. The cataloguer cannot always depend upon the wording of the producer/ manufacturer in determining volumes or parts. Generally speaking, a volume wilt have a separate title, possibly be labeled as a volume, and be a unique, separate item with a distinct beginning and ending.

A part, on the other hand, may be labeled as such, not have a separate title, and not possess a distinguishable end/credits. Many television miniseries now released on video in multiple cassettes of two or more, such as North and South, should be considered parts rather than volumes. When parts constitute more than two physical videocassettes, a decision as to whether they should be circulated separately or as one unit must be made. All parts must be consistently labeled and/ or relabeled so that shelvers and other public service staff, as well as patrons, know what they are handling.

Format Integration

Final implementation of LC's format integration for MARC records is set for 1995, but there are many bugs to work out. Simply

Put, format integration will allow cataloguers the necessary freedom to do a full description of the item and include coded data elements for all aspects of materials, especially useful for kits containing multimedia such as an audiocassette, videocassette, compact disc, books and manuals, and so on. The [740] field will become obsolete, reassigned to 246 [VARYING FORM OF TITLE] and a repeatable 006 [FIXED-LENGTH DATA ELEMENTS-ADDITIONAL MATERIAL CHARACTERISTICS] will be available for different media.

Cataloguers will not have to determine which type of media is the primary type from which to catalogue. While this is an important step in media catalogue advancement, it will no doubt cause chaos within a local database. Profiles must be modified to search not only existing [740] fields, but also new [246] fields, or programmes globally written to change [740] fields into [246]. Additionally, a 546 [LANGUAGE NOTE] has been added (formerly placed in [500]) as well as a 511 [PARTICIPANT OR PERFORMER NOTE]. Lastly, a 521 field [TARGET AUDIENCE] has been added. Search profiles must be modified and consistent language developed, to reflect these changes and them for local database use."

Trial by Fire-Tales of Public Access Catalogues, Patrons, and Staff

In order to develop a useful card catalogue, there must be a good match between the needs of the patron and staff and the demands and limitations of the system. This match involves an introspective examination of what the library's clientele and staff need from the catalogue and how they perform routine searches. The best way to find out what patrons want is to talk to them about how they use the materials. What would be useful in a catalogue that is not there now? What is good (*i.e.*, useful) about what is already in use?

Informal conversations with patrons utilizing reference interview techniques will provide surprising insights. Formal in-house use surveys can also be helpful and produce hard evidence to support changes and cataloguing policy/procedural modifications. Talking to staff who deal with the patrons on the front line is probably going to produce the most pertinent information.

Surveying the staff can also be helpful, especially if they can anonymously and objectively critique current practices. This information gathering is the most important step in the initial planning process and will be very time-consuming and tedious, but will ultimately reap benefits in information access for the staff and patrons. Having a cataloguing staff who actually work a public service desk occasionally will help sensitize them to the needs of the patrons as well as make them acquainted with the searching limits and capabilities of the on-line catalogue and patron searching patterns and methods. By far the most difficult procedure in computerizing a library collection is setting up a system profile, or searching programme/parameters so that the computer will search, compile, and list the correct MARC record fields for the specific search selected by the user and disregard/not display duplicated information.

The computer display must be "user friendly" in that it should display information in an easy-to-read, easily recognizable fashion, such as in standard catalogue card format rather than in delineated MARC fields. It should also give the patron information about the media type, displaying the GMD whenever the title is displayed. The inclusion of subfield h in [730] and [7401 is vitally important so that all video titles display a GMD.

Today's cataloguer of videocassettes must possess an in-depth knowledge of the local computer searching capabilities, but also be able to think like a patron when videographic information must be created, modified, and placed into discrete computer/database fields for search access points. For example, if a user selects a title or title keyword search, the profile might command the computer to search the [245] and [740] fields, as well as the [505) fields. Likewise, series searches might access the [245] and [730], but omit the [505] fields of the videographic record. For the above stated reasons, it is imperative that, whenever . MARC records are downloaded into a,ny local system, they are immediately checked for datal field inclusion as well as for field standardization and modified accordingly.

Local standardization and record modification can be extremely complex, or as simple as adding a space before and after the GMD so that it does not adversely effect the title filing order. Cataloguers control the search pattern in their inclusion and arrangement of data, as well as in their knowledge of how the local database will search, limit, and display that data. In particular, cataloguers should be aware of how their local public access catalogue searches data through answers to the following questions and characteristics:

1. Does the system have the following capabilities?

   A. Keywords in titles, summaries, subject headings, and other fields.

   B. Word truncation.

   C. Do browsable and permuted indexes exist?

   D. Does the computer allow stop words to be added (words such as a, an, and the) which are not searched?

   E. Are Boolean operators used; if so, which ones and how (and, or, not, etc.)?

2. If the MARC record contains the same word, phrase, title, or name in more than one field, and those fields are accessed in the same search, will that search bring up duplicated listings referring back to the same title? This may indicate unwanted duplication in specific fields (*e.g.*, (7401 and [505]).

3. How are titles Wed on screen as the result of a search? Is GMD (general media designator) shown? Is all, or ,a portion, thereof, of the [245] subfield b, subtitle shown? How many titles/entries are listed on a single screen, and can screens be saved and/ or combined?

   What information stays on the screen during a hierarchical search? How easy/difficult is it to branch out on a search or retrace steps? 4. Can "see" and "see also" references be placed in these searches?

The trick to having patron-usable cataloguing, regardless of what rules and standards are applied, is to choose only one set of rules and standards and stick to them and be consistent in their application. When modifications to those rules are made, they should be documented. Records should be modified globally, if possible, so that access points remain consistent throughout the database, or the entire structure will suffer.

The problem with large national and regional databases is that, although they try to adhere to various standards, the sheer number of disparate cataloguers inputting records into the database makes' conformity impossible. For any given videocassette, there may be as many as eight to ten different bibliographic records for the same item-just catalogued differently. On the local level, the cataloguer must search out the title, look at the various record options, and choose the one record that both best suits the needs of the library and will need the least amount of local modification, or choose to perform original cataloguing.

An on-line circulation, public access database is usually setup or "profiled" to search specific MARC record fields for specific searches, rather than searching the entire MARC record for every search. It is vitally important that the cataloguer know what MARC/ OCLC fields are used in different searches and, if modified, how that modification will effect other searches and still provide the searcher with succinct, intelligible information.

A Case for Subject Headings

After the video has been physically described, 'its contents must be conveyed to tile user in some fashion. Historically, the contents of any item have been described through subject headings called tracings, which can be terms, word combinations, or phrases. Cataloguers have always felt that the distillation of film contents into discrete subject headings was more difficult than describing their book counterparts. Actually, films and videocassettes are not more complex than books to catalogue; it is the simple fact that the former can be easily pursued for subject content while the latter must be viewed through a VCR-a time consuming process.

Most videocassettes are packaged with attractive and descriptive cover art, similar to a book jacket, making content information readily attainable. In 1979, in an attempt to address the complexity of assigning subject headings to films, the National Film Board of Canada developed the PRECIS method. PRECIS was itself a complex system, utilizing keywords from the title and other sources, recombined to produce multiple key phrases.

The problem with this system was that there was little consistency or uniformity in phrases and, with so many descriptive terms, a printed catalogue quickly developed into a huge, unwieldy, and unusable monster. Today the most commonly used lists are the following: The ERIC List of Descriptors, The Library of Congress Subject Headings, and Sears List of Subject Headings. For an extremely up-to-date, popular listing of subject headings, the reader might try the Hennepin County (MN) Library's Subject Authorities List (Minnetonka, MN: the Library).

Without the analytic subject headings of the various activities in The Mac-Millan Video Almanac for Kids, this information would be inaccessible to patrons in a card catalogue environment. In a computerized PAC environment, if the [505] fields were searched along with the subject heading fields [650] using subject keyword or subject exact searches, the various information included in the summary would not necessarily need to be detailed through subject headings. The development of an up-to-date Subject thesaurus which lists terms and phrases in a consistent, standardized fashion is a necessity to accessible subject cataloguing. In the omnimedia, integrated catalogue environment, it is vitally important that these subject headings be used consistently with nonprint and print titles.

Four subject headings for videocassettes teaching a foreign language have been chosen to describe the Berlitz video. It is important that cataloguers follow this example in duplicating this consistent use of those subject headings for other Spanish language videocassettes as well as any other foreign language videos. In this way, all languages will utilize the same subject headings and will be easily accessible.

Genre Headings for Feature Films

Audiovisual cataloguers agree that previously mentioned subject and genre lists do not provide adequate subject headings to describe film genres. In fact, these headings are inconsistent within their own framework. Take, for example, The Library of Congress Subject Headings entry for Romance, Historical, Science fiction and Westerns as a Comparison:

Romance drama	Historical drama
Romance fiction	Historical fiction
Romance literature	Historical films
Romances	Historical television programmes
Science fiction	Western stories
Science fiction films	Western television programmes
Science fiction television programmes	

There is little uniformity or standardization across genres in Historical television programmes and Western (television programmes). Romance does not even possess a film or television programme equivalent. Thus, libraries have had to create their own genre lists. As with subject headings, it is important that the structure be derived from an existing subject heading, fitting within that genre hierarchy, but modified to fit the genre. The following list details one such genre list currently used by the Elkhart (IN) Public Library to describe genre videocassettes. When questions arise as to what genre(s) a certain film should be categorized into, it is highly recommend that the following genre guides be consulted: Mick Martin and Marsha Porter's The Video Movie Guide, Bowker's Complete Video Directory, and The Video Source Book.

Two of the most extensive reference sources this author has found for classifying movies by genre are The Motion Picture Guide (Bowker/CineBooks, 1985+), which is also available on CD-ROM, and Films by Genre by Daniel Lopez (Jefferson, NC: McFarland & Co. Publishers, 1993). Remember that the entire purpose of genre categorization is to allow patrons to access smaller groups of the larger video collection whole through standardized topics which are meaningful to them.

Genre Headings for Feature Videos

Action Films. This includes films where the main plot and characters are involved in relentless action/adventure regardless of the time period (historical period). Includes films with such actors as Clint Eastwood, Chuck Norris, Charles Bronson, Jean-Claude Van Damme, and Arnold Schwarzenegger. Includes spy and espionage films like The Eiger Sanction, if action, rather than the solving of the mystery or crime, is the ultimate goal or if there are sufficient "shoot 'em up" action sequences.

Adventure Films. This includes films with adventure, especially outdoor adventure, as the primary plot/source of action. Includes films such as Grizzly Adams, White Fang, White Fang 2, Courage Mountain, Swiss Fandly Robinson, Moby Dick, The Incredible Journey, and The Adventures of Milo and Otis.

Animated Films. A full-length feature which uses animated settings and characters exclusively-no (or very little) live action. (I would not put Who Framed Roger Rabbit? here!) Full-length and the style of animation (not cartoonish) are keys here. Examples include The Hobbit, Gulliver's Travels, Fantasia, 101 Dalmatians, Pinnochio, Snow White and the Seven Dwarfs, Beauty and the Beast, and Winnie the Pooh.

Children s Films. Use this heading for full-length films that do not fit into any other genre (using the subhead "Juvenile") but target children as their main audience. (I can't think of any feature which would not fit into a genre category. This heading should be used sparingly.)

Cartoon Films. Basically, what distinguishes an animated feature from a cartoon are three things: the duration of the film (most cartoons are short), the unrealistic, cartoonish drawing style, and the exaggerated intent to make the viewer laugh. All Warner Brothers, MGM, and Disney short compilations (under 30 minutes).

Comedy Films. Where the main characters are involved in a comedic plot and comedy is not an incidental part, but rather an intrinsic whole. Includes 'Me Three Stooges, The Marx Brothers Laurel & Hardy, and so on. Also includes crossover genres like romantic comedies, musical comedies, and others. However, comedy drama, class in Dramatic Films. Examples include With Six You Get Egg Roll, Which Way to the Forum?, The Pink Panther, Arthur, Bringing UP Baby, Mr. Blandings Builds His Dream House, Oh, God, The Apple Dumpling Gang, The Naked Gun, Blazing Saddles, Young Frankenstein, and What's Up Doc?

Definition of Feature (Film). For purposes of cataloguing, a full-length feature is defined as being a movie released on video that is at least 60 minutes in length, and which has previously been in theatrical release, or is a made-for-video. Made-for-television movies should fall under their appropriate genres, with "Television programmes" phrase added to each. We will use the term FILM after each genre type instead of videorecording, feature, or other format indicator.

Dramatic Films. A film that does not easily fit into any of the other genres and may contain elements of any or all genres. Examptes include Anastasia, Barry Lyndon, Blackboard Jungle, Champion, The Champ, Giant, and Cat on a Hot Tin Roof.

Detective Films. Involves a plot revolving around some type of crime, criminals, and the crime's solution. Characters frequently are police, detectives, private eyes, and other nosy people." Examples include The Adventures of Sherlock Holmes, The Alphabet Murders, Double Indemnity, Fatal Attraction, Madame X, and Gree for Danger.

Family Films. Both "Children's Films" and this subject heading are not necessarily genre-related; rather, they indicate a particular audience. Unlike "Children's Films", "Family" should be used in conjunction with other genre subject headings if possible. All MP AA Grated films (live action and animated), and possibly some PG films, should fall into the "Family" category.

Judgement should be used in assessing whether included titles are appropriate for viewing by the entire family. They should be nonviolent, nosex, no-blood, and possibly underscore a positive life-skills lesson or message. Examples include The Bear, Milo and Otis, The Incredible Journey, Seven Alone, White Fang, and all Disney films (animated or live-action).

Fantasy Films. Fantasy strictly follows a set of laws to create an imaginary world. The rules used may not agree with logic or the laws of nature. Nonrational happenings occur without scientific basis, with magic and the supernatural present. Include films involving mythology here. Examples include The Neverending Story, Alice in Wonderland, The Adventures of Sinbad, The Dark Crystal, The Hobbit, Watership Down, Time Bandits, Hercules, and Jason and the Argonauts.

Foreign Films (Country). A film produced in a country other than the United States. Many will have narration/dialog in the original language (other than English) and or be sublitled. Others may be dubbed in English. Examples include Dos Bool, Babette's Feast, The 400 Blows, Ran, Intermezzo, and Knife in the Water.

Folk and Fairy Tale Films. Adaptations of or works based on folk and fairy tales by authors such as Hans Christian Anderson and The Brothers Grimm. Includes The Little Mermaid, Sleeping Beauty, and Pinocchio.

Historical Films. A feature whose plot revolves around an historic event as a central point, using characterizations of real-life people. The story line tries to be as close to the real telling as possible but may take dramatic liberties. Examples include Lion in Winter,

King Lear, Abe Lincoln in Illinois, The Alamo, Henry V, Peter the Great, Quo Vadis, Ben Hur, Martin Luther, Joan of Arc, The Last of the Mohicans, and Columbus.

Horror Films. The matter of horror films is derived from the supernatural and the occult exhibited in very overt terms-ghosts and ghouls, witches and warlocks, vampires and werewolves, monsters and mummies, demonology, black magic and voodoo, and other forms of occult magic. Examples include The Bride of Frankenstein, Dracula, The Pit and the Pendulum, Fright Night, The Invisible Man, and all Stephen King movie adaptations.

Mystery Films. A mystery is a story of a crime and its investigation involving the police, detectives private eyes, or other amateur sleths. The solving of the crime is the main plot while the detective is the main character. All Agatha Christie and Sherlock Holmes movies fall into this category. Also included are Patriot Games, The Big Sleep, D.O.A., The Ipcress File, Klute, and The Conversation.

Musical Films. A feature where the music is an intrinsic and intregal part for the furthering of the plot (story line). Involves not only orchestral music but singing as well. This does not include music videos or operas. Examples include Band Wagon, Camelot, Carousel, Funny Face, Easter Parade, and Sweeney Todd.

Romance Films. A romance is a story (dramatic or comedic) in which the plot revolves around the main character's pursuit of lasting happiness and romantic fulfillment with the opposite sex, regardless of the time period (historical period). Examples include Idiot's Delight, It Happened One Night, Pillow Talk, The French Lieutenant's Woman, Black Orchid, and Tire Ghost and Mrs. Muir.

Religious Films. A dramatic or comedic film where religion (or religious figures, such as King David, Jesus, etc.) plays a prominent and plot-determinant role. Examples include Moses, The Ten Commandments, The Bible, The Robe, Barabbas, The Lost Temptation of Christ, Sister Act, and The Bells of St. Mary's.

Short Films. This would be analogous to the term "Featurette" used in the early movie days, where shorter films were butted together or used as a leader into the main feature film. A feature film is over one hour long; anything else is a short. Examples include The Little Rascals (Out Gang is a Comedy television programme), We. Fields shorts, and some Laurel and Hardy.

Science Fiction Films. Science fiction is speculative fiction pertaining to potential uses of science and the future of mankind, with its characters and plot obeying all the laws of nature and with scientific knowledge as the base. Examples include Blade Runner, THX 1138, all Star Wars and Star Trek films, Alien, 2001, and 2010.

Suspense Films. Similar to horror films and possibly involving a mystery and/or the occult, but not relying on overt horror, the suspense film places characters in plots involving extreme physical and psychological tension and terror, and or danger. All Film Noir and the Hitchcock films are examples of this genre. Others include Basic Instinct, The Silence of the Lambs, Final Analysis, Jacob's ladder, DOA, North by Northwest, The Birds, Double Indemnity, The Parallax View, Vertigo, Tightrope, and The Mechanic.

Silent Films. Used for films released without a soundtrack, circa 1898-1928. Videos now include added musical soundtrack but no narration or dialog. These include films like The Great Train Robbery, Charlie Chaplin films, Buster Keaton films, and Harold Lloyd films.

Television Programmes. Omitting feature films that have been theatrically released and later shown on television, this heading is to be used for till television broadcast shows such as made-for-TV -movies, variety shows, TV specials, miniseries, serial compilations and anthologies, and other shows. Examples include Monty Python's Flying Circus, Black Adder, I Love Lucy, The Jackie Gleason Show, Christmas with the Carpenters, Lonesome Dove, 0 Pioneers!, Sarah Plain and Tall, all Wonderworks Family Movies, The Twilight Zone, The Outer Limits, Roots, and The Blue and the Gray (the latter might be described as an Historical Television Programme, a Romance Television programme and a War Television Programme).

Sub-division. If a television show is a particular genre as described within the enclosed defintions, that genre should be placed ahead of the 'heading in the following manner: Western Television Programmes, Science Fiction Television Programmes, Family Television Programmes, etc. In a similar fashion, Children's television programmes should be categorized one of two ways: *(1)* If the genre cannot be easily ascertained: Television Programmes (Juvenile); *(2)* If a genre(s) can be identified: Western Television Programmes (Juvenile) Horror Television Programmes (Juvenile), etc.

Western Films. Primarily, the Western is an adventure involving cowboys, the frontier, and Indians and outlaws, with the setting and time period set in the American Old West, c. 1789-1900. Examples include Abilene Town, Big Jake, Comancheros, High Plains Drifter and Angel and the Badman.

War Films. A war film is primarily an adventure story set in a period of war (any period using a recognized war or military action, *i.e.*, Korea and Vietnam) and involving armies, soldiers, and organized military fighting. The war must be the focal point, not just the background, and actions should have military consequences. For example, Lord Jim involves an insurrection, but should not be considered a war movie because it is not the focal point of the movie. Examples include The Eagle Has Landed, The Green Berets, The Killing Fields, Platoon, War and Peace, Tora! Tora! Tora! Back to Bataan Plat and Full Metal Jacket.

Special Subject Headings

Described Videos. Used as above, this heading delineates those videos having a "described narration" overlaying the soundtrack. Currently, produced by DVS, Inc.

Public Performance Films. Used in similar fashion to the subject headings "Video recordings for the hearing impaired" or

"Closed captioned videos," this heading delineates and groups those titles possessing public performance rights.

Video-recordings. While this heading is currently in use in many MARC records, no other material such as audio-cassettes, art prints, or books are so delineated by a similar subject heading. This heading will accomplish one feat-to bring together all titles of one format. However, a search under the [505] field "VHS" string or the [GMD] would yield the same result. Video Recordings for the Hearing Impaired. Used in place of Films for the Hearing Impaired, Video recordings for the Hearing Impaired, or Closed Captioned Video-cassettes. Use this beading for all videos displaying the CC (closed captioned) trademark. Note that "Closed Captioned for the Hearing Impaired" is appearing much more in both the local SH and notes field than before.

Classification System

Basically, there are two types of classification arrangements: alphabetic and classified. An alphabetic arrangement usually alphabetizes by title. The listing is simple and straightforward, but fragments related genres and subjects. Exact titles are easy to locate but similar genres and subjects cannot be found easily.

A classified arrangement shows subject and genre hierarchies, locates related subjects, and allows greater subject depth to be expressed, but searchers must be knowledgeable about the system or first consult an alphabetic index for location information. Many libraries simply throw videocassettes on the shelf in random order; others use an alphabetic arrangement for features and a classified arrangement for subject-oriented video-cassettes. Still other libraries may divide their collections between Children's and Adult, further breaking down each of those collections into broad genreclassified arrangement for features and a number classified system for subject video-cassettes.

In situations where a two-box system or flat browser-paks (Chicago-One Stop) are used, a classified arrangement many be used with a straight numeric accession system. By using such a system, patrons can easily access titles by genre and subject and staff can maximize space by simply "adding on" to the ends of rows rather than creating space between them for new acquisitions. However, in such a system, care must be taken to identify both dummy and live item with both accession and classified numbers.

This text advocates the use of the same subject classification system used for the book collection at any library for subject "nonfiction" videocassettes. Advantages from using the same system include the cataloguer's, processor's, and public desk staff's familiarity with the current system, achievement of consistency between collections, and the patron's possible familiarity with the system. Genre arrangements are fine for libraries with enough space to shelve materials and expand their collection at the same time. However, locating a specific title involves not only knowing the title but also determining the genre designation..

The practical purpose of any alphabetic or classified arrangement of materials is to provide some type of logical, repeatable order to a group of materials. To this practical end, they provide an orderly shelving arrangement which accomplishes three functions:

1. facilitates ease of browsing and title location;
2. is organized in a logical manner which is readily apparent to patrons and staff; and
3. is kept as simple as possible but with subjcct/genre areas sufficiently delineated so as to avoid confusion.

The advantage of using the Dewey Decimal Classification system (DOC) or Library of Congress Classification system (LC) is that staff and patrons will already by familiar with it. A videocassette on travel in Hawaii will have the same DOC number as a book on the same subject. If a library decided to go to an integrated collection, the use of one of these systems would certainly be necessity.

Classification schemes for feature films is more problematic for libraries. DC and LC leave a lot to be desired as far as public libraries a concerned. The fact is that library patrons also use video stores and are used to genre groupings. While librarians may turn up their collective noses at this type of scheme, is it really any different from book collections, where mysteries are frequently pulled out of the fiction $ection and classified and shelved separately. It is not unusual to find science fiction, short stories, fantasy, and young aduft novels separated from the fiction collection in libraries.

Genre classifications are user friendly and are particularly appealing for browsing collections. Obviously, if the feature film collection is part of a university collection that serves a film school, different needs will exist that will necessitate a different approach. American films classed in DOC could go in 813, English films in 823, and so on. Or all the films could go into the 790s An excellent example of using the DOC number for videocassettes occurs regularly with two series titles, "The American Short Story series" and "Reading Rainbow series." The first series is often classed in 808 and the latter series in 372.6. The cataloguer must realize that any classification scheme will have hundreds of videocassettes with numbers that are basically only a few digits apart Workmarks and Cutter numbers with the first four letters of the title might end up being the only descernable difference for many titles. Librarians possessing small collections may feel that a classified system such as LC or DDC is too complex and may choose to use a few broad subject categories such as feature films, music, documentary, instructional, and children's films.

The DDC system provides for an orderly shelf arrangement of subject videos and facilitates transitional continuity from print to nonprint. Alternately, arranging feature films alphabetically by title with genres denoted using colored labels also seems to work well. Genre labels are available from traditional library supply vendors like Demco and Gaylord, as well as video store supply companies such as Video Store Services (6115 Monroe Court, Morton Grove, IL 60053; (800) 325-6867), The Video Store Shopper (8100 Remmet A venue, Canoga Park, CA 91304; (800) 325-6867) and United Ad Label

Company (650 Columbia Street, Brea, CA 92621; (714) 990-2700). These labels facilitate easy location and patron browsing.

Whatever system is decided upon, it is imperative that the selector/acquisitions librarian and the cataloguer be on the same wavelength concerning how these materials will be handled as well as who will have the final say on disputed titles.

Options for Cataloguing and Conversion

In the preparation for establishing a cataloging conversion project (or just implementing cataloguing for a new collection), it is important to be aware of what choices can be made. Basically there are two options: the library catalogues the materials or an outside contractor does the work.

A library's cataloguing department is the first obvious choice for any cataloguing. However as mentioned before, backlogs, staffing, or lack of experienced staff may hinder their function as a practical idea. Often, as new materials alive, they can be more easily catalogued and processed; but conversion of older titles may have to be done on an "as time allows" schedule. If at all possible, it is best to set up monthly quotas and a schedule of which subject areas or titles are to be priorities.

A time/motion study might be done to determine an average cost per record for in-house conversion versus the item cost for an outside vender to do the same task. In many instances, the outside vendor is cheaper; however, quality control is a big issue. Therefore, serious consideration should be given to having an outside cataloguing service convert all current holdings with new materials done by in-house staff. It is very important to consider the cataloguing staff's experience and/or expertise in nonprint formats. Before any project can get off the ground, cataloguers may have to have some training. The On Line Audio Visual-Cataloguers group (OLAC) holds annual workshops; the annual ALA conference frequently has cataloguing. programmes; and most states have some sort of local cataloguing network that hosts training workshops.

Cataloguing Vendor Services

As library videocassette collections proliferated, the services offered by cataloguing vendors increased to include video as well as books and audio matet:ials. The services available range from the traditional packs of printed catalogue cards to full MARC records on tape/disk ready to be loaded onto a local library's automated system. Some of the vendors also sell nonprint materials and ship them to libraries already catalogued and processed, and ready to be shelved. If a library has limited cataloguing staff this may be a valid option. It is important to analyze costs compared with the cost of a vendor cataloguing and/or processing versus the library doing the work itself. Following is a selective list of conversion vendors and CD-ROM products that are above average in the media cataloguing field.

The vendors provide full cataloguing and/or processing services, and the CD-ROM products allow low-cost uploading of videographic records because there are no on-line or telecommunications charges, only one time equipment and subscription fees. Rates will vary and services change from time to time, and the best rule of thumb is to call and get their basic print information and follow up with a telephone call if their services look viable for the library's needs.

Gutenberg and the Printed Catalogue

Once upon a time, in 16mm film library land, there was the printed catalogue. This catalogue, approximately the size of the New York City white pages, was an alphabetically arranged-by-title body with descriptive annotations, including a complex subject index, which was distributed to schools, YMCAs, community centers, churches, schools, and individuals.

Many libraries and media centers did not perform traditional cataloguing of films and videocassettes, this was the only point of access to the collection. Now as more libraries put their collection "on line" via automated systems and/or media booking systems, the question arises about the need for a printed catalogue. With the number of videos being collected increasing dramatically, the ability to keep a print catalogue current becomes problematic. Also, the cost of printing a large catalogue with full annotations and subject index can become too expensive. After all, there is not a printed catalogue of the book collection, and no longer even printed catalogue cards.

The arrival of the personal computer certainly made it easier for libraries to add to and delete materials from a master list of materials. Many libraries make money producing and selling simple title lists of their videocassette holdings. Automated booking (aka media scheduling) systems, such as Tek Data's DMAX and Paulmar's SAM systems, usually provide an option for easily printing out a camera-ready copy for duplication. For stand-alone media centers such as school cooperatives and some college/university centers, either of these options may be perfectly suited to their needs. The problem arises when the collection becomes so large that printing a catalogue is no longer feasible.

A printed catalogue must not be just an 8 1/2" by 11" duplication of catalogue cards, which would be entirely too unwieldy. In order to be viable, it must be physically pleasing and easily handled, presenting selected information to the reader. Annotations are very important; series titles and their groupings, along with separate titles, are also valuable. Audience indicators and a usable subject index that is sufficiently descriptive, grouping titles into broad categories rather than disparate, isolated subject headings, is vital to patron satisfaction. An index without "see" and "I see also" references is not much use. Buying an automated system with home computer dial-access 'capabilities which permit both database searching and online scheduling, holds and/or reserves is one of the technological options toward circumventing the traditional printed catalogue. The hard-line fact is that, at some point, printed catalogues will no longer be available because of increased production costs and update difficulties.

Patrons will have to either dial into the database and search for the materials they need and place the reserve/ booking themselves or they will have to come to the library and use the catalogue oil site to find their materials. For those librarians and patrons used to having a printed catalogue in hand, this seems like a step backward; the counterbalance being the availability of much more information on a professionally produced, dynamic database possessing many more search options than are available in a static printed catalogue.

This chapter has attempted to outline and discuss some of the problems in cataloguing videocassettes and also provide some solutions. The cataloguer's role in making videographic information available in a palatable and usable form for both patrons and public services staff is a crucial one. Videographic records unloaded onto local databases are most often not complete or correct and may need substantial modification to meet local needs and system profile standards.

The cataloguer must carefully match the actual item in hand to the video graphic record, viewing it if necessary. The cataloguing of videocassettes involves more "exceptions to the rule" and rule interpretations than most print materials; therefore, it is a more detail oriented, exhaustive, time-consuming process. Audiovisual cataloguers must become proficient in knowing and applying those rules on a daily basis, as well as developing an in-depth knowledge of the library's local database structure and search engine methods.

❑